BEYOND TALENT

BEYOND TALENT

Become Someone Who
Gets Extraordinary Results

John C.
Maxwell

Thomas Nelson
Since 1798

NASHVILLE   DALLAS   MEXICO CITY   RIO DE JANEIRO

Published in Nashville, Tennessee, by Thomas Nelson. Thomas Nelson is a registered trademark of Thomas Nelson, Inc.

Published in association with Yates & Yates, www.yates2.com.

Thomas Nelson, Inc., titles may be purchased in bulk for educational, business, fund-raising, or sales promotional use. For information, please e-mail SpecialMarkets@ThomasNelson.com.

ISBN: 978-1-4002-0357-4 (trade paper)

Library of Congress has cataloged the hardcover edition, *Talent Is Never Enough*, as follows

Maxwell, John C., 1947–
    Talent is never enough : discover the choices that will take you beyond
your talent / John C. Maxwell.
      p. cm.
    Includes bibliographical references.
    ISBN: 978-0-7852-1403-8 (hardcover)
    ISBN: 978-0-7852-8896-1 (IE)
    1. Ability. 2. Success. I. Title.
BF431.M393 2006
650.1—dc22

2006024658

Printed in the United States of America

11 12 13 14 15 RRD 5 4 3 2 1

Beyond Talent is dedicated to John Porter Maxwell, our third grandchild. His ready smile and desire to be with Papa and Mimi have stolen our hearts. We pray that as he grows older, he will make the right choices enabling him to be a talent-plus person.

CONTENTS

It's called the guarantee. At the time, many people said it was just big talk. Not true. It was a mark of the confidence possessed by the person who uttered it. That strong sense of belief made him a legend and his team members champions. What could it do for you?

Why would a barber receive a prestigious fellowship, be recognized by the U.S. Small Business Administration, and be awarded an honorary doctorate? Hint: it has little to do with barbering and everything to do with his passion to change the world.

No one can make the most of his talent in the midst of bureaucratic red tape, especially in the fallout of natural disaster. Right? You might be surprised. Because of its initiative, this company was able to do the seemingly impossible in a remarkable sixty-six days.

What do you get when you put two unfocused and inexperienced hunters in one of the most bountiful hunting regions in the world? Comedy! Learn where and how to focus your efforts so that you get much better results than these hunters did.

ACKNOWLEDGMENTS

Thank you to
Charlie Wetzel, my writer
Stephanie Wetzel, who proofs and edits the manuscript
Linda Eggers, my assistant

WHEN IS TALENT ALONE ENOUGH?

Talent is often overrated and frequently misunderstood. French poet and dramatist Edouard Pailleron pointed out, "Have success and there will always be fools to say that you have talent." When people achieve great things, others often explain their accomplishments by simply attributing everything to talent. But that is a false and misleading way of looking at success. If talent alone is enough, then why do you and I know highly talented people who are not highly successful?

Many American business leaders are obsessed with talent. Some think talent is the answer to every problem. Malcolm Gladwell, author of *The Tipping Point* and *Blink*, notes that many companies and consultants put finding people with talent ahead of everything else. He says, "This 'talent mind-set' is the new orthodoxy of American management." Certain companies hire dozens of MBAs from top universities, promote them quickly, reward them lavishly, and never accurately assess their performance. The prime example he gives is Enron. Its talent focus was legendary. For example, Lynda Clemmons, who started Enron's weather derivatives business, went from trader to associate to manager to director to head of her own business unit in only seven years! Gladwell asks, "How do you evaluate someone's performance in a system where no one is in a job long enough to allow such evaluation?"[1]

Talent is never enough. Peter Drucker, the father of modern management, said, "There seems to be little correlation between a man's effectiveness and his intelligence, his imagination, or his knowledge . . . Intelligence, imagination, and knowledge are essential resources, but only effectiveness converts them into results. By themselves, they only set limits to what can be contained." If talent were enough, then the most effective and influential people would always be the most talented ones. But that is often not the case. Consider this:

- More than 50 percent of all CEOs of Fortune 500 companies had C or C- averages in college.
- Sixty-five percent of all U.S. senators came from the bottom half of their school classes.
- Seventy-five percent of U.S. presidents were in the Lower-Half Club in school.
- More than 50 percent of millionaire entrepreneurs never finished college![2]

Clearly talent isn't everything.

THE HIGH-JUMP PRINCIPLE

This is not an anti-talent book. I believe in the importance of talent. How could I not? All successful leaders understand its importance. Legendary college football coach Lou Holtz once told me, "John, I've coached teams with good players and I've coached teams with bad players. I'm a better coach when I have good players!" The more talent that a sports, business, or service team possesses, the greater potential it has—and the better its leader can be.

Most leaders understand the dynamics of ownership, shared responsibility, division of labor, committee governance, and delegation. Often leaders accomplish great tasks by dividing a job into its parts and coordinating the whole effort. Remarkable feats, such as the building of the pyramids or the Great Wall of China, were accomplished in that fashion. However, there are some tasks that are not improved by adding more people. Brooks's Law states, "Adding people to a late software project makes it later." More isn't always better, and some things are best done by an individual.

A wonderful, simple illustration of the importance of talent can be seen in a sports event like the high jump. Winning the high jump requires one person who can jump seven feet, not seven people who can jump one foot. Such an example may seem obvious, yet don't we often believe that we can accomplish more by throwing more people at a task? That isn't always the right solution. In fact, there are many tasks that call for talent more than numbers. Like high jumping, they require the extraordinary talent of one person, not the mediocre talent of many.

Putting Talent into Perspective

As I said, I don't mean to minimize the importance of talent. Talent is a God-given gift that should be celebrated. When we observe talented people . . .

1. We Should Marvel at Their Giftedness

Reading leadership books by Jack Welch, I am amazed by his deep wisdom mixed with common sense. It is no surprise that he was able to turn around GE and lift it to a dominant position in corporate America. He is a born leader.

Every time I have the opportunity, I go to Sarah Brightman's concerts. I find that her voice sets her apart from other vocal artists. I often close my eyes and just listen to her sing, marveling at the giftedness of this diva. Sarah Brightman is a born vocalist.

Professional football in Atlanta rose to a new level when Michael Vick came to town. His ability to run a football is guaranteed to thrill the crowd every game. He has lifted his team and the Falcons' fans with his extraordinary gifts. Michael Vick is a born athlete.

Talent can enable people to do extraordinary things, and we should acknowledge people's talent and marvel at their accomplishments.

2. We Should Recognize Their Contribution to Society

When we observe talented people, we should note their impact. Where would America be today if it had not been formed by talented leaders? I have been reading *Booknotes Life Stories: Notable Biographers on the People Who Shaped America* by Brian Lamb, the founding CEO of C-SPAN and host of C-SPAN's *Booknotes* program. The book has reminded me of the talent of America's Founding Fathers:

- THOMAS JEFFERSON, the nation's third president and primary writer of the Declaration of Independence, was a Renaissance man: He invented the first modern plow, was the president of the American Philosophical Society, sent Lewis and Clark on the country's first scientific expedition, redesigned Washington, D.C., so that the president in the White House would have to look up to see Congress on Capitol Hill, and offered his 6,500-volume personal library so that it could become the foundation of the U.S. Library of Congress.

- THOMAS PAINE produced the nation's first bestseller when he penned *Common Sense*. It sold half a million copies in a country of three million people.

- JAMES MADISON, the country's fourth president, was the primary thinker behind the U.S. Constitution. He was the MVP of the fifty-five men who created that world-changing document. He was a better thinker than Jefferson.

- HENRY CLAY, orator, statesman, and lawyer, was a mentor to Abraham Lincoln and prevented a move by the southern states to secede in 1850. Many historians believe that the decade-long delay gave the Union enough time to build its industrial base, thus leading to the preservation of the United States.

The course of history the world over has been changed by talented men and women who have maximized their skills.

3. We Should Separate What They Can Do from Who They *Are*

Fred Smith, author and former president of Fred Smith Associates, shared a bit of wisdom with me many years ago. He said, "The giftedness is usually greater than the person." By that he meant that the talent of some people is greater than other important personal attributes, such as character and commitment. As a result, they often fail to rise to the level of their talent. Talented people are always tempted to coast on their abilities. Or they want others to recognize their skills but overlook their deficiencies.

Haven't you known people who should have risen to the top but didn't? They had all the talent they should ever need, but they still didn't succeed. Philosopher Ralph Waldo Emerson must have known people like that, too, because he said, "Talent for talent's sake is a bauble and a show. Talent working with joy in the cause of universal truth lifts the possessor to a new power as a benefactor."

So is talent ever enough? Yes, but only in the very beginning. Novelist Charles Wilson says, "No matter the size of the bottle, the cream always rises to the top." Talent stands out. It gets you noticed. In the beginning, talent separates you from the rest of the pack. It gives you a head start on others. For that reason, natural talent is one of life's greatest gifts. But the advantage it gives lasts only a short time. Songwriter Irving Berlin understood this truth when he said, "The toughest thing about

> "The toughest thing about success is that you've got to keep on being a success. Talent is only a starting point in business. You've got to keep working that talent."
>
> —Irving Berlin

success is that you've got to keep on being a success. Talent is only a starting point in business. You've got to keep working that talent."

Too many talented people who start with an advantage over others lose that advantage because they rest on their talent instead of raising it. They assume that talent alone will keep them out front. They don't realize the truth: if they merely wing it, others will soon fly past them. Talent is more common than they think. Mega-best-selling author Stephen King asserts that "talent is cheaper than table salt. What separates the talented individual from the successful one is a lot of hard work." Clearly, more than just talent is needed for anyone who wants to achieve success.

Do You Have What It Takes?

So what does it take to succeed? Where does that leave you and me? Can anyone be successful? And where does talent fit in? Here's what I believe:

1. Everyone Has Talent

People have equal value, but not equal giftedness. Some people seem to be blessed with a multitude of talents. Most of us have fewer abilities. But know this: all of us have something that we can do well.

In their book *Now, Discover Your Strengths*, Marcus Buckingham and Donald O. Clifton state that every person is capable of doing something better than the next ten thousand people. And they support that assertion with solid research. They call this area the strength zone, and they encourage everyone to find it and make the most of it. It doesn't matter how aware you are of your abilities, how you feel about yourself, or whether you previously have achieved success. You have talent, and you can develop that talent.

2. Develop the Talent You Have, Not the One You Want

If I asked you who would be more successful, the person who relies on his talent alone or the person who realizes his talent and develops it, the answer would be obvious. Then I'll ask you this question: Why do most people spend the majority of their time focused on strengthening their weaknesses?

One thing I teach people at my conferences is to stop working on their weaknesses and start working on their strengths. (By this I mean abilities, not attitude or character issues, which *must* be addressed.) It has been my observation that people can increase their ability in an area by only 2 points on a scale of 1 to 10. For example, if your natural talent in an area is a 4, with hard work you may rise to a 6. In other words, you can go from a little below average to a little above average. But let's say you find a place where you are a 7; you have the potential to become a 9, maybe even a 10, if it's your greatest area of strength and you work exceptionally hard! That helps you advance from 1 in 10,000 talent to 1 in 100,000 talent—but only if you do the other things needed to maximize your talent.

3. Anyone Can Make Choices That Will Add Value to Talent

The question remains: What creates the effectiveness that Peter Drucker says is necessary for converting talent into results? It comes from the choices you make. *The key choices you make—apart from the natural talent you already have—will set you apart from others who have talent alone.* Orator, attorney, and political leader William Jennings Bryan said, "Destiny is not a matter of chance, it is a matter of choice; it is not a thing to be waited for, it is a thing to be achieved."

> The key choices you make—apart from the natural talent you already have—will set you apart from others who have talent alone.

I've discovered thirteen key choices that can be made to maximize any person's talent:

1. Belief lifts your talent.
2. Passion energizes your talent.
3. Initiative activates your talent.
4. Focus directs your talent.
5. Preparation positions your talent.
6. Practice sharpens your talent.
7. Perseverance sustains your talent.
8. Courage tests your talent.
9. Teachability expands your talent.
10. Character protects your talent.
11. Relationships influence your talent.
12. Responsibility strengthens your talent.
13. Teamwork multiplies your talent.

Make these choices, and you can become a talent-plus person. If you have talent, you stand alone. If you have talent *plus*, you stand out.

YOU CAN DO IT!

I believe the ideas in this book can help you. *Beyond Talent* was inspired by something that happened to me in 2004. Coach Jim Tressel asked me to speak to the Ohio State football team on the weekend that they played Michigan. It was more than just a speaking engagement for me—it was a dream come true! I grew up in Ohio, and I have been a lifelong Buckeye fan.

Coach Tressel had read my book *Today Matters*. Because his players were very young and he wanted to teach them to keep their focus on the 2004 football season, the team studied the book throughout the year. Coach Tressel wanted me to speak to the team on the last and most important game of their regular season schedule. It was an unforgettable experience. I spoke to the Buckeyes on Friday night, walked with them to the stadium on Saturday, and went into their locker room where I saw a countdown clock for the Michigan game that also said, "Today Matters."

Could it get any better? Yes! Coach Tressel turned to me while we were still in the locker room and said, "John, you and I will lead the team out on the football field."

In front of one-hundred thousand screaming fans, we ran onto the field. I'll never forget that moment. Could it get any better? Yes! I was on the sidelines with the team for the entire game. And it got even better than that! Ohio State won!

How does this relate to *Beyond Talent?* Prior to my visit, Coach Tressel had sent me some information on Ohio State football to help me prepare. One item was "The Winner's Manuel," which contained an article titled "Things That Do Not Require Talent." It emphasized that characteristics such as punctuality, effort, patience, and unselfishness were important to the OSU football program. Not one of those things required any talent. Coach Tressel told me that he and his staff were trying to help their talented players realize that their talent alone was not enough.

I loved the article and thought that if I wrote a book on the subject, it could help a lot of people. You see, people who neglect to make the right choices to release and maximize their talent continually underperform. Their talent allows them to stand out, but their wrong choices make them sit down. Their friends, families, coaches, and bosses see their giftedness, but they wonder why they so often come up short of expectations. Their talent gives them opportunity, but their wrong choices shut the door. Talent is a given, but you must earn success.

In contrast, talent-plus people come as close as humanly possible to achieving their potential. They frequently overperform. People see their giftedness and are amazed at how they continually rise above expectations. Their talent gives them opportunity, and their right choices open the door for even greater success.

Life is a matter of choices, and every choice you make makes you. What will you do for your career? Who will you marry? Where will you live? How much education will you get? What will you do with today? But one of the most important choices you will make is *who will you become!* Life is not merely a matter of holding and playing a good hand as you would hope to do in a card game. What you start with isn't up to you. *Talent* is God-given. Life is playing the hand you have been dealt well. That is determined by your choices.

TALENT + *RIGHT CHOICES* = A TALENT-PLUS PERSON

The talent-plus people are the ones who maximize their talent, reach their potential, and fulfill their destiny.

I was reading a book by Dr. Seuss to my grandchildren called *Oh, The Places You'll Go!* In it, I found a wonderful truth. It said,

> You have brains in your head.
> You have feet in your shoes.
> You can steer yourself
> Any direction you choose.

I believe that with all my heart. My prayer is that *Beyond Talent* will help you to steer yourself in the right direction and make right choices that will empower you to become a talent-plus person, build upon the foundation of your abilities, and live your life to its fullest potential.

1
BELIEF LIFTS
YOUR TALENT

The first and greatest obstacle to success for most people is their belief in themselves. Once people figure out where their sweet spot is (the area where they are most gifted), what often hinders them isn't lack of talent. It's lack of trust in themselves, which is a self-imposed limitation. Lack of belief can act as a ceiling on talent. However, when people believe in themselves, they unleash power in themselves and resources around them that almost immediately take them to a higher level. Your potential is a picture of what you can become. Belief helps you see the picture and reach for it.

MORE THAN JUST GREAT TALENT

It has become an American sports legend. People call it the guarantee. At the time, it seemed like little more than an outrageous statement— bravado from a high-profile athlete whose team was the underdog before the big game. It occurred on January 9, 1969, just three days before the third world championship game of football, the first that was called the Super Bowl. And it was just eight simple words uttered by the Jets' quarterback, Joe Namath: "The Jets will win Sunday. I guarantee it."

That boastful statement may not seem remarkable today. Ever since the career of Muhammad Ali, bold statements by athletes have been commonplace. But people didn't hear those kinds of boasts from anyone playing in the upstart American Football League (AFL). The eight-year-old AFL was considered to be inferior, and in the previous two world championship football games, the AFL teams had been trounced. Most experts believed it would be many years before an AFL team could compete at the level of any NFL team. The NFL's Colts were favored to win this third championship game by 18 or 19 points.

Namath's guarantee might have seemed outrageous, but it was more than a hollow boast. It wasn't out of character for him either. Despite the fact that Namath was often quick to take the blame in interviews when the Jets lost, he always displayed a powerful self-confidence. He believed in himself, his team, and their ability to win the game. That ability to believe in himself was something that could be traced all the way back to his childhood.

EARLY SIGNS

Joe Namath always possessed athletic talent. He came from a family of athletes. His first coaches were his family members. John, his father, spent a lot of time showing him how to throw, hit, and field a baseball and teaching him what to do in various game situations. His brothers contributed too. His brother Bobby started teaching him the position of quarterback when Joe was only six. And brother Frank drilled him and pounded him if he didn't perform well in their family practices.

Growing up, Joe was small and light for his age. Sometimes people underestimated him because of that. When he was in elementary school, a group of kids from an even tougher neighborhood than his own challenged his friend Linwood Alford to a game of two-on-two basketball. Linwood and Joe showed up to play, and Linwood recalled, "They were all laughing like: who's this little scrawny kid? How you gonna win with this guy?" Joe might have looked like an easy kid to beat, but he wasn't. "You knocked him down, he got right back up," observed Alford. "Joe wasn't no pretty boy."[1] Joe and Linwood beat the other kids and quickly earned their respect.

Joe had a certain fearlessness. He and Linwood used to go to a train trestle near their home, and they would hang from the trestle as the locomotive and its cars thundered overhead. But at first, that fearlessness didn't translate onto the athletic field. The key to unleashing the belief that lifted his talent occurred when Joe Namath was eight years old. He came home with his first team uniform for the Elks' Little League baseball team. Namath's biography recounts the exchange that occurred between young Joe and his father, John:

"That's real nice, son. Fits you good."

Joey was the smallest kid on that team. He was the youngest, too, probably by a year. "You know, Daddy, those other kids are so good," he said. "They're bigger than I am . . . I don't have a chance."

"Well, you take that uniform off right now," his father said. "Take it back to the manager and tell him that you can't make the team because the other boys are better than you are."

Joey looked at his father with those sad, dreamy eyes. "Oh, no, Daddy. I can't do that."

"If you can't make the team, what's the use of keeping the uniform?"

"But, Daddy," he said, "they're so good."

"You're good, too. You can field grounders. You can hit the ball. You know where to make the plays."

John gave the boy a choice: return the uniform or practice with the team. If, after the practice, he didn't feel that he was better than every other kid, he should quit.

Joey said he'd try.

As it happened, he turned out to be the best player on that Elks team.[2]

The belief that John Namath tried to instill in his son was not misplaced. The father used to sum up Joe's Little League career by telling about a particular game that represented his son's ability. John arrived late and asked about the score from someone who was at all of the games. There were no outs, the score was tied at 3, and all and the bases were loaded. "But don't worry," the man said. "They just put the little Namath kid in to pitch." Joe got three quick outs, including striking out the opposing team's best player, a boy who was two years older than Joe (and who later played football at Pitt). Then when Joe got up to bat, he hit the winning home run.[3]

BUSINESS AS USUAL

That kind of confident performance became the norm for Namath. As a high school basketball player, he was fast, he could shoot, and unlike most of his opponents and teammates, he could dunk. As a football player, he led his Beaver Falls team to win the Western Pennsylvania Interscholastic Athletic League championship. Before one of the games when Joe had a sore ankle, the confident quarterback, who also punted for the team, assured his worried coach, "Don't worry, coach, we won't have to punt."[4]

Namath was heavily recruited out of high school, and some referred to him as the best quarterback in the country. He ended up at the University of Alabama, where he became a star and led the Crimson Tide to a national championship.

Entering the pros, Namath was again considered the best quarterback of his class. It's said that the NFL's New York Giants wanted him badly, but the AFL's New York Jets got him. Namath signed a contract in 1965 whose terms dwarfed anything previously seen in professional football—in any professional sport, for that matter.

For three years, Namath played his heart out, broke passing records, underwent knee surgeries, and led his team to losing seasons. But he never lost his belief in himself. He knew he could play and lead his team to victory. In the 1968 season, his fourth, he finally led his team to a winning season and a victory in the AFL championship. He didn't care that nobody gave the Jets a chance to win against the NFL team. He believed in himself and his ability to win. He also convinced his team. What most people didn't know was that Namath had watched hours of film on the Colts, as he did for every opponent. "The one-eyed monster—it never lies," Namath used to say, referring to the projector he kept in his apartment.[5] He showed his teammates what he saw. They could win that game. And that's exactly what they did. The Jets beat the Colts 16 to 7. Most people consider it to be the biggest upset in Super Bowl history.

What would have happened to Joe Namath if his father hadn't challenged him to believe in himself and his ability when he was only eight years old? Maybe he would have ended up like his brothers, talented athletes who dropped out of high school or college to work in the local mill or machine shop. Or maybe he would have ended up a pool hustler. It's hard to say. But one thing is certain: he wouldn't have ended up in the Pro Football Hall of Fame in Canton, Ohio. It takes more than talent to end up there; it also takes belief.

BELIEFS WORTH BUYING INTO

I don't know what your talent is, but I do know this: it will not be lifted to its highest level unless you also have belief. Talent alone is never enough. If you want to become your best, you need to believe your best. You need to . . .

1. Believe in Your Potential

Your potential is a picture of what you can become. Inventor Thomas Edison remarked, "If we did all the things we are capable of doing, we would literally astonish ourselves."

Too often we see what is, not what could be. People looked at Joe Namath when he was young, and they saw a skinny, undersized kid. They looked at him when he was in high school, and they saw a kid who hung around with the wrong crowd and didn't do his homework. They looked at him when he was in the pros, and they saw a guy with bad knees. But he saw himself as a champion. If you could see yourself in terms of your true potential, you wouldn't recognize yourself.

When my daughter, Elizabeth, was in high school, she had a "glamour shot" taken of herself to give me as a gift. That was the rage at the time. A person would go into the photo studio and be made up to look like a movie star. When I first saw the picture, I thought, *That's not the way she looks every day, but that's Elizabeth. That's truly her.* Likewise, that's what it's like when you see and believe in your potential. If you were to see yourself as you could be, you would look better than you ever imagined. I just wish I could show you a picture of yourself with your potential intact.

Indian statesman Mohandas Gandhi said, "The difference between what we do and what we are capable of doing would suffice to solve most of the world's problems." Closer to home, it would also suffice to solve most of our *individual* problems. We must first believe in our potential if we are to do what we're capable of.

Too many people fall far short of their real potential. John Powell, author of *The Secret of Staying in Love*, estimates that the average person reaches only 10 percent of his potential, sees only 10 percent of the beauty that is all around him, hears only 10 percent of its music and poetry, smells only 10 percent of its fragrance, and tastes only 10 percent of the deliciousness of being alive. Most neither see nor seize their potential.

Executive coach Joel Garfinkle recounts a story by writer Mark Twain in which a man died and met Saint Peter at the pearly gates. Immediately realizing that Saint Peter was a wise and knowledgeable individual, the man inquired, "Saint Peter, I have been interested in military history for many years. Tell me who was the greatest general of all time?"

Saint Peter quickly responded, "Oh, that's a simple question. It's that man right over there."

"You must be mistaken," responded the man, now very perplexed. "I knew that man on earth and he was just a common laborer."

"That's right, my friend," assured Saint Peter. "He would have been the greatest general of all time, if he had been a general."[6]

Cartoonist Charles Schulz offered this comparison: "Life is a ten-speed bike. Most of us have gears we never use." What are we saving those gears for? It's not good to travel through life without breaking a sweat. So what's the problem? Most of the time it's self-imposed limitations. They limit us as much as real ones. Life is difficult enough as it is. We make it more difficult when we impose *additional* limitations on ourselves. Industrialist Charles Schwab observed, "When a man has put a limit on what he *will* do, he has put a limit on what he *can* do."

> "Life is a ten-speed bike. Most of us have gears we never use."
>
> —Charles Schulz

In *If It Ain't Broke . . . Break It!* Robert J. Kriegel and Louis Patler write,

> We don't have a clue as to what people's limits are. All the tests, stopwatches, and finish lines in the world can't measure human potential. When someone is pursuing their dream, they'll go far beyond what seems to be their limitations. The potential that exists within us is

limitless and largely untapped . . . When you think of limits, you create them.[7]

We often put too much emphasis on mere physical challenges and obstacles, and give too little credence to psychological and emotional ones. Sharon Wood, the first North American woman to climb Mount Everest, learned some things about that after making her successful climb. She said, "I discovered it wasn't a matter of physical strength, but a matter of psychological strength. The conquest lay within my own mind to penetrate those barriers of self-imposed limitations and get through to that good stuff—the stuff called potential, 90 percent of which we rarely use."

> "When a man has put a limit on what he *will* do, he has put a limit on what he *can* do."
>
> —Charles Schwab

In 2001, I was invited to Mobile, Alabama, to speak to six hundred NFL coaches and scouts at the Senior Bowl. That's the game played by two teams of college seniors who have been invited to participate because they are believed to have NFL potential. In the morning I taught from *The 17 Indisputable Laws of Teamwork,* which had just been published. And in the afternoon, I attended a workout session in which the players were tested for running speed, reaction time, jumping ability, and so forth.

One of the coaches in attendance, Dick Vermeil, chatted with me as I watched. At some point he said, "You know, we can measure many of their skills, but it's impossible to measure the heart. Only the player can determine that."

Your potential is really up to you. It doesn't matter what others might think. It doesn't matter where you came from. It doesn't even matter what you might have believed about yourself at a previous time in your life. It's about what lies within you and whether you can bring it out.

There's a story about a farm boy from Colorado who loved to hike and rock climb. One day while climbing in the mountains, he found an eagle's nest with an egg in it. He took the egg from the nest, and when he got home, he put it under a hen along with her other eggs.

Since he hatched among chicks, the eagle thought he was a chicken. He learned chicken behavior from his "mother" and scratched in the chicken yard along with his "siblings." He didn't know any better. And when he sometimes felt strange stirrings within him, he didn't know what to do with them, so he ignored them or suppressed them. After all, if he was a chicken, he should behave like a chicken.

Then one day an eagle flew over the farm, and the chicken-yard eagle looked up and saw him. In that moment, he realized he wanted to be like that eagle. He wanted to fly high. He wanted to go to the mountain peaks he saw in the distance. He spread his wings, which were much larger and stronger than those of his siblings. Suddenly he understood that he was like that eagle. Though he had never flown before, he possessed the instinct and the capabilities. He spread his wings once more, and he flew, unsteadily at first, but then with greater power and control. As he soared and climbed, he knew that he had finally discovered his true self.

Phillips Brooks, writer of the song "O Little Town of Bethlehem," remarked, "When you discover you've been leading only half a life, the other half is going to haunt you until you develop it." Not only is that true, but I'd also say this: Not reaching your potential is a real tragedy. To reach your potential, you must first believe in your potential, and determine to live way beyond average.

2. Believe in Yourself

It's one thing to believe that you possess remarkable potential. It's another thing to have enough faith in yourself that you think you can fulfill it. When it comes to believing in themselves, some people are agnostic! That's not only a shame; it also keeps them from becoming what they could be. Psychologist and philosopher William James emphasized that "there is but one cause of human failure. And that is man's lack of faith in his true self."

People who believe in themselves get better jobs and perform better in them than those who don't. Martin Seligman, professor of psychology at the University of Pennsylvania, did some research at a major life insurance company and found that the salespeople who expected to succeed sold 37 percent more insurance than those who didn't.[8] The impact of belief in self begins early.

> When it comes to believing in themselves, some people are agnostic!

Some researchers assert that when it comes to academic achievement in school, there is a greater correlation between self-confidence and achievement than there is between IQ and achievement.

Attorney and marketing expert Kerry Randall observed, "Successful people believe in themselves, especially when others do not." That's no more evident than in sports. Coaches have told me that self-confidence within players is especially important in tight ball games. During crunch time, some players want the ball. Others want to hide. The ones who want the ball are the self-confident ones, like Namath, who held the ball down to the last second during a high school basketball game in which his team was one point behind. While his team's leading scorer kept shouting, "Give me the ball!" Namath was as cool as ever and sank the winning shot as the buzzer sounded.[9]

People with confidence live by a credo that is said to hang in the office of golfer Arnold Palmer. It reads,

> If you think you are beaten, you are.
> If you think you dare not, you don't.
> If you'd like to win, but think you can't
> It's almost certain you won't . . .

Life's battles don't always go
To the stronger or faster man,
But soon or late, the man who wins
Is the man who thinks he can.[10]

Only with belief in yourself will you be able to reach your potential.

3. Believe in Your Mission

What else is necessary to lift a person's talent? Believing in what you are doing. In fact, even if the odds are against your accomplishing what you desire, confidence will help you. William James asserted, "The one thing that will guarantee the successful conclusion of a doubtful undertaking is faith in the beginning that you can do it." How does this kind of belief help?

Belief in your mission will empower you. Having confidence in what you are doing gives you the power to achieve it. Architect Frank Lloyd Wright noted, "The thing always happens that you really believe in; and the belief in a thing makes it happen." Confident people can usually evaluate a task before undertaking it and know whether they can do it. In that belief is great power.

Belief in your mission will encourage you. A woman with a will to win will have her naysayers. A man on a mission will have his critics. What often allows such people to keep going in a negative environment? Belief in the mission.

Playwright Neil Simon advises, "Don't listen to those who say, 'It's not done that way.' Maybe it's not, but maybe you'll do it anyway. Don't listen to those who say, 'You're taking too big a chance.' Michelangelo would have painted the Sistine floor, and it would surely be rubbed out today." Simon should know. He has been awarded seventeen Tony Awards, five Drama Desk Awards, and two Pulitzer Prizes.

Obviously he believes in what he does.

Belief in your mission will enlarge you. The more you believe in your potential, yourself, and your mission, the more you will be able to accomplish. If you keep believing, you will someday find yourself doing what you once considered impossible.

Actor Christopher Reeve had that perspective, and it carried him far. He once told an audience,

America has a tradition many nations probably envy: we frequently achieve the impossible. That's part of our national character. That's what got us from one coast to another. That's what got us the largest economy in the world. That's what got us to the moon. On the wall of my room when I was in rehab was a picture of the space shuttle blasting off, autographed by every astronaut now at NASA. On top of the picture says, "We found nothing is impossible." That should be our motto . . . It's something that we as a nation must do together. So many of our dreams at first seem impossible, then they seem improbable, and then, when we summon the will, they soon become inevitable. If we can conquer outer space, we should be able to conquer inner space, too. The frontier of the brain, the central nervous system, and all the afflictions of the body that destroy so many lives, and rob . . . so much potential.[11]

Do you believe in your mission? Are you confident that you can accomplish great tasks? Do you expect to achieve your goals? These are necessary ingredients to lift your talent from potential to fruition.

I need to say one more thing about mission. It needs to include people. Only a life lived for others is worthwhile. As you fulfill your mission, will others around you say . . .

"My life is *better* as a result," or
"My life is *worse* as a result"?

If you think it won't be the former, then the mission may not be worth doing.

One of my prized possessions is a simple crystal paperweight. It doesn't have an especially artistic design. It's not especially valuable monetarily. But it means a lot to me because of what is engraved in it and who gave it to me. It says,

> John—
> Pastor, Mentor, Friend
> "Thank you for believing in me."
> Love,
> Dan

It was a gift from Dan Reiland, who worked with me for twenty years as a staff member, as my second in command, and then as a senior vice president at one of my companies. Dan is someone I would go to battle with. He's like a kid brother to me. The mission we pursued together made *both* of us better. That's the kind of person you want working with you—and the kind of result.

TALENT + *BELIEF* = A TALENT-PLUS PERSON
PUTTING THE TALENT-PLUS FORMULA INTO ACTION

So how do you become a talent-plus person? You tap into a natural chain of actions that begins with belief and ends with positive action:

Belief Determines Expectations

If you want your talent to be lifted to its highest level, then you don't begin by focusing on your talent. You begin by harnessing the power of your mind. Your beliefs control everything you do. Accomplishment is more than a matter of working harder or smarter. It's also a matter of believing positively. Someone called it the "sure enough" syndrome. If you expect to fail, sure enough, you will. If you expect to succeed, sure

> You will become
> on the outside
> what you believe
> on the inside.

enough, you will. You will become on the outside what you believe on the inside.

Personal breakthroughs begin with a change in your beliefs. Why? Because your beliefs determine your expectations, and your expectations determine your actions.

A belief is a habit of mind in which confidence becomes a conviction that we embrace. In the long run, a belief is more than an idea that a person possesses. It is an idea that possesses a person. Benjamin Franklin said, "Blessed is he who expects nothing, for he shall never be disappointed." If you want to achieve something in life, you have to be willing to be disappointed. You need to expect to succeed. Does that mean you always will? No. You will fail. You will make mistakes. But if you expect to win, you maximize your talent, and you keep trying. Then like Joe Namath, you will eventually succeed.

Attorney Kerry Randall said, "Contrary to popular opinion, life does not get better by chance, life gets better by change. And this change always takes place inside; it is the change of thought that creates the better life." Improvement comes from change, but change requires confidence. For that reason, you need to make confidence in yourself a priority. You need to put believing in your potential, yourself, your mission, and your fellow human beings at the top of your list. President Franklin Delano Roosevelt asserted, "The only limit to our realization of tomorrow will be our doubts of today." Don't let your doubts cause your expector to expire.

Harvey McKay tells the story of a professor who stood before a class of thirty senior molecular biology students. Before he passed out the final exam, he stated, "I have been privileged to be your instructor this semester, and I know how hard you have worked to prepare for this test. I also know most of you are off to medical school or grad school next fall. I am well aware of how much pressure you are under to keep your GPAs up, and because I am confident that you know this material, I am prepared to offer an automatic B to anyone who opts to skip taking the final exam."

The relief was audible. A number of students jumped up from their desks, thanking their professor for the lifeline he had thrown them.

"Any other takers?" he asked. "This is your last opportunity."

One more student decided to go.

The instructor then handed out the final exam, which consisted of two sentences. "Congratulations," it read, "you have just received an A in this class. Keep believing in yourself."[12] It was a just reward for the students who had worked hard and believed in themselves.

Expectations Determine Actions

Fred Smith Sr., one of my mentors and the author of *Leading with Integrity*, says that a linguist with Wycliffe Bible translators told him that in twenty of the world's most primitive languages, the word for *belief* is the same as the word for *do*. It is only as people become more "sophisticated" that they begin to separate the meaning of one word from the other. That insight is very telling because most people separate belief from action. So how can we bring these two things back together? Through our expectations.

We cannot live in a way that is inconsistent with our expectations for ourselves. It just doesn't happen. I once heard a story that I have not been able to confirm about an aviation pioneer who built a plane the year before the Wright brothers made their historic flight in Kitty Hawk. The plane sat in this inventor's barn because he was afraid to fly it. Maybe it was because it had never been done before. Maybe it was because he expected it to fail—I don't know. It's said that after the news reached him about Orville and Wilbur Wright, the man flew his plane. Before then, he didn't believe in himself enough to take the risk.

> We cannot live in a way that is inconsistent with our expectations for ourselves.

There are two kinds of people in this world: those who want to get things done and those who don't want to make mistakes. The Wright brothers were of the first type. The would-be aviation pioneer was of the

> There are two kinds of people in this world: those who want to get things done and those who don't want to make mistakes.

second. If you're of the first type, then you already expect to believe in yourself and take risks. But what if you're of the second type? There's good news: you can grow.

A story in Robert Schuller's book *Tough Times Never Last, but Tough People Do!* is about Sir Edmund Hillary, who was the first person to reach the summit of Mount Everest along with Tibetan Tenzing Norgay. Prior to his success on Everest, Hillary had been part of another expedition, in which the team not only had failed to reach the summit but also had lost one of its members. At a reception for the expedition members in London, Hillary stood to address the audience. Behind the platform was a huge photograph of Everest. Hillary turned to face the image of the mountain and exclaimed, "Mount Everest, you have defeated us. But I will return. And I will defeat you. *Because you cannot get any bigger, and I can.*"[13]

I don't know what challenges you face. They may be getting bigger every day, or they may already be as big as they can get, like Mount Everest. But I do know this: the only way you can rise to meet the challenges effectively is to expect to. You don't overcome challenges by making them smaller. You overcome them by making yourself bigger!

Actions Determine Results

Results come from actions. That may seem obvious in the physical realm. Sir Isaac Newton's third law of motion states that for every action, there is an equal and opposite reaction. However, in the human realm, many people don't make the connection. They simply hope for good results. Hope is not a strategy. If you want good results, you need to perform good actions. If you want to perform good actions, you must have positive expectations. To have positive expectations, you have to first believe. It all goes back to that. Radio personality Paul Harvey observed, "If you don't live it, you don't believe it." It all starts with belief.

A popular activity for tourists in Switzerland is mountain climbing—not the type of climbing that the world-class mountaineers do to scale the world's highest peaks. Maybe it would be more accurate to call it high-altitude hiking. Groups depart from a "base camp" early in the morning with the intention of making it to the top of the mountain by mid-afternoon.

I talked to a guide about his experiences with these groups, and he described an interesting phenomenon. He said that for most of these expeditions, the group stops at a halfway house where the climbers have lunch, catch their breath, and prepare themselves for the last leg of the rigorous climb. Invariably some members of the group opt for the warmth and comfort of the halfway house and decide not to climb to the

> "If you don't live it, you don't believe it."
>
> —Paul Harvey

top. As the rest of the group leaves, the ones who stay are happy and talkative. It's a party. But when the shadows begin to lengthen, many make their way over to the window that looks up the mountain. And the room gets quiet as they wait for the climbers to return. Why is that? They realize they've missed a special opportunity. Most of them will never be in that part of the world again. They won't ever have a chance to climb that mountain again. They missed it.

That's what it's like when people don't make the most of their talent, when they don't believe in themselves and their potential, when they don't act on their belief and try to make the most of every opportunity.

Don't allow that to happen to you! Live the life you were meant to. Try to see yourself as you could be, and then do everything in your power to believe that you can become that person. That is the first important step in becoming a talent-plus person.

TALENT + *BELIEF* APPLICATION EXERCISES

At the end of each chapter of this book, you will find application exercises like the ones below to help you put into practice the ideas contained in the chapter. *Learning* an idea isn't enough to make a person grow; you must *put ideas into practice* to make the most of your talent and become a talent-plus person. I encourage you to create a growth journal and use it as you answer questions and record observations as you do assignments. It will help you to stay focused and chart your progress.

1. Write a short description of yourself as you are today.

2. What are your top five talents? If you have not explored them before, you may have to do some work to answer this question. If necessary, buy a book like *Now, Discover Your Strengths* by Marcus Buckingham and Donald O. Clifton and take the Strengths Finder quiz, or do the exercises in *What Color Is Your Parachute?* by Richard Nelson Bolles. In addition, think about your most significant and fulfilling accomplishments. And interview colleagues, family, and close friends to get their input concerning your talents. When you have completed your research, list those strengths.

3. List the three activities you are most passionate about.

4. Think about what opportunities may be presenting themselves to you. They may be related to where you live, where you work, who you know, or what's happening in your industry or area of interest. List as many opportunities as you can.

5. Take some time to consider what kind of picture emerges based on these talents, interests, and opportunities. How might they come together for someone other than you, someone with few obstacles or limitations—someone who was in the right place at the right time? Dream big—no idea is too outrageous. Brainstorm what someone in that situation might be able to do, what he or she could become. What would be this person's mission? Using a phrase or short description, write down these things.

6. What you just wrote is a description of who you could be. It is a picture of your potential. How does it compare with the description you wrote in Exercise 1? Believe in your potential, yourself, your mission, and your fellow human beings. How can you light the fire of your belief and increase your expectations to become that person? Give yourself an action plan to do it. Enlist the help of others if needed.

2

PASSION ENERGIZES YOUR TALENT

W hat carries people to the top? What makes them take risks, go the extra mile, and do whatever it takes to achieve their goals? It isn't talent. It's passion. Passion is more important than a plan. Passion creates fire. It provides fuel. I have yet to meet a passionate person who lacked energy. As long as the passion is there, it doesn't matter if they fail. It doesn't matter how many times they fall down. It doesn't matter if others are against them or if people say they cannot succeed. They keep going and make the most of whatever talent they possess. They are talent-plus people and do not stop until they succeed.

LOOKING FOR DIRECTION

What does a boy like Rueben Martinez do in a place like Miami, Arizona? Miami is a small mining town of two thousand people in the southeastern part of Arizona that has changed little since its founding in 1907. When Rueben was growing up in the 1940s and 1950s, most of the town's jobs came from the copper mining industry, as they still do. Rueben's parents, who were Mexican immigrants, worked in the mines.

There wasn't much to do in Miami. But Rueben had a curious mind, and he found his passion in books—not necessarily an easy task when your parents aren't big readers and your town is so small that it doesn't even have a public library.

"My mother always wanted me to put down my books and clean the yard," recalls Rueben. "So I would hide in the outhouse and read because no one would bother me there."[1]

The child was so desperate for reading material that he became very industrious. "Every morning at 6:45," he says, "the newspaper boy would deliver the newspaper and, when it hit my neighbor's side of the house, I would wake up, go out the back door, lean against my neighbor's house and read the newspaper every morning thoroughly. Then I'd fold that newspaper and put it back as neatly as I could."[2]

Eventually Rueben got caught. But his neighbor didn't mind and encouraged him to keep reading. Rueben was also inspired and assisted by two of his teachers. They continually encouraged his love of reading and loaned him books.

NEW DIRECTION

When he was seventeen, Rueben moved to Los Angeles to find greater opportunities. The moment he saw the Pacific Ocean, he knew he'd never live in Arizona again. He took whatever jobs he could. He worked as a grocery clerk, crane operator, and factory worker, including at the Bethlehem Steel Mill in Maywood. But then one day he saw an ad for a barber college, and he was captivated by the idea of attending. "I saw those smocks they wore, so white," says Martinez. "It was the opposite of the dirt of the mining world. I wanted clean."[3]

In the 1970s, Rueben Martinez opened his own barbershop and became his own boss. He was making a better life for himself. But he never lost his passion for reading, a passion he wanted to pass on to others, especially young people in the Hispanic and Latino communities. According to a National Endowment for the Arts survey, the reading level among Hispanics is half that of non-Hispanic whites.[4] Martinez wanted to change that.

He started out by lending volumes from his two-hundred-book collection to people waiting for a haircut. The books ranged from Spanish-language masterpieces like *One Hundred Years of Solitude* by Gabriel Garcia Marquez and *Don Quixote* by Cervantes, to American books by Hemingway or Silverstein translated into Spanish, to a signed autobiography by actor Anthony Quinn. But often his patrons forgot to return the books, which frustrated Martinez and diminished his supply for other patrons. His solution? Start selling books. In 1993, Martinez offered books for sale for the first time. He started out with two titles. But it didn't take long for sales to increase, and he started carrying more titles. He became an advocate for literacy. He talked to parents about reading to their children. He talked to young people about diving into books. And he contacted high-profile authors, such as Isabel Allende, and invited them to his shop. Martinez recalls Allende's reaction when she showed up. "When she came into the barbershop bookstore, she said, 'Is this it?' And I said, 'This is it.' Because I only had two book shelves. I had art. I had a barber chair . . . And she said, 'I like it.' And we had a good time. But we also had one of the biggest audiences that ever came to see an author in the city of Santa Ana. We had quite a few people . . . about 3,000."[5]

A few years later, the barbershop with books became a bookstore with a symbolic barber chair. Martinez called his store Librería Martínez Books and Art Gallery. "We started out with two books," says Martinez, "then 10, then 25. Little by little, we've sold over 2 million books. That's what happens if you dare to dream."[6] The store now stocks seventeen thousand titles and has become one of the country's largest collections of Spanish-language books. Martinez opened a second store in 2001 and also a third store just for children. He tells parents, "Do you want your child to be ahead of the line or at the back of the line, moms and dads?

You have to support, endorse, and read to your kid . . . if you do that, your kid will be at the head of the line . . . and be someone special in this world. Reading does it."[7]

Momentum

Rueben Martinez's talent for promoting literacy has blossomed as he has allowed his passion to explode. He started hosting a weekly cable show on Univision. He cofounded the Latino Book Festival with actor Edward James Olmos. And he started speaking at schools and to other groups to promote literacy. He advises his audiences to read twenty minutes a day so that they consume one million words a year. One of his favorite sayings is that books can take a person all over the world—a library card will take you farther than a driver's license.

"I started reading at a very, very young age," says Martinez, "and I still do. I read a lot every day. I look forward to that. I love literature."[8]

People are starting to recognize Martinez's talent. In 2004, he won a MacArthur Foundation fellowship—often called a "genius grant"—for "fusing the roles of marketplace and community center to inspire appreciation of literature and preserve Latino literary heritage." He became the U.S. Small Business Administration's 2004 Minority Business Advocate of the Year. He received an honorary doctorate in humane letters from Whittier College in 2005 and was also named one of Inc.com's twenty-six most fascinating entrepreneurs. Carlos Azula of Random House points out that "Rueben isn't just selling books; he's selling reading."[9]

Martinez isn't stopping. In his midsixties, he has no intention of resting on his laurels. He is energized by what he does.

"I made more money cutting hair than selling books," notes Martinez, age sixty-four. "But the joy of my life is what I'm doing now."[10] Martinez wants to create a bilingual Borders-style chain of bookstores across the nation, hoping to establish twenty-five stores by 2012.

"If I had stayed with my factory jobs," observes Martinez, "I would have been living a comfortable retirement now. But I chose to go on my own as a barber. Now with the bookstores, I'm going to work for the rest of my life. My kids think I'm crazy."[11] No, he's not crazy. He's just filled with passion!

Your Passion Can Empower You

Passion can energize every aspect of a person's life—including his talent. Have you ever known a person with great passion who lacked the energy to act on what mattered to her? I doubt it. A passionate person with limited talent will outperform a passive person who possesses greater talent. Why? Because passionate people act with boundless enthusiasm, and they just keep on going! Talent plus passion energizes.

Authors Robert J. Kriegel and Louis Patler cite a study of 1,500 people over twenty years that shows how passion makes a significant difference in a person's career:

At the outset of the study, the group was divided into Group A, 83 percent of the sample, who were embarking on a career chosen for the prospects of making money now in order to do what they wanted later, and Group B, the other 17 percent of the sample, who had chosen their career path for the reverse reason, they were going to pursue what they wanted to do now and worry about the money later.

The data showed some startling revelations:

- At the end of the 20 years, 101 of the 1,500 had become millionaires.
- Of the millionaires, all but one—100 out of 101—were from Group B, the group that had chosen to pursue what they loved![12]

The old saying is true: "Find something you like to do so much that you'd gladly do it for nothing, and if you learn to do it well, someday people will be happy to pay you for it." When that's the case, then true are the words of a motto that Dr. Charles Mayo kept on his office wall: "There's no fun like work."

THE POWER OF PASSION

There really is no substitute for passion when it comes to energizing your talent. Take a look at what passion can do for you:

1. Passion Is the First Step to Achievement

Loving what you do is the key that opens the door for achievement. When you don't like what you're doing, it really shows—no matter how hard you try to pretend it doesn't. You can become like the little boy named Eddie whose grandmother was an opera lover. She had season tickets, and when Eddie turned eight, she decided to take him to a performance of Wagner—in German—as his birthday present. The next day, at his mother's prompting, the child wrote the following in a thank-you note: "Dear Grandmother, Thank you for the birthday present. It is what I always wanted, but not very much. Love, Eddie."

It's difficult to achieve when you don't have the desire to do so. That's why passion is so important. There is a story about Socrates in which a proud and disdainful young man came to the philosopher and, with a smirk, said, "O great Socrates, I come to you for knowledge."

Seeing the shallow and vain young man for what he was, Socrates led the young man down to the sea into waist-deep water. Then he said, "Tell me again what you want."

"Knowledge," he responded with a smile.

Socrates grabbed the young man by his shoulders and pushed him down under the water, holding him there for thirty seconds. "Now, what do you want?"

"Wisdom, O great Socrates," the young man sputtered.

The philosopher pushed him under once again. When he let him up, he asked again, "What do you want?"

"Knowledge, O wise and . . . ," he managed to spit out before Socrates held him under again, this time even longer.

"What do you want?" the old man asked as he let him up again. The younger man coughed and gasped.

"Air!" he screamed. "I need air!"

"When you want knowledge as much as you just wanted air, then you will get knowledge," the old man stated as he returned to shore.

The only way you can achieve anything of significance is to really want it. Passion provides that.

2. Passion Increases Willpower

One of my roles as a motivational teacher is to try to help people reach their potential. For years, I tried to inspire passion in audiences by going about it the wrong way. I used to tell people about what made me passionate, what made me want to get out and do my best. But I could see that it wasn't having the effect I desired—people just didn't respond. I couldn't ignite others' passion by sharing my own.

I decided to change my focus. Instead of sharing my passion, I started helping others discover their passion. To do that, I ask these questions:

What do you sing about?
What do you cry about?
What do you dream about?

The first two questions speak to what touches you at a deep level today. The third answers what will bring you fulfillment tomorrow. The answers to these questions can often help people discover their true passion.

> The secret to willpower
> is what someone once
> called *wantpower*.

While everybody can possess passion, not everyone takes the time to discover it. And that's a shame. Passion is fuel for the will. Passion turns your have-to's into want-to's. What we accomplish in life is based less on what we want and more on how much we want it. The secret to willpower is what someone once called *wantpower*. People who want something enough usually find the willpower to achieve it.

You can't help people become winners unless they want to win. Champions become champions from within, not from without.

3. Passion Produces Energy

When you have passion, you become energized. You don't have to produce perseverance; it is naturally present in you. It helps you to enjoy the journey as much as reaching the destination. Without it, achievement becomes a long and difficult road.

For many years my wife, Margaret, has called me the Energizer Bunny because of the commercials where the battery-operated rabbit keeps going and going. I guess she does so with good reason. I do have a lot of energy. There are always things I hope to do, people I want to see, and goals I want to reach. The reason is passion! We often call people high energy or low energy based on how much they do, but I have come to the conclusion that it might be more appropriate to call them high or low *passion*.

During a Q-and-A session at a conference, an attendee once asked me, "What is the secret of your passion?" It took me only a moment to be able to articulate it:

1. I am gifted at what I do (strength zone).
2. What I do makes a difference (results).
3. When I do what I was made to do, I feel most alive (purpose).

I believe all passionate people feel that way. Aviation pioneer Charles Lindbergh observed, "It is the greatest shot of adrenaline to be doing what you've wanted to do so badly. You almost feel like you could fly without the plane."

Some people say that they feel burned out. The truth is that they probably never were on fire in the first place. Writer and editor Norman Cousins said, "Death isn't the greatest loss in life. The greatest loss is what dies inside of us while we live." Without passion, a part of us does becomes dead. And if we're not careful, we could end up like the person whose tomb-stone read, "Died at 30. Buried at 60." Don't allow that to happen to you. Be like Rueben Martinez who is still going strong beyond age sixty. People often describe him as acting half his age. What gives him such energy? His passion!

> "Death isn't the greatest loss in life. The greatest loss is what dies inside of us while we live."
>
> —Norman Cousins

4. Passion Is the Foundation for Excellence

Passion can transform someone from average to excellent. I can tell you that from experience. When I was in high school, I wasn't a great student. My priorities were basketball first, friends second, and studies a distant third. Why? Because playing basketball and spending time with friends were things I was passionate about. I studied, but only to please my parents. School held little appeal for me.

Everything changed when I went to college. For the first time I was studying subjects that mattered to me. They were interesting, and they would apply to my future career. My grades went up because my passion did. In high school I was sometimes on the principal's "list" (which was not a good thing), but in college I continually made the *dean's* list. Passion fired my desire to achieve with excellence.

Civil rights leader Martin Luther King Jr. asserted, "If a man hasn't discovered something that he will die for, he isn't fit to live." When you find purpose, you find passion. And when you find passion, it energizes your talent so that you can achieve excellence.

5. Passion Is the Key to Success

People are such that whenever anything fires their souls, impossibilities vanish. Perhaps that's why philosopher-poet Ralph Waldo Emerson wrote, "Every great and commanding movement in the annals of the world is the triumph of enthusiasm."

> "Every great and commanding movement in the annals of the world is the triumph of enthusiasm."
>
> —Ralph Waldo Emerson

I read about two hundred executives who were asked what makes people successful. The number one quality they cited was enthusiasm, not talent—80 percent of them recognized that there needed to be a fire within to achieve success.

The most talented people aren't always the ones who win. If they did, how could anyone explain the success of the 1980 U.S. Olympic hockey team, which was depicted in the movie *Miracle*, or the Hall of Fame careers of basketball's Larry Bird or football's Joe Montana? Of Montana, teammate Ronnie Lott said, "You can't measure the size of his heart with a tape measure or a stopwatch." It takes more than talent to create success. It takes passion.

6. Passion Makes a Person Contagious

Writer and promotional publicist Eleanor Doan remarked, "You cannot kindle a fire in any other heart until it is burning within your own." I believe that's true. One of my favorite subjects is communication. I have studied and taught it for years, and I always enjoy observing great communicators in action. I believe that people are instructed by reason, but they are inspired by passion.

Even a brief review of effective leaders and businesspeople through-out history illustrates that their passion "caught on" with others. One of my favorites is Winston Churchill. In the 1930s, Churchill was begin-ning to fade from view in British politics. But with the rise of Hitler came a rise in Churchill's passion. Long before others did, Churchill spoke out against the Nazis. He had a passion to protect freedom and democracy. And when Hitler declared war and sought to conquer Europe and crush England, Churchill's passion for resistance became infused in the people of Britain and eventually the United States. Without Churchill, the fate of the free world might have turned out to be quite different.

TALENT + PASSION = A TALENT-PLUS PERSON
PUTTING THE TALENT-PLUS FORMULA INTO ACTION

If you don't possess the energy that you desire, then you need to fire up your passion. Here is how I suggest you proceed:

1. Prioritize Your Life According to Your Passion

People who have passion but lack priorities are like individuals who find themselves in a lonely log cabin deep in the woods on a cold snowy night and then light a bunch of small candles and place them all around the room. They don't create enough light to help them see, nor do they produce enough heat to keep them warm. At best, they merely make the room seem a bit more cheerful. On the other hand, people who possess priorities but no passion are like those who stack wood in the fireplace of that same cold cabin but never light the fire. But people who have passion with priorities are like those who stack the wood, light the fire, and enjoy the light and heat that it produces.

In the early 1970s, I realized that my talent would be maximized and my potential realized only if I matched my passion with my priorities. I was spending too much of my time doing tasks for which I possessed nei-ther talent nor passion. I had to make a change—to align what I felt strongly about with what I was doing. It made a huge difference in my life. It didn't eliminate my troubles or remove my obstacles, but it empowered me to face them with greater energy and enthusiasm. For more than thirty years, I have worked to maintain that alignment of priorities and passion. And as I have, I've kept in mind this quote by journalist Tim Redmond, which I put in a prominent place for a year to keep me on track: "There are many things that will catch my eye, but there are only a few that catch my heart. It is those I consider to pursue."

> "There are many things that will catch my eye, but there are only a few that catch my heart. It is those I consider to pursue."
>
> —Tim Redmond

Prioritizing your life according to your passion can be risky. For most people, it requires a major realignment in their work and private lives. But you can't be a talent-plus person and play it safe. Advertising agency president Richard Edler stated this:

Safe living generally makes for regrets later on. We are all given talents and dreams. Sometimes the two don't match. But more often than not, we compromise both before ever finding out. Later on, as successful as we might be, we find ourselves looking back longingly to that time when we should have chased our *true* dreams and our *true* talents for all they were worth. Don't let yourself be pressured into thinking that your dreams or your talents aren't prudent. They were never meant to be prudent. They were meant to bring joy and fulfillment into your life.[13]

If your priorities are not aligned with your passion, then begin thinking about making changes in your life. Will change be risky? Probably. But which would you rather live with? The pain of risk or the pain of regret?

2. Protect Your Passion

If you've ever built a fire, then you know this: the natural tendency of fire is to go out. If you want to keep a fire hot, then you need to feed it, and you need to protect it. Not everyone in your life will help you do that when it comes to your passion. In truth, there are two kinds of people: fire*lighters*, who will go out of their way to help you keep your fire hot, and fire*fighters*, who will throw cold water on the fire of passion that burns within you.

How can you tell the firelighters from the firefighters? Listen to what they say. Firefighters use phrases like these:

- "It's not in the budget."
- "That's not practical."
- "We tried that before and it didn't work."
- "We've never done that before."
- "Yeah, but . . ."
- "The boss won't go for it."
- "If it ain't broke, then don't fix it."
- "That's not the way we do things around here."
- "It'll never work."
- "But who will do all the extra work?"
- "You're not _____ [smart, talented, young, old, etc.] enough."
- "You're getting too big for your britches."
- "Who do you think you are?"

If you've heard one or more of these phrases coming from people you know, you may want to create some distance between yourself and them. These firefighters focus on what's wrong rather than what's right. They find the cloud that comes with every silver lining. They doubt. They resist change. They keep people from reaching their potential by trying to put out the fire of their passion. Stay away from them. Instead, spend more time with people who see you not just as you are but as you could be; people who encourage your dreams, ignite your passion. I try to schedule a lunch or two with firelighters like these every month. They really fire me up and energize me to do what I know is best for me.

3. Pursue Your Passion with Everything You've Got

Rudy Ruettiger, upon whose life the movie *Rudy* was based, observed, "If you really, really believe in your dream, you'll get there. But you have to have passion and total commitment to make it happen. When you have passion and commitment, you don't need a complex plan. Your plan is your life is your dream."

What do you want to accomplish in your lifetime? How do you want to focus your energy: on survival, success, or significance? We live in a time and place with too many opportunities for survival alone. And there's more to life than mere success. We need to dream big. We need to adopt the perspective of someone like playwright George Bernard Shaw, who wrote,

> I am convinced that my life belongs to the whole community; and as long as I live, it is my privilege to do for it whatever I can, for the harder I work the more I live. I rejoice in the life for its own sake. Life is no brief candle to me. It is a sort of splendid torch which I got hold of for a moment, and I want to make it burn as brightly as possible before turning it over to future generations.

Shaw had passion—for life and his work. Your passion has the potential to provide you energy far beyond the limitations of your talent. In the end, you will be remembered for your passion. It is what will energize your talent. It is what will empower you to make your mark.

TALENT + PASSION
APPLICATION EXERCISES

1. To get a better handle on what you are passionate about, answer these questions:

    What makes you sing?

    What makes you cry?

    What makes you dream?

2. Make a list of the people in your life who try to put out the fire of your passion. If you can simply stop spending time with some of them, then plan to distance yourself. For those with whom you *must* spend time, create a strategy for minimizing the damage they can do to you. If you're married and your spouse is on this list, then seek help from a professional to help you repair the damage and rebuild relational bridges.

3. Think about key firelighters in your life, both past and present. Make spending time with some current firelighters a priority in the coming weeks. Write a note to a firelighter from your past to thank him or her for inspiring you to succeed.

4. Spend some time identifying the top priorities in your life. Think broadly and include the areas of work, family, recreation, health, and so on. Try to write out the priorities in order of importance.

5. Compare what you have written about your passions and talent from Chapter 1 and the priority list you just completed. How do they

match up? What could you change to help align them? What price will you likely pay if you neglect to make changes?

6. For whom can you be a firelighter? Where and when is your passion contagious? How can you add value to others by helping to light their fire?

3

INITIATIVE ACTIVATES YOUR TALENT

It's a cliché to say that every journey begins with the first step, yet it is still true. Talent-plus people don't wait for everything to be perfect to move forward. They don't wait for all the problems or obstacles to disappear. They don't wait until their fear subsides. They take initiative. They know a secret that good leaders understand: momentum is their friend. As soon as they take that first step and start moving forward, things become a little easier. If the momentum gets strong enough, many of the problems take care of themselves and talent can take over. But it starts only after you've taken those first steps.

DISASTER

On January 17, 1994, at 4:30 in the morning, a 6.7 magnitude earthquake struck the Los Angeles area. The earthquake was considered moderate (in contrast, the San Francisco earthquake of 1906 was believed to be more than ten times as powerful), but it still did an incredible amount of damage. More than 50 people died and 9,000 were seriously injured.[1] More than 22,000 people were left homeless, and

7,000 buildings were judged uninhabitable with an additional 22,000 sustaining major damage. The quake closed 9 hospitals, ruined several freeways, and collapsed 9 bridges.

The disaster, called the Northridge earthquake, was centered beneath the San Fernando Valley and did $44 billion in damage. Some experts considered the people who lived in the area to be fortunate because the earthquake occurred so early in the morning and on a holiday—Martin Luther King Day. Yet it was still the most monetarily costly earthquake in the history of the United States.

BREAKING GRIDLOCK

Los Angeles typically has the worst congestion and traffic delays of any large city in the nation. The effects of the Northridge earthquake made them worse. One of the most problematic areas was a section of Interstate 10 called the Santa Monica Freeway in the heart of Los Angeles—the most heavily used highway in the world. Every day it carries as many as 341,000 vehicles. Estimates were that it would cost California $1 million a day in lost wages, added fuel costs, and depressed business activity for every day it was closed.[2]

Environmental reviews and permitting requirements in California routinely take eighteen to twenty-four months. And construction on a project this size usually takes well over six months. At a cost of $1 million a day, that would mean the closure of the Santa Monica Freeway alone could create a negative impact costing Los Angeles more than $900 million!

Governor Pete Wilson knew that he needed to act to solve the problem. He initiated a plan to clear the way for quick reconstruction. Wilson recounts, "I issued an executive order suspending all statutes and regulations related to state contracting . . . My goal was to reopen I-10 within 6 months. Each contract included an incentive. If the work was late, we charged a fine, and if it was completed early, we paid a bonus."[3]

Demolition and removal work had begun a mere six hours after the earthquake. And on Monday, January 31, just two weeks after the earthquake, CalTrans, the state's agency responsible for freeway construction, invited five contractors to bid on the job of rebuilding the Santa Monica Freeway. Preliminary plans were made available to the contractors that night. But bids would be due Friday, February 4, at 10:00 a.m., just four days later! The contract would be awarded that night, and construction would commence on Saturday, February 5. And there were two other important pieces of information. First, the maximum amount of time allowed for construction was 140 days. Second, the financial stakes for finishing the project on time were high. If the winning contractor finished the project late, there would be a penalty of $200,000 per day. However, the contractor would receive $200,000 per day over the bid for each day it finished ahead of schedule.

STEPPING FORWARD

One company that received the offer to bid was C. C. Myers, which had completed several CalTrans projects in the past. The company bid the project at $14.7 million with the promise to finish in 140 days.[4] However, the management team privately set the goal of completing it in 100 days. If all went well, the company could make an additional $8 million.

But of course, everything didn't go well. C. C. Myers planned to work its crews in twelve-hour shifts, twenty-four hours a day, seven days a week. The crews quickly became fatigued. The solution? The managers hired more workers. A job that size usually required 65 carpenters. They hired 228. Instead of 15 iron workers, they employed 134. They continually initiated steps to speed up the project, such as using an expensive fast-drying concrete rather than their usual material. And when the company was informed that the railroads would require three weeks to deliver the steel beams needed for the project, C. C. Myers chartered its own trains to get the supplies from Arkansas and Texas to Los Angeles.[5]

C. C. Myers's initiative paid off. The company didn't just beat the 140-day deadline or even its own internal goal of 100 days. The crews finished the job in a mere 66 days—74 days ahead of schedule. And in the process the organization earned bonuses totaling $14.5 million, nearly the amount of the original bid.

The C. C. Myers organization had expertise, experience, and a proven track record. But the leaders didn't rely on those things alone. Why? They knew that talent alone is never enough. They knew they needed talent plus! To complete the Santa Monica Freeway project, they needed to show initiative in the bidding process, in the leadership of their people, and in the management of the details. That initiative brought them great success. And the company continues to show initiative. In the wake of the Northridge earthquake, Myers began working with engineers at the University of Southern California on innovations to strengthen existing freeways against earthquake damage.

Insights on Initiative

If you want to reach your potential, you have to show initiative, just as Governor Pete Wilson and the leaders at C. C. Myers did. Here's why:

1. Initiative Is the First Step to Anywhere You Want to Go

A tourist paused for a rest in a small town in the mountains. He sat down on a bench next to an old man in front of the town's only store. "Hi, friend," he said, "can you tell me something this town is noted for?"

"Well," answered the old man after a moment's hesitation, "you can start here and get to anywhere in the world you want."

That's true of nearly every location. Where you finish in life isn't determined so much by *where* you start as by *whether* you start. If you're willing to get started and keep initiating, there's no telling how far you might go.

That was the case for Les Brown. Les and his brother, Wes, were adopted when they were six weeks old, and they grew up in Liberty City, a poor section of Miami, Florida. As a child, Les was branded a slow learner and given little chance of success by many of his teachers. But with the encouragement of one of his high school teachers, who told him, "Someone else's opinion

> Where you finish in life isn't determined so much by *where* you start as by *whether* you start.

of you does not have to become your reality," Les managed to graduate from high school and later got a job as a radio DJ. With much hard work, he became a broadcast manager. He got involved in his community, became a community activist and leader, and eventually was elected to the state legislature for three terms. And then he turned his attention to public speaking, where he received the National Speakers Association's highest honor and was named one of the world's top five speakers according to Toastmasters in 1992. He has written books, hosts his own syndicated television show, owns a business, and commands $25,000 per appearance as a public speaker.

When he started life, most people wouldn't have given him much of a chance to succeed. Few thought he had talent. But he just kept moving forward, and he has since moved far beyond his detractors. Successful people initiate—and they follow through.[6]

2. Initiative Closes the Door to Fear

Author Katherine Paterson said, "To fear is one thing. To let fear grab you by the tail and swing you around is another." We all have fears. The question is whether we are going to control them or allow them to control us.

In 1995, my friend Dan Reiland and his wife, Patti, went skydiving along with a group of friends (including my writer, Charlie Wetzel). They approached the event with a mixture of excitement and fear. At the skydiving center in Southern California, they received only a few minutes of training to prepare them for their tandem jumps. Dan said they were feeling pretty good about the whole thing until a guy walked into the room and made a pitch to sell them life insurance.

As the plane ascended to 11,000 feet, they became increasingly nervous. Then they opened the sliding door at the back of the plane, at which point the fear factor went through the roof. Wishing they had worn rubber pants, they approached the door, each of them harnessed to a jumpmaster, and then launched themselves out of the plane.

Within seconds, they were hurtling toward the earth at 120 miles an hour. And after a free fall of 6,000 feet, they pulled their rip cords. When the canopy opened, with a forceful jolt they went from 120 miles an hour to 25 miles an hour. Dan said, "It made my underwear find places it had never found before!"

I laugh whenever Dan tells the story, but I was really surprised to learn from Dan and Patti that as petrified as they were before they jumped, all their fear was gone the second they left the plane.

Author and pastor Norman Vincent Peale asserted, "Action is a great restorer and builder of confidence. Inaction is not only the result, but the cause, of fear. Perhaps the action you take will be successful; perhaps different action or adjustments will have to follow. But any action is better than no action at all." If you want to close the door on fear, get moving.

3. Initiative Opens the Door to Opportunity

Benjamin Franklin, one of our nation's Founding Fathers, advised, "To succeed, jump as quickly at opportunities as you do at conclusions." People who take initiative and work hard may succeed, or they may fail. But anyone who doesn't take initiative is almost guaranteed to fail. I'm willing to bet that you have . . .

> a decision you should be making,
> a problem you should be solving,
> a possibility you should be examining,
> a project you should be starting,
> a goal you should be reaching,
> an opportunity you should be seizing,
> a dream you should be fulfilling.

No one can wait until everything is perfect to act and expect to be successful. It's better to be 80 percent sure and make things happen than it is to wait until you are 100 percent sure because by then, the opportunity will have already passed you by.

4. Initiative Eases Life's Difficulties

Psychiatrist M. Scott Peck famously stated, "Life is difficult." That's not most people's problem. Their response to life's difficulties is. Too many people wait around for their ship to come in. When they take that approach to life, they often find it to be hardship. The things that simply come to us are rarely the things we want. To have a chance at getting what we desire, we need to work for it.

> "Nothing is so fatiguing
> as the hanging on
> of an uncompleted task."
>
> —William James

Philosopher and author William James said, "Nothing is so fatiguing as the hanging on of an uncompleted task." The longer we let things slide, the harder they become. The hardest work is often the accumulation of many easy things that should have been done yesterday, last week, or last month. The only way to get rid of a difficult task is to do it. That takes initiative.

5. Initiative Is Often the Difference Between Success and Failure

A man who was employed by a duke and duchess in Europe was called in to speak to his employer.

"James," said the duchess, "how long have you been with us?"

"About thirty years, Your Grace," he replied.

"As I recall, you were employed to look after the dog."

"Yes, Your Grace," James replied.

"James, that dog died twenty-seven years ago."

"Yes, Your Grace," said James. "What would you like me to do now?"

Like James, too many people are waiting for someone else to tell them what to do next. Nearly all people have good thoughts, ideas, and intentions, but many of them never translate those into action. Doing so requires initiative.

Most people recognize that initiative is beneficial, yet they still frequently underestimate its true value. Perhaps the best illustration of the power of initiative is a story about the patenting of the telephone. In the 1870s, two men worked extensively on modifying and improving tele-graphy, which was the current technology. Both had ideas for transmitting sounds by wire, and both explored the transmission of the human voice electrically. What is remarkable is that both men— Alexander Graham Bell and Elisha Gray—filed their ideas at the patent office on the same day, February 14, 1876. Bell was the fifth person on record that day who filed for a patent. Gray, on the other hand, sent his attorney, and the man arrived more than an hour after Bell, applying for a caveat, a kind of declaration of intention to file for a patent. Those minutes cost Gray a fortune. Bell's claim was upheld in court, even though Gray complained that he had come up with the idea first.

Talent without initiative never reaches its potential. It's like a caterpillar that won't get into its cocoon. It will never transform, forever relegated to crawling on the ground, even though it had the potential to fly.

PEOPLE WHO LACK INITIATIVE

When it comes to initiative, there are really only four kinds of people:

1. People who do the right thing without being told

2. People who do the right thing when told

3. People who do the right thing when told more than once

4. People who never do the right thing, no matter what

Anyone who wants to become a talent-plus person needs to become the first kind of person. Why doesn't everyone do that? I think there are several reasons.

1. People Who Lack Initiative Fail to See the Consequences of Inaction

King Solomon of ancient Israel is said to have been the wisest person who ever lived. Every time I read Proverbs, which he is believed to have authored, I learn something. In recent years, I've enjoyed reading his words in a paraphrase called *The Message:*

> You lazy fool, look at an ant.
>> Watch it closely; let it teach you a thing or two.
> Nobody has to tell it what to do.
>> All summer it stores up food;
>> at harvest it stockpiles provisions.
> So how long are you going to laze around doing nothing?
>> How long before you get out of bed?
> A nap here, a nap there, a day off here, a day off there,
>> sit back, take it easy—do you know what comes next?
> Just this: You can look forward to a dirt-poor life,
>> poverty your permanent houseguest![7]

British civil servant and economist Sir Josiah Stamp remarked, "It is easy to dodge our responsibilities, but we cannot dodge the consequences of dodging our responsibilities." That is true. Whatever we do—or neglect to do—will catch up with us in the end. Those who never initiate often end up like the subject of English playwright James Albery's verse,

> He slept beneath the moon;
> He basked beneath the sun.
> He lived a life of going-to-do;
> And died with nothing done.[8]

Don't let that happen to you.

2. People Who Lack Initiative Want Someone Else to Motivate Them

There's a silly story of a man in a small town who was known as a great fisherman. Every morning he went out on a lake in his small boat, and in a short time, he returned with his boat loaded with fish.

One day a stranger showed up in town and asked if he could accompany the man the next time he went out. The fisherman said, "Sure, you can come. Meet me at the dock at five a.m."

The next morning the two men went far out into the lake and made their way to a remote cove. As they traveled, the stranger noticed that the fisherman didn't have any poles or other equipment—just a rusty tackle box and a scoop net.

After the fisherman shut off the motor, he opened the tackle box and pulled out a stick of dynamite. He struck a match, lit it, and then tossed it into the water. After a deafening explosion, he grabbed his net and started scooping up fish.

With a hard look, the stranger reached into his pocket and pulled out a badge with the words *game warden* on it. "You're under arrest," he said evenly.

His words didn't faze the fisherman. He simply reached into the tackle box again, lit another stick of dynamite, and held it while the fuse burned down. He then handed it to the game warden and said, "So, are you going to just sit there, or are you going to fish?"

Successful people don't need a lighted fuse to motivate them. Their motivation comes from within. If we wait for others to motivate us, what happens when a coach, a boss, or other inspirational person doesn't show up? We need a better plan than that.

Tom Golisano, founder of Paychex, Inc., offered this considered opinion: "I believe you don't motivate people. What you do is hire motivated people, then make sure you don't demotivate them." If you want to get ahead, you need to light your own fire.

3. People Who Lack Initiative Look for the Perfect Time to Act

Timing is important—no doubt about that. The Law of Timing in my book The 21 Irrefutable Laws of Leadership states, "When to lead is as important as what to do and where to go." But it's also true that all worthwhile endeavors in life require risk. I love this Chinese proverb: "He who deliberates fully before taking a step will spend his entire life on one leg." For many people, the tragedy isn't that life ends too soon; it's that they wait too long to begin it.

> "He who deliberates fully before taking a step will spend his entire life on one leg."
>
> —Chinese proverb

4. People Who Lack Initiative Like Tomorrow Better Than Today

One of the reasons noninitiators have such a difficult time getting started is that they focus their attention on tomorrow instead of today. Jazz musician Jimmy Lyons remarked, "Tomorrow is the only day in the year that appeals to a lazy man." But that attitude gets us into trouble because the only time over which we have any control is the present.

Edgar Guest wrote a poem that captures the fate of those who have this problem. It is appropriately titled "To-morrow":

> He was going to be all that a mortal should be
> To-morrow.
> No one should be kinder or braver than he
> To-morrow.
> A friend who was troubled and weary he knew,
> Who'd be glad of a lift and who needed it, too;
> On him he would call and see what he could do
> To-morrow.
> Each morning he stacked up the letters he'd write
> To-morrow.
> And thought of the folks he would fill with delight
> To-morrow.
> It was too bad, indeed, he was busy to-day,
> And hadn't a minute to stop on his way;
> More time he would have to give others, he'd say
> To-morrow.
> The greatest of workers this man would have been
> To-morrow.
> The world would have known him, had he ever seen
> To-morrow.
> But the fact is he died and he faded from view,
> And all that he left here when living was through
> Was a mountain of things he intended to do
> To-morrow.[9]

The idea of tomorrow can be very seductive, but the promise that it holds is often false. I heard about a customer who went into a furniture store in Santa Fe, New Mexico, and saw an old, faded sign on the wall that said, "Tomorrow we will give away everything in the store." For a moment, the customer got excited. Then he realized the sign would say the same thing tomorrow—putting off the giveaway another day and then another day. That particular *tomorrow* would never come.

Spanish priest and writer Baltasar Gracian said, "The wise man does at once what the fool does finally." Anything worth doing is worth doing immediately. Remember that for people who never start, their difficulties never stop.

TALENT + *INITIATIVE* = A TALENT-PLUS PERSON PUTTING THE TALENT-PLUS FORMULA INTO ACTION

To be honest, all of us are plagued by procrastination in some area of our lives. If something is unpleasant, uninteresting, or complex, we tend to put it off. Even some things we *like* doing can cause us difficulty. Johann Wolfgang von Goethe observed, "To put your ideas into action is the most difficult thing in the world." Yet to reach our potential and become talent-plus people, we must show initiative. Here are some suggestions to help you as you strive to become a talent-plus person in this area:

1. Accept Responsibility for Your Life

Greek philosopher Socrates said, "To move the world we must first move ourselves." Show me those who neglect to take responsibility for their own lives, and I'll show you people who also lack initiative. Responsibility and initiative are inseparable.

Everyone experiences setbacks. We all face obstacles. From time to time, we all feel that the deck is stacked against us. We need to show initiative anyway. Dick Butler asserted, "Life isn't fair. It isn't going to be fair. Stop sniveling and whining and go out and make it happen for

> "To move the world we must first move ourselves."
>
> —Socrates

you. In business I see too many people who expect the financial tooth fairy to come at night and remove that ugly dead tooth from under the pillow and substitute profitability just in the nick of time at the end of the fiscal year." There's a saying that great souls have wills but feeble ones have only wishes. We cannot wish our way to success. We need to take responsibility and act.

2. Examine Your Reasons for Not Initiating

Chinese philosopher Mencius made this point: "If your deeds are unsuccessful, seek the reason in yourself. When your own person is correct, the whole world will turn to you." If you lack initiative, the only way you will be able to change is to first identify the specific problem. Think about the reasons people lack initiative already outlined in this chapter. Are you in denial about the consequences of not taking initiative and responsibility for yourself? Are you waiting for others to motivate you instead of working to motivate yourself? Are you waiting for everything to be perfect before you act? Are you fantasizing about tomorrow instead of focusing on what you can do today? Or is there some other issue that is preventing you from taking action?

What's important is that you separate legitimate reasons from excuses. An excuse puts the blame on someone or something outside you. Excuses are like exit signs on the road of progress. They take us off track. Know this: it's easier to move from failure to success than from excuses to success. Eliminate excuses. Once you've done that, you can turn your attention to the reasons—and how to overcome them.

3. Focus on the Benefits of Completing a Task

It is extremely difficult to be successful if you are forever putting things off. Procrastination is the fertilizer that makes difficulties grow. When you take too long to make up your mind about an opportunity that presents itself, you will miss out on seizing it. In the previous chapter, I wrote about the importance of aligning your priorities with your passion. To become effective and make progress in your area of talent or responsibility, you can't spend your valuable time on unimportant or unnecessary tasks. So I'm going to make an assumption that if you do procrastinate about a task, it is a necessary one. (If it's not, don't put it off; eliminate it.) To get yourself over the hump, focus on what you'll get out of it if you get it done. Will completing the task bring a financial benefit? Will it clear the way for something else you would *like* to do? Does it represent a milestone in your development or the completion of something bigger? At the very least, does it help to clear the decks for you emotionally? If you seek a positive reason, you are likely to find one.

Once you find that idea, start moving forward and act decisively. U.S. admiral William Halsey observed, "All problems become smaller if you don't dodge them, but confront them. Touch a thistle timidly, and it pricks you; grasp it boldly, and its spines crumble."

4. Share Your Goal with a Friend Who Will Help You

No one achieves success alone. As the Law of Significance states in my book *The 17 Indisputable Laws of Teamwork*, "One is too small a number to achieve greatness." Lindbergh didn't fly solo across the Atlantic without help, Einstein didn't develop the theory of relativity in a vacuum, and Columbus didn't discover the New World on his own. They all had help.

My primary partner in life has been my wife, Margaret. She has been a part of every significant goal that I have achieved. She is the first to know when I identify a goal, and she is both the first and the last to support me along the way. And of course, many others have helped me and encouraged me along the way, particularly my parents and my brother, Larry.

In recent years, a key person in supporting me has been John Hull, the president and CEO of EQUIP. When I set the goal of EQUIP to train one million leaders around the globe, the task seemed formidable.

As much as I was dedicated to that vision, I had moments when I wondered if it were really possible. John not only was encouraging, but he took ownership of the vision and launched the plan to accomplish it. As you read this book, we have surpassed the goal of training one million leaders and are now working on training another million. One of the reasons I love and admire John is his initiative.

There is no way to put a value on the assistance that others can give you in achieving your dreams. Share your goals and dreams with people who care about you and will encourage and assist you in accomplishing them. It means taking a risk because you will have to be vulnerable in sharing your hopes and ambitions. But the risk is worth taking.

5. Break Large Tasks Down into Smaller Ones

Once you remove some of the internal barriers that may be stopping you from taking initiative and you enlist the help of others, you're ready to get practical. Many times large tasks overwhelm people, and that's a problem because overwhelmed people seldom initiate.

Here's how I suggest you proceed in breaking an intimidating goal into more manageable parts:

Divide it by categories. Most large objectives are complex and can be broken into steps for functions. The smaller pieces often require the effort of people with particular talents. Begin by figuring out what skill sets will be required to accomplish the smaller tasks.

Prioritize it by importance. When we don't take initiative and prioritize what we must do according to its importance, the tasks begin to arrange themselves according to their urgency. When the urgent starts driving you instead of the important, you lose any kind of initiative edge, and instead of activating your talent, it robs you of the best opportunities to use it.

Order it by sequence. Dividing the task according to its categories helps you to understand *how* you will need to accomplish it. Prioritizing by importance helps you to understand *why* you need to do each part of it. Ordering by sequence helps you to know *when* each part needs to be done. The important thing here is to create a timetable, give yourself deadlines, and stick to them. The biggest lie we tell ourselves when it comes to action is, "I'll do it later."

Assign it by abilities. When you divide the large task into smaller ones by category, you begin to understand what kinds of people you'll need to get the job done. At this stage, you very specifically answer the *who* question. As a leader, I can tell you that the most important step in accomplishing something big is determining who will be on the team. Assign tasks to winners and give them authority and responsibility, and the job will get done. Fail to give a specific person ownership of the task or give it to an average person, and you may find yourself in trouble.

Accomplish it by teamwork. Even if you break a task down, strategically plan, and recruit great people, you still need one more element to succeed. Everyone has to be able to work together. Teamwork is the glue that can bring it all together.

6. Allocate Specific Times to Tasks You Might Procrastinate

Dawson Trotman, author and founder of The Navigators, observed, "The greatest time wasted is the time getting started." Haven't you found that to be true? The hardest part of writing a letter is penning the first line. The hardest part of making a tough phone call is picking up the receiver and dialing the number. The most difficult part of practicing the piano is sitting down at the keyboard.

> "The greatest time wasted is the time getting started."
>
> —Dawson Trotman

It's the start that often stops people. So how do you overcome that difficulty? Try scheduling a specific time for something you don't like doing. For example, if dealing with difficult people is a regular part of your job, but you tend to avoid doing it, then schedule a set time for it. Maybe the best time would be between two and three o'clock every day. Treat it like an appointment, and when three o'clock rolls around, stop until tomorrow.

7. Remember, Preparation Includes Doing

One of the questions I often hear concerns writing. Young leaders frequently ask me how I got started, and I tell them about my first book, *Think on These Things*. It's a small book comprised of many three-page chapters, but it took me nearly a year to write it. I remember many nights when I spent hours scribbling on a legal pad only to have a few sentences to show for my effort.

"I want to sell a lot of books and influence a lot of people like you do," these young leaders will declare.

"That's great," I'll answer. "What have you written?"

"Well, nothing yet" is typically the response.

"Okay," I say. "What are you working on?" I ask the question hoping to give some encouragement.

"Well, I'm not actually writing yet, but I have a lot of ideas," they'll say, explaining that they hope they'll have more time next month or next year or after they get out of school. When I hear an answer like that, I know that it will never happen. Writers write. Composers compose. Leaders lead. You must take action in order to become who you desire to be. Novelist Louis L'Amour, who wrote more than 100 books and sold more than 230 million copies, advised, "Start writing, no matter about what. The water does not flow until the faucet is turned on."

> "The water does not flow until the faucet is turned on."
>
> —Louis L'Amour

Desire isn't enough. Good intentions aren't enough. Talent isn't enough. Success requires initiative. Michael E. Angier, founder of SuccessNet, stated, "Ideas are worthless. Intentions have no power. Plans are nothing . . . unless they are followed with action. Do it now!"

TALENT + *INITIATIVE* APPLICATION EXERCISES

1. Spend some time creating a list of all the reasons why you do not display greater initiative. Be thorough and list everything you can think of. Once the list is complete, go through and mark each entry with either an *E* for excuse or an *R* for reason.

   Now, create three new lists from your original list. The first is to be called "No More Excuses." On it, rewrite each excuse as a statement of responsibility. For example, if one of your excuses stated, "I don't have enough money," rewrite it to say, "I will no longer blame not having enough money." Post this list where you can see it every day.

   The second list comes from the remaining reasons on your original list and will be called "Facts of Life." Anything you have no control over and cannot change—such as the actions of others, your age, or the economy—is to go on this list. These are things you must simply accept.

   Whatever remains from your list of reasons goes on the third list called "My Responsibility." Since these things are your responsibility, you must solve them. Put them on your to-do list and get to work.

2. What causes you to procrastinate?
   - Are you in denial about the consequences of not taking initiative and responsibility for yourself?
   - Are you waiting for others to motivate you instead of working to motivate yourself?

- Are y ou waiting for everything to be perfect before you act?
- Are you fantasizing about tomorrow instead of focusing on what you can do today?
- Are you trying to go it alone?

Identify a specific action you can take to overcome your procrastination, designate a specific time on your calendar to take it, and if needed, enlist someone to help you follow through.

3. Think about something you strongly desire to do but are currently afraid of. As Dan Reiland did when he jumped out of the plane, what step can you take to put yourself into action mode, thus taking your focus off your fear?

4. What are you currently neglecting that is preventing your talent from becoming activated? Is it a decision you should be making? A problem you should be solving? A possibility you should be examining? A project you should be starting? A goal you should be reaching? An opportunity you should be seizing? A dream you should be fulfilling? Figure out what it is and determine to tackle it using the steps outlined in the chapter:

- Divide it by categories.
- Prioritize it by importance.
- Order it by sequence.
- Assign it by abilities.
- Accomplish it by teamwork.

4

FOCUS DIRECTS YOUR TALENT

Watch small children playing, and what do you see? They move quickly from one toy to another and from activity to activity. They expend tremendous amounts of energy but get little done. That's to be expected. They are exploring their world and learning by doing.

Focus does not come naturally to us, yet it is essential for anyone who wants to make the most of his talent. Having talent without focus is like being an octopus on roller skates. You can be sure that there will be plenty of movement, but you won't know in what direction it will be. Talent with focus directs you and has the potential to take you far.

In 2004, I traveled to Buenos Aires, Argentina, to do leadership training for a group of about seven thousand people. Whenever I travel to a part of the world that is new to me, I do some research to find out what's unique about the area. I always want to visit special places or engage in experiences that aren't available anywhere else in the world.

I learned that Argentina has the greatest dove hunting in the world. There is a place about seventy-five to one hundred miles north of Buenos Aires where there are literally millions upon millions of doves, and anybody who hunts loves to go there for the experience.

A-Hunting We Will Go

Although I have been hunting before, I'm not really a hunter. Some people are passionate about it, and they enjoy hunting game of all kinds. I go mostly because I love a new experience. So when I went to Argentina, I talked one of my team members, Ray Moats, into going with me. We planned to fly up and go hunting together.

When the guide picked us up from the airport, he took one look at me and said, "You're not a hunter, are you?" I confessed that I wasn't. "That's what I thought. The first thing we'll have to do is get rid of that red jacket you're wearing. Even doves will see that. We'll get you some camouflage."

The guide got Ray and me all set up, and there we were, in a beautiful valley. And sure enough, flocks of doves flew over our heads along the valley. In an hour's time, at least fifty thousand doves flew over us. There were moments when the sky was black with them. So for an hour I shot . . . and shot . . . and shot. It was one of those situations where there are so many that you say to yourself, *How can I miss?* And you just start shooting everywhere.

But do you know how many doves I hit in that hour? None! I was surrounded by empty shotgun shells, and I didn't have a single dove to show for it.

Intervention

After an hour of watching my technique and seeing me come up empty-handed, my guide finally couldn't take it anymore. At that rate, we were on track to break a record—for the fewest doves ever shot on a hunt. So he tried to help me.

"Your problem is, you are trying to shoot *all* of the doves," he said. "You don't try to shoot all the doves. You don't even worry about the doves that get away. Trust me," he continued, "in another twenty-five to thirty seconds another whole flock of doves will come. So don't worry about the doves; they'll keep coming all day. Quit worrying about what you lost. Focus on getting *one*."

While the guide was saying all this, Ray was right there beside me soaking it in. Why? Because he wasn't a hunter either, and he was doing as poorly as I was.

MEET SOME REAL HUNTERS

A couple of hours later, our guide decided it was time for us to take a break, and we went back to camp for lunch. There we met some good ol' boys from Arkansas who were real hunters. You could tell by taking one look at them. They were wearing camouflage—and not something they had just bought for the trip. Their clothes, like their shotguns, were well broken in. And these boys were talking very seriously about their hunting experience.

Ray and I sat down across from the Arkansans, and one of them looked at us and said to Ray, "Say, son, how many did you shoot this morning?"

"Three," Ray answered kind of sheepishly.

"Three, huh? Well, you shouldn't feel bad," he said. "Three hundred's not bad at all. Really, that's pretty good. We got about four hundred fifty, but three hundred's not bad, especially if it's your first time down here."

"No, you don't understand," Ray said. "We got three. Not three hundred. You know, *three!*" Ray counted on his fingers. "One. Two. Three."

For a moment, the boys from Arkansas just stared at us. "Son, son," one finally said, "you don't even have to *aim* to get three. You just shoot in the air and you're gonna get three. Heck, you can't get just three *on purpose*. You can only get three *by accident*."

> If you want
> to be successful,
> you must focus
> on what you
> *can* do, not on
> what you can't.

After lunch, we did a little better, but not much. It's true that Ray and I are not good hunters, so that was definitely a problem. In an area where there is little talent, you can't expect much success. However, our hunting trip is a great example of a situation where there are so many opportunities that you miss all of them. In hunting as in anything else, what we should have done was focus on the few that we could hit and forget about any opportunities we missed. If you want to be successful, you must focus on what you *can* do, not on what you can't.

THE POWER OF FOCUS

Focus can bring tremendous power. Without it, you will often feel drained and unable to accomplish much. With it, you will find that your talents and abilities gain direction and intentionality. And those qualities pay off by producing results.

Here are some facts you need to know about focus:

1. Focus Does Not Come Naturally to Most People

We live in a culture with almost infinite choices and opportunities, and because of that, most people find themselves pulled in dozens of directions. What's worse is that people often find themselves expending much of their time and energy on things they don't really care about. Don Marquis, author of *Archy and Mehitabel*, put it this way: "Ours is a world where people don't know what they want and are willing to go through hell to get it."

The solution to such a predicament is focus. Poet William Matthews wrote, "One well-cultivated talent, deepened and enlarged, is worth 100 shallow faculties. The first law of success in this day, when so many things are clamoring for attention, is concentration—to bend all the energies to one point, and to go directly to that point, looking neither to the right nor to the left."

I try to maintain my focus in the moment by heeding the advice of the martyred missionary Jim Elliott, who said, "Wherever you are, be all there." But I also look at the bigger picture. As a leader, I am always asking myself, *Am I helping others make progress?* I am vigilant about how I spend my time, with whom I am spending it, how it fits into the bigger picture, and whether it produces results. And my assistant, Linda Eggers, also keeps me on track by overseeing my calendar. She is a tremendous asset for helping me maintain my priorities. If I feel that I'm not moving forward and helping others throughout the day, then I know that I'm off track in some way. Linda helps me monitor that.

2. Focus Increases Your Energy

If you desire to achieve something, you first need to know what your target is. That's true even when it comes to personal development. If you lack focus, you will be all over the place. Attempting everything, like attempting nothing, will suck the life out of you. It will sap you of energy and new opportunities. And whatever momentum you have going for you will be diminished.

In contrast, focus gives you energy. Polar explorer Admiral Richard E. Byrd asserted, "Few men during their lifetime come anywhere near exhausting the resources dwelling within them. There are deep wells of strength that are never used." One of the reasons that those wells often go untapped is lack of focus. Something wonderful happens when we narrow our focus and set goals. That is where the real magic starts. The mind doesn't reach toward achievement until it has clear objectives.

After American astronauts successfully landed on the moon, Albert Siepert, deputy director of the Kennedy Space Center, attributed their success, at least in part, to NASA's focus. For a decade, the organization

> Attempting everything,
> like attempting nothing,
> will suck the life out of you.

put nearly all of its time and energy into reaching the moon. Siepert observed, "The reason NASA has succeeded is because NASA had a clear-cut goal and expressed its goal. By doing this, we drew the best of men to our goal and the support of every phase of government to reach our goal."

3. Focus Lifts You

Scholar and educator David Star Jordan said, "The world stands aside to let anyone pass who knows where he or she is going." In a sea of mediocrity, just knowing what you want to do and then making an effort to pursue it distinguishes you from almost everybody else.

The plain-spoken American writer Henry David Thoreau asked, "Did you ever hear of a man who had striven all his life faithfully and singly toward an object, and in no measure obtained it? If a man constantly aspires, is he not elevated?" Focus always has an impact. Just by striving to become better than you are, you become elevated—even if you don't accomplish what you desire, and even if others *don't* step aside for you. You can't shoot for the stars and remain unaffected by the effort.

4. Focus Expands Your Life

A few years ago, I wrote a book called *Thinking for a Change* in which I described the various thinking skills that can help a person become more successful. Included was a chapter on focused thinking, the ability to remove distractions and mental clutter so that a person can concentrate with clarity. In it I explained how I often bring together a team of people to help me brainstorm when working on a project. Because we focus our attention on the subject at hand, we are able to expand ideas in a way that we wouldn't be able to do otherwise.

Mike Kendrick asserts, "What you focus on expands." That may seem ironic, but it's true. Have you noticed that if you consider buying a particular kind of car, you begin seeing them everywhere? Narrowing your view widens your perspective. On the other hand, if you actually try to expand your view, instead of taking more in, it simply wears you out. If you want to expand your capacity, then focus.

5. Focus Must Be Intentionally Sustained

People do not naturally remain focused. Just as light naturally loses its focus and gets diffused, so does a person's attention. It takes a lot of effort, but the payoff is significant. Hall of Fame baseball player Hank Aaron says, "I think what separates a superstar from the average ballplayer is that he concentrates just a little bit longer." Aaron demonstrated that he was able to sustain his concentration. He holds the major-league baseball record for the most home runs hit in a career.

> "I think what separates a superstar from the average ballplayer is that he concentrates just a little bit longer."
>
> —Hank Aaron

In his book *Laughter, Joy, and Healing,* Donald E. Demaray wrote about a young journalist who was receiving tough criticism from his father because he didn't seem to be making much progress in his career. Undaunted, the young man wrote back to his father explaining that he had a plan for success upon which he was focused. His intentions were as follows:

- At 30, he would be a great newspaper reporter.
- At 40, he would be a great editor.
- At 50, he would be a great story writer.
- At 60, he would be a great fiction writer.

- At 70, he would be a great grandfather.

- At 80, he would be a great admirer of beautiful women.

- At 90, he would be a great loss to the community.

Demaray said that the father got a good laugh from the letter and was gratified when he began to see that his son's career was progressing along those lines.[1]

Several years ago, I memorized a definition of success to help me in my career: "Success is the progressive realization of a predetermined worthwhile goal." What I learned most from that definition is that success is not an event; it is a process. And anytime you engage in a process that takes time, focus is essential. Only people capable of remaining focused can expect to direct their talent and achieve a level of success.

TALENT + *FOCUS* = A TALENT-PLUS PERSON
PUTTING THE TALENT-PLUS FORMULA INTO ACTION

If you desire to become a talent-plus person, you need to make focus your friend. Here's how:

1. Be Intentional—Make Every Action Count

A family who had moved to a new neighborhood got a late start one morning, and as a result their six-year-old missed her bus to school. Though it would make him late for work, the father agreed to take her to school if she could give him directions.

They left their neighborhood, and the young girl began directing her father to take one turn after another. Following twenty minutes of circuitous driving, they arrived at the school, which turned out to be only eight blocks away. Steaming, the father asked the kindergartener why she had him drive all over the place when the school was so close to home.

"We went the way the bus goes," she said. "That's the only way I know."

If you want to maximize your talent and become a talent-plus person, you need to make every action count. You must determine where you want to go and

> "You've removed most of the roadblocks to success when you know the difference between motion and direction."
>
> —Bill Copeland

how to get there. You cannot be like Alice in Lewis Carroll's *Through the Looking Glass*, who asks for directions in this way during her encounter with the Cheshire Cat:

> "Would you tell me please, which way ought I to go from here?" she asks.
>
> "That depends a good deal on where you want to get," the cat replies with a grin.
>
> "I don't care much where," she answers.
>
> "Then it doesn't matter which way you go," the cat responds.

People who are undecided about what they want to do or where they want to go cannot tap into their strength of will—or their talent. As a result, they will merely drift along.

Private investigator and author Bill Copeland advises, "You've removed most of the roadblocks to success when you know the difference between motion and direction." Have you asked yourself what you really want to do? And have you determined that you will pursue it against the odds, despite the obstacles, and regardless of the circumstances? Being intentional is about focusing on doing the right things, moment by moment, day to day, and then following through with them in a consistent way. As President John F. Kennedy asserted, "Efforts and courage are not enough without purpose and direction."

2. Challenge Your Excuses

A sign on the desk of an officer who works at the Pentagon reads, "The secrecy of my job does not permit me to know what I'm doing." It's a clever joke, but it's not funny when it's actually true. People who don't know what they're doing soon become frustrated.

We all have reasons for not doing what we ought to do. We don't have enough time. We don't have enough resources. We don't have enough help. We have problems. We have shortcomings. We have distractions. Should we let these things get us off track? No!

3. Don't Let Yesterday Hijack Your Attention

Humorist and entertainer Will Rogers shared this thought: "Don't let yesterday take up too much of today." I've never known a person focusing on yesterday who had a better tomorrow. Too many people *yearn* for the past and get stuck in it. Instead, they should *learn* from the past and let go of it.

Alvin Dark, who was once the manager of the Kansas City Athletics, used to say, "There's no such thing as taking a pitcher out. There's only bringing another pitcher in." That runs contrary to what you hear during most baseball broadcasts, but here's the point. When you say you're going to take a pitcher out, you're probably focused on the mistakes he made—the players he walked, the hits he allowed. That doesn't help you win the game. In contrast, when you say you're putting a pitcher in, you are focusing on what that new pitcher is going to do now to try to help you beat the other team. That can make a big difference in your team's attitude—and in the players' ability to succeed.

> "Don't let yesterday take up too much of today."
> —Will Rogers

Editor and publisher Elbert Hubbard wrote,

A retentive memory may be a good thing, but the ability to forget is the true token of greatness. Successful people forget. They know the past is irrevocable. They're running a race. They can't afford to look behind. Their eye is on the finish line. Magnanimous people forget. They're too big to let little things disturb them. They forget easily. If anyone does them wrong, they consider the source and keep cool. It's only the small people who cherish revenge. Be a good forgetter. Business dictates it, and success demands it.

If you desire to make the most of your talent and achieve success, then you need to make what you're doing now your focus. Striving for achievements is a lot like driving a car. It's a good idea to check your rearview mirror occasionally, but not to give it your complete attention. If you do, you will eventually be incapable of moving forward at all.

4. Focus on the Present

Just as you should keep your focus off yesterday, you shouldn't have it on tomorrow. If you're always thinking about tomorrow, then you'll never get anything done today. Your focus needs to remain in the one area where you have some control—today. What's ironic is that if you focus on today, you get a better tomorrow.

I try to do certain things every day to help me in this area. I read daily to grow in my personal life. I listen to others daily to broaden my perspective. I spend time thinking daily to apply what I am learning. And I try to write daily so that I can remember what I've learned. I also try to share those lessons with others. (Today's lessons become tomorrow's books.) Every day I read aloud to myself the daily dozen list from my book *Today Matters* to help me focus and have the right mind-set.

You should do something similar. You can't change yesterday. You can't count on tomorrow. But you can choose what you do today. Giving it your focus will pay dividends.

5. Stay Focused on Results

Anytime you concentrate on the difficulty of the work at hand instead of its results or rewards, you're likely to become discouraged. Dwell on the difficulties too long and you'll start to develop self-pity instead of self-discipline, and your attention will become scattered instead of focused. As a result, you will accomplish less and less. By focusing on results, you will find it easier to stay positive and encouraged.

Another thing that can distract you from results is interaction with difficult people. You will come in contact with a lot of people who can impact your efforts as you work on achieving your dreams— some in a negative way. Here are five types of people you are likely to encounter:

- *Refreshers*—they inspire your dreams and energize your talents.
- *Refiners*—they sharpen your ideas and clarify your vision.
- *Reflectors*—they mirror your energy, neither adding nor subtracting from it.
- *Reducers*—they try to reduce your vision and efforts to their comfort level.
- *Rejecters*—they deny your talent, hinder your efforts, and impede your vision.

If you remain focused on results, you will stay grounded. The praise of others is less likely to go to your head, and the negative impact of people such as the reducers and rejecters will be minimized.

6. Develop and Follow Your Priorities

There's an old saying that if you chase two rabbits, both will escape. Unfortunately that is what many people seem to do. They don't focus their attention, and as a result, they become ineffective. Perhaps the reason is that people in our culture have too many choices—nearly unlimited options. Management expert Peter Drucker recognized this phenomenon. He said, "Concentration is the key to economic results. No other principle of effectiveness is violated as constantly today as the basic principle of concentration . . . Our motto seems to be, 'Let's do a little bit of everything.'"

If you want to develop your talent, you need to focus. If you're going to focus, you need to work on knowing what your true priorities are and then following them. This is something I have learned to do over time. I love options. I like to have the freedom to pursue the best course of action at any given moment. When I was in my twenties, I spent a lot of time doing things that had little return. In my thirties, I did better, but I still wasn't as focused as I should have been. It wasn't until I reached forty that I started to become highly selective about where I spent my time and energy. Today, as I approach sixty, I filter just about everything I do through my top priority: *Am I adding value to people?* For me, it all comes down to that.

7. Focus on Your Strengths, Not Your Weaknesses

There's a story about a couple who bought a new piece of property upon which they intended to establish a farm. It was good land, and they could hardly wait to move there and get started. As they made plans for the move one night, they began to argue about what to do first. The wife wanted to build the house first. After all, once they moved, the new property would be their home. The husband, who had grown up working on a farm, wanted to build the barn first to house their animals. They went back and forth for a while until the man finally said, "Look, we have to build the barn first—because the barn will build the house, and the garage, the silo, the kids' swing set, and everything else!" When you focus on your priorities and put first things first, everything else is more likely to fall into place.

Anthony Campolo, professor emeritus of sociology at Eastern University in Pennsylvania, says,

What you commit yourself to will change what you are and make you into a completely different person. Let me repeat that. Not the past but the future conditions you, because what you commit yourself to become determines what you are—more than anything that ever happened to you yesterday or the day before. Therefore, I ask you a very simple question: What are your commitments? Where are you going? What are you going to be? You show me somebody who hasn't decided, and I'll show you somebody who has no identity, no personality, no direction.

Focusing on weaknesses instead of strengths is like having a handful of coins—a few made of pure gold and the rest of tarnished copper—and setting aside the gold coins to spend all your time cleaning and shining the copper ones in the hopes of making them look more valuable. No matter how long you spend on them, they will never be worth what the gold ones are. Go with your greatest assets; don't waste your time.

8. Delay Rewards Until the Job Is Done

One of the tricks I've used with myself for years is to reward myself when I've done something that I ought to do. My father taught me that when I was a kid—pay now and play later. I think too often people want the rewards before the results, and for that reason they don't stay as focused as they could.

One secret of a life well lived is making every action count—being intentional. That kind of focus helps people live without regrets because it directs and makes the most of their talent and their opportunities. If you know that you have talent, and you are energetic and active, but you don't see concrete results, then lack of focus is likely your problem. It takes talent plus focus to reach your potential and become the person you desire to be.

TALENT + *FOCUS*
APPLICATION EXERCISES

1. In what area has lack of focus tapped your energy in the past? Is this a recurring problem? If so, try to determine why.

2. Give an example of a time when your ability to focus well helped you to achieve excellent results. What helped you to maintain your focus? What can you learn from that experience?

3. Where have you been putting your focus? Do you spend a great part of your time thinking about what happened in the past? Are you placing much hope in the future, when you hope to get a raise, establish a relationship, take a vacation, or enjoy retirement? Or are you concentrating on the here and now? Try to break down your thinking time according to percentages and write them here (making sure they total 100 percent):

    _____ Past
    _____ Present
    _____ Future

I believe it is healthy to spend 90 percent of your time focused on the present. Considering the past 5 percent of the time is useful if you learn from your successes and mistakes. Contemplating the future 5 percent of the time is useful to make sure your current activities are pointed in the right direction. Anything more may be detrimental to your productivity. You will have to begin making adjustments to refocus yourself on the present.

4. At the end of Chapter 1, I asked you to identify your strengths. Do you typically focus on developing and maximizing them? Or do you gravitate to shoring up your weaknesses? What can you do to place an even greater emphasis on your strengths? What can you give up that is undermining your focus? What untapped strength or talent do you suspect that you possess but have neglected? What concrete step can you take to start utilizing it?

5. Since the present is the only time over which you have any control, how can you "up the ante" and make your activities even more focused? Your goal should be to make every action count toward the results you desire.

6. Think about something you would like to have. It can be any-thing—a book or CD, a set of golf clubs, a vacation, or even a new car. Instead of just buying it, consider making it a reward that you will allow yourself to have once you have earned it by producing some kind of desired result. Make sure that the effort matches the reward. (If you're not sure about whether they match, ask a friend or your spouse.)

5

PREPARATION POSITIONS YOUR TALENT

What happens when you don't prepare? Things you hoped *won't* happen do happen—and they occur with greater frequency than the things you hoped *would* happen. The reason is simple: being unprepared puts you out of position. Ask negotiators what happens at the bargaining table when they are out of position. Ask athletes what happens when they are out of position. They lose. Preparation positions people correctly, and it is often the separation between winning and losing. Talent-plus people who prepare well live by this motto: "All's well that begins well."

GREAT CHALLENGES

What was the greatest adventure humankind faced in the twentieth century? Exploring the polar ice caps? Conquering the world's highest mountains? Sending ships into space and landing people on the moon? Good cases could be made for each adventure.

How about in the nineteenth century? It was undoubtedly the exploration of the interior of Africa, Australia, and the Americas. Much global exploration had occurred from 1492 to 1800. Bold adventurers had explored the globe and been able to map and define all the continents in broad strokes, having accurately mapped their shorelines. But what lay within the boundaries of some of those continents remained a mystery.

In North America, the leaders of the newly formed United States were anxious to know details about the interior of their continent. Much of the territory between the Atlantic Ocean and the Mississippi River (south of St. Louis) had been explored, but in 1801 when Thomas Jefferson became president of the United States, two-thirds of the nation's 5.3 million occupants lived within fifty miles of the coast, and few had traveled west of the Appalachian Mountains. The land west of the Mississippi River was unknown and still up for grabs. The fate of the nation would be determined by who controlled that land—the United States, France, England, Spain, or the native populations who inhabited it.

No American leader was more interested in knowing about North America than was Thomas Jefferson. Historian Stephen E. Ambrose asserts that Jefferson's interest in exploration began in the 1750s. Ambrose writes, "In the decade following the winning of independence, there were four American plans to explore the West. Jefferson was the instigator of three of them."[1] In the 1790s, as a member of the American Philosophical Society, Jefferson tried to launch an exploratory expedition. He knew the key to its success would be selecting the right leader. He chose a trained scientist from France named André Michaux and directed him to find the shortest route between the United States and the Pacific Ocean, presumably up the Missouri River and somehow connected to the Columbia River in the West. In 1793, Michaux made it as far as Kentucky before Jefferson recalled the mission after discovering that the scientist was a secret agent of the French government given the mission to incite people to attack Spanish possessions in the West.

THE RIGHT PERSON FOR THE JOB

Jefferson's best opportunity to launch the expedition of the American West wouldn't come until he became president of the United States. The key still would be the leader of the expedition. It would require an extremely talented person. And Jefferson thought he knew who that would be: Meriwether Lewis.

Ironically, back in 1792, when Jefferson and the American Philosophical Society were preparing the ill-fated expedition that would be headed by Michaux, one of the people who asked to be selected to lead it was Lewis. Like Jefferson, Lewis was born in Albemarle County, Virginia, but at that time Lewis was only eighteen years old. It was true that Lewis had lived on the frontier in Georgia for three or four years where he had learned many frontier skills. As a boy of eight, he was known to go out hunting in the middle of the night on his own. Lewis's cousin, Peachy Gilmer, described the young Lewis as "always remarkable for persevereance [sic], which in the early period of his life seemed nothing more than obstinacy in pursuing the trifles that employ that age; a martial temper; great steadiness of purpose, self-possession, and undaunted courage."[2] Lewis also already had experience as a leader. Because of his father's early death, Lewis had taken charge of a two-thousand-acre plantation when he was still a teenager. But back then he didn't have the wherewithal to lead an expedition. He was talented but green.

Years later, Jefferson explained why he selected Lewis instead of a credentialed scientist. He said it was impossible to find a person possessing "a compleat science in botany, natural history, mineralogy & astronomy" who could add to it "the firmness of constitution & character, prudent, habits adapted to the woods, & a familiarity with the Indian manners & character, requisite for this undertaking. *All the latter qualifications Capt. Lewis has.*"[3]

Lewis further honed those character qualities and frontier skills during six years in the army where he rose from the rank of private to captain. He served much of his time on the frontier as far west as Ohio and Michigan. At one point as a regimental paymaster, he traveled extensively, learned to understand much about the Native Americans in that part of the country, and refined his leadership skills.

What Lewis most lacked was formal education. His other responsibilities kept him from studying as much as he would have liked. Why would that matter? The expedition to the West that Jefferson envisioned would be more than just the search for an all-water route to the Pacific Ocean. It was also to be a scientific and diplomatic mission. The president wanted to know the quality of the land for farming and for the support of future settlers. He wanted reliable information on previously unknown plants, animals, and fossils from the regions, and he expected many specimens to be collected, catalogued, and brought back east.

Jefferson directed the party to create accurate maps of previously unexplored regions. He wanted to know about the geography and weather. He desired facts concerning the culture and habits of the native populations. He also intended the party to initiate friendly relations with those populations and convince them of the value of trading with the United States. It was to be so much more than a mere trailblazing adventure.

EARLY PREPARATION

The way Jefferson decided to deal with Lewis's raw but still largely undeveloped talent was characteristic of the president's leadership and genius. As Jefferson prepared to assume his role as president, he invited Lewis to become his personal secretary, telling him it "would make you know & be known to characters of influence in the affairs of our country, and give you the advantage of their wisdom."[4] Lewis's time at the White House did that and much more. The young man was treated as a member of Jefferson's family, and he was, in fact, the only resident of the White House along with Jefferson, a widower, besides the servants.

Lewis's first task was to help Jefferson as he reduced the size of the nation's army. He frequently gathered information for the president, and he also copied and drafted documents. He was a frequent messenger to Congress. He functioned as the president's aide-de-camp. They spent long hours working together, Lewis read extensively from Jefferson's library, and the young captain always dined with Jefferson as he entertained the great thinkers, scientists, and leaders of the day. Lewis biographer Richard Dillon states that his experience in the White House functioned as "an ideal finishing school for Lewis."[5]

But Jefferson wasn't finished getting Lewis ready. In the summer of 1802, Jefferson procured and read a copy of *Voyages from Montreal, on the River St. Lawrence, Through the Continent of North America, to the Frozen and Pacific Ocean*, an account of Scotsman Alexander Mackenzie's exploration across Canada. It spurred Jefferson's desire to launch an American expedition. And it prompted him to become highly intentional in Lewis's preparation. Jefferson helped Lewis study geography, botany, celestial observation with a sextant, and more. Ambrose says, "In short, between the time Mackenzie's book arrived at Monticello [August 1802] and December 1802, Jefferson gave Lewis a college undergraduate's introduction to the liberal arts, North American geography, botany, mineralogy, astronomy, and ethnology."[6] Their preparations for the expedition had formally begun.

BECOMING MORE INTENTIONAL

Two kinds of preparations were going on in the months prior to Lewis's departure. The first was Lewis's gathering and preparing the supplies and equipment for the trip. The second was Lewis's preparation of himself. It's hard for us in the age of Internet communication, worldwide overnight

delivery services, and corner convenience stores to imagine how complex
the logistical and physical preparations were. Today if you go on vacation
and discover that you forgot to pack a book, you simply buy one. If you get
sick, you visit a drugstore. If your clothes get lost or ruined, you buy new
ones. If you forget your glasses, you can ask someone at home to overnight
them to you. It may cost you more than you would like to spend, but in a
pinch you can always charge it. These problems are solvable.

In the age before motorized transportation or rapid communication,
mistakes of preparation could be devastating. In addition, the logistical
preparations of Lewis were massive. He had to secure *tons* of supplies
from an amazing variety of manufacturers and purveyors, everything
from rifles and ammunition to delicate scientific equipment to paper
and ink to medical supplies to food to gifts for the Native Americans
they would encounter. He had to have a keel boat built for travel up the
Mississippi and Missouri Rivers (which he designed himself). He had to
select the members of the expedition.

As daunting as those tasks were, they paled in comparison to the
importance of the preparation of the man. If Lewis was not ready for the
task, then the entire expedition—no matter how well planned and
equipped—would be a failure. Lewis spent months with some of the top
experts in America continuing to learn scientific skills and to prepare
himself for his mission. Here is a list of the most notable ones along with
how they helped Lewis:

- ALBERT GALLATIN, map collector—knowledge of the
  geography of western North America

- ANDREW ELLICOTT, astronomer and mathematician—skill in
  celestial observation using the sextant, chronometer, and other
  instruments

- ROBERT PATTERSON—additional assistance with celestial observation and with the purchase of the chronometer for the journey

- DR. BENJAMIN RUSH, physician—medical matters, the selection and purchase of medicines, and the creation of questions to be asked of the native populations

- DR. BENJAMIN SMITH BARTON, botany professor—skill in preserving specimens and properly labeling them, and knowledge of botanical terminology (later experts judge Lewis's knowledge to have been remarkable for an amateur)

- DR. CASPAR WISTAR, anatomy professor and expert on fossils—fossil discovery and collection[7]

All the preparation paid off. Ambrose describes the result:

Two years of study under Thomas Jefferson, followed by his crash course in Philadelphia, had made Lewis into exactly what Jefferson had hoped for in an explorer—a botanist with a good sense of what was known and what was unknown, a working vocabulary for description of flora and fauna, a mapmaker who could use celestial instruments properly, a scientist with keen powers of observation, all combined in a woodsman and an officer who could lead a party to the Pacific.[8]

The final pieces in the preparation process were the selections of a fellow officer and the men who would become members of the "corps of discovery." That was no small task. Lewis knew who the officer should be: William Clark, a captain under whom Lewis had served while in the army and with whom he had developed a remarkable friendship. Assembling the twenty-nine men who would make the trip took more time since, as Clark and Lewis agreed, "a judicious choice of our party is of the greatest importance to the success of this vast enterprise."[9] As Lewis traveled west from Philadelphia toward St. Louis, he continued collecting supplies, searching for suitable men, and making financial arrangements. It was during this phase that he got word from Jefferson that Jefferson had transacted the Louisiana Purchase.

Finally Getting Out!

On May 22, 1804, Lewis and Clark set off up the Missouri River from their winter camp just north of St. Louis where they had completed the last of their preparations. Counting from the time Lewis began working for the president in April of 1801, the preparations had taken a little more than three years for a trip that they hoped could be completed in eighteen to twenty-four months. Actually the trip took longer than that. The explorers made it to the Pacific and back to St. Louis in two and a half years, and to Washington four months later.

The expedition was an amazing success. The corps of discovery made their way across the continent. They skirted or passed through modern-day Missouri, Kansas, Iowa, Nebraska, South Dakota, North Dakota, Montana, Idaho, Washington, and Oregon. They were the first non-indigenous people to see and cross the Rocky Mountains. James P. Ronda, the H. G. Barnard Professor of Western American History at the University of Tulsa, points out that they strengthened the claims of the United States in the West. They established peaceful contact with many groups of Native Americans. They set the pattern for scientific exploration in the U.S. They discovered 122 animal species or subspecies and 178 new plant species. And Ronda says, "The journals, maps, plant and animal specimens, and notes on Native American societies amounted to a Western encyclopedia."[10] Ambrose goes even farther: "Since 1803 and the return of the expedition in 1806, every American everywhere has benefited from Jefferson's purchase of Louisiana and his setting in motion the Lewis and Clark Expedition."[11]

> Spectacular achievement comes from unspectacular preparation.

What's sad is that as prepared as Lewis was for his expedition and as well as he performed, he was not prepared for life after its completion. Jefferson made Lewis governor of Louisiana, a task for which he was *not* prepared, and he did not succeed in that post. As much as he tried to work on his extensive journals, he never completed their preparation for publication. Others had to work on them after his death. Lewis began to drink heavily. And when he was ill, he began taking medicine laced with opium or morphine, a practice he continued, though he vowed to stop. On October 11, 1809, in a bout of despair, Lewis shot himself and died a few hours later.

WHY PEOPLE FAIL TO PREPARE

The life of Meriwether Lewis shows a truth about preparation: spectacular achievement comes from unspectacular preparation. Talent, much like the eighteen-year-old Lewis, wants to jump into action, but preparation positions talent to be effective. Talent plus preparation often leads to success. Talent minus preparation often leads to disaster.

In hindsight, it's easy to recognize the value of preparation. So why do so many people fail to prepare?

They Fail to See the Value of Preparation Before Action

Authors Don Beveridge Jr. and Jeffrey P. Davidson believe that lack of preparation is the primary reason for business failure today. "Poorly educated, poorly prepared, and poorly trained people fail because they do not have the skills or expertise to perform," they say. "Inadequate financing, the number-one reason businesses fail, can also be traced to lack of preparation."[12]

> Talent may be a given, but success you must earn.

In the introduction to this book I wrote about how talent early in life or in the beginning of a career makes a person stand out—but only for a short time. Why? Talent may be a given, but success you must earn. Proverbs 18:16 states, "A man's gift makes room for him."[13] In other words, your talent will give you an opportunity. But you must remember that the room it makes is only temporary.

Preparation is a major key to achieving any kind of success. It alone can position your talent to achieve its potential. Military people know this. General Douglas MacArthur said, "Preparedness is the key to success and victory." He also stated it more bluntly: "The more you sweat in peace, the less you bleed in war." The actions of Meriwether Lewis demonstrated that he had a similar attitude. Despite all the dangers and deprivations, the brutal weather and hostile Native Americans, Lewis lost only one member of his party, Sergeant Charles Floyd, probably from peritonitis cause by a ruptured appendix. No preparation on Lewis's part could have saved him from that. In fact, in 1804, Floyd probably would have died under the care of a trained physician.

They Fail to Appreciate the Value of Discipline

It's been said that discipline is doing what you really *don't want* to do so that you can do what you really *do want* to do. Meriwether Lewis's most evident weakness was a tendency to be a bit rash and take offense. In fact, one of Jefferson's serious concerns was that Lewis might alienate the Native Americans and either start a war or get himself and his party killed. Lewis came close several times, including a tense standoff with the Teton Sioux. The explorers were one wrong move away from being wiped out and becoming little more than an obscure footnote in American history. What saved the day? Ambrose says Lewis's rashness was compensated by his tremendous self-discipline. With guns loaded and aimed and dozens of arrows pointed in their direction, Lewis waited out the situation. Eventually a Sioux chief managed to get the angry braves to stand down and defuse the conflict. Lewis understood the value of discipline.

A frustrating thing about preparation is that it usually takes much more time than the actual event one prepares for. Musicians may practice many hours preparing to perform a three-minute piece. Stage actors practice for weeks to prepare for a performance that lasts two hours. I know that when I create a leadership lesson that may take me less than an hour to deliver, it usually takes me eight to ten hours to write it. Discipline is required to keep preparing long hours for something that will be over quickly.

Alexander Hamilton, a Founding Father of the United States and its first secretary of the treasury, said, "Men give me credit for genius; but all the genius I have lies in this: When I have a subject on hand I study it profoundly." Hamilton was a disciplined and highly productive man. He understood that no matter your circumstances, resources, or natural talent, certain things were always within your control—your ability to work harder and smarter than anybody else. That bears remembering as you prepare yourself for the challenges that lay ahead of you.

PREPARATION PRINCIPLES

Automaker Henry Ford observed, "Before everything else, getting ready is the secret of success." Ford understood the power of preparation and all the things it can do for someone:

1. Preparation Allows You to Tap into Your Talent

While I was working on this book, I was scheduled to make a trip to Latin America to teach leadership and meet national leaders in Guatemala, El Salvador, Honduras, Panama, Venezuela, Bolivia, and Peru. I would be gone more than ten days, so before I left, I spent an entire day making sure I had the materials I would need to keep working on the book. I reviewed the chapter outlines, gave some thinking time to the subject of the first couple of chapters, and pulled quotes and other materials from my files to take with me. And of course, I packed several new legal pads!

I also wrote the book's introduction. A group of excellent leaders and thinkers would be accompanying me on the trip, and I wanted their comments on the direction I was taking the book. I had copies made of that introduction so that I could hand them out to my fellow travelers, and I asked everyone to give me feedback and ideas. (I'm a strong believer in teamwork when related to talent too. I'll write more about that in Chapter 13.) And since we spent a lot of hours flying on a plane, during much of that time I pulled out the materials I had packed and did some writing.

As the trip concluded and we were flying back home, one of my travel mates, David McLendon, said to me, "I've learned a valuable lesson on this trip. You came prepared to maximize your time because you knew what you wanted to accomplish. While the rest of us read and talked, you got a lot of work done. You outlined two chapters. You even engaged all of us in the writing of your book!"

What he observed was possible because I had prepared. "You know, David," I replied, "I've found that every minute spent in preparation saves ten in execution." And that had been the case here. Because I spent a day preparing, I was able to work for ten days on that trip. It's not difficult; it just takes planning. The questions I ask myself before a trip like this are really very simple:

- *What work is to be done?*

- *How is it to be done?*

- *When is it to be done?*

- *Where is it to be done?*

- *How fast can it be done?*

- *What do I need to get it done?*

Answering these questions prepares me for what lies ahead. And when I am prepared, my talent is positioned for maximum effect.

2. Preparation Is a Process, Not an Event

We live in a quick-fix society. We think in terms of events and instant solutions. But preparation doesn't work that way. Why? Because it's about you. Anything having to do with people is process-oriented. The Law of Process in *The 21 Irrefutable Laws of Leadership* states, "Leadership develops daily, not in a day." The same can be said of maximizing your talent.

Legendary UCLA basketball coach John Wooden says that the best way to improve your team is to improve yourself. He learned that lesson from his father, Joshua Wooden, who used to tell young John, "Don't try to be better than somebody else, but never cease trying to be the best you can be." That's good advice whether you're playing basketball, parenting, or conducting business.

In 1983, I began teaching and recording monthly leadership lessons. Today, more than two decades later, I am still teaching them, and I have produced more than three hundred different leadership lessons. How was I able to do it? By continually feeding my mind and adding to my pool of resources. Every day, I read and file quotes, stories, and idea starters. Every month, I draw upon those filed resources. Every year, I use some of those lessons to write new books. My productivity comes more from my preparation than anything else. That positions whatever talent I have so that I can use it to my maximum potential. It is an ongoing process. And if the daily learning and preparation ever stop, so will my productivity.

> The best way to improve your team is to improve yourself.

3. Preparation Precedes Opportunity

There's an old saying: "You can claim to be surprised once; after that, you're unprepared." If you want to take advantage of opportunities to use your talent, then you *must* be prepared when the opportunities arise. Once the opportunity presents itself, it's too late to get ready.

If you study the lives of dynamic men and women, you will find that preparation for opportunity is a common theme. President Abraham Lincoln said, "I will prepare and some day my chance will come." Prime Minister Benjamin Disraeli of England remarked, "The secret of success

> You can claim
> to be surprised once;
> after that,
> you're unprepared.

in life is for a man to be ready for his time when it comes." Oprah Winfrey asserted, "Luck is a matter of preparation meeting opportunity." And President John F. Kennedy observed, "The time to repair the roof is when the sun is shining." All of these people had talent, prepared themselves, and then made the most of their opportunities when they arose. Many people believe that their greatest barrier to opportunity is having one, but the reality is that their greatest barrier is being ready when one arrives.

4. Preparation for Tomorrow Begins with the Right Use of Today

Recently, a few friends and I were privileged to have dinner with former New York City mayor Rudy Giuliani and his wife, Judith, in Orlando after a speaking engagement. I found the mayor to be a very warm and personable man who was an easy conversationalist. During our conversation, I of course asked him about his experience during 9-11. He talked about his impressions from that day and how the event impacted him as a leader. He said that leaders need to be ready for anything. They need to study, acquire skills, and plan for every kind of situation.

"Your success will be determined by your ability to prepare," he said. He went on to explain that when a situation like that on September 11 occurs—for which there was no plan in place—leaders must take action and rely on whatever preparation had taken place. In his case, it was the emergency drills they had followed. Both helped during the crisis.

Preparation doesn't begin with what you do. It begins with what you believe. If you believe that your success tomorrow depends on what you do today, then you will

> If you are *preparing* today, chances are, you will not be *repairing* tomorrow.

treat today differently. What you receive tomorrow depends on what you believe today. If you are *preparing* today, chances are, you will not be *repairing* tomorrow.

5. Preparation Requires Continually Good Perspective

When I was a kid, my first love was basketball. From the time I was ten until I graduated from high school, I was shooting hoops at every free moment. One thing that I still enjoy about basketball is how quickly one player can change the tempo and momentum of a game. That's true not only of the stars and starters but also of the players who come off the bench. That's why the "sixth man," the player of starting caliber who is often the first substitute in the game, is so important. Former Boston Celtics coach Tom Heinsohn observed, "The sixth man has to be so stable a player that he can instantly pick up the tempo or reverse it. He has to be able to go in and have an immediate impact. The sixth man has to have the unique ability to be in a ball game while he is sitting on the bench." What makes the sixth man capable of that? Perspective. He has to have both a coach's mind-set as he watches the game from the bench and a player's ability once he steps into it. If he does, then he is prepared to impact the game.

Howard Coonley, the executive after whom the American National Standards Institute named its award honoring service to the national economy, stated, "The executive of the future will be rated by his ability to anticipate his problems rather than to meet them as they come."

Perspective not only helps people prepare, but it can also *motivate* them to prepare. I love the quote from Abraham Lincoln, who said, "If I had eight hours to chop down a tree, I'd spend six sharpening my ax." Lincoln had split rails with an ax as a young man, so he knew the value of a sharp ax. Perspective always prompted him to prepare—whether he was getting ready to cut wood, study law on his own to pass the bar, or lead the country.

6. Good Preparation Leads to Action

What value has preparation if it never leads to action? Very little. As William Danforth, former chancellor of Washington University in St. Louis, noted, "No plan is worth the paper it is printed on unless it starts you going."

People who enjoy preparation sometimes find themselves caught in the trap of overpreparing, and they sometimes do so to the point that they fail to act. Kathleen Eisenhardt, professor of management science and engineering at Stanford University, studied the decision-making process at twelve technology companies. She found that the fast deciders, who took two to four months to make major decisions, were much more effective than their slower counterparts who wanted to get all the facts of their

> "No plan is worth the paper it is printed on unless it starts you going."
> —William Danforth

situation and create consensus. The slower group took up to eighteen months to plan and decide, and by the time they did find resolution, the decision they made was often irrelevant.

Preparation does not mean mastery of the facts. It does not mean knowing all the answers. It does not necessarily mean achieving consensus. (Former British prime minister Margaret Thatcher remarked that "consensus is the negation of leadership.") It means putting yourself in a better position to succeed.[14]

TALENT + PREPARATION = A TALENT-PLUS PERSON
PUTTING THE TALENT-PLUS FORMULA INTO ACTION

Sports have always been an area in which you can see the value of preparation. It doesn't matter what sport—good athletes talk about it all of the time. Tennis champion Arthur Ashe explained, "One important key to success is self-confidence. An important key to self-confidence is preparation." Quarterback Joe Namath said simply, "What I do is prepare myself until I know I can do what I have to do."

Friend and fellow golfer Rick Bizet once told me that his golf coach taught him that the only thing that relieves pressure is preparation. If you want to see that preparation in action, observe any professional golfer's pre-shot routine. I particularly appreciate the routine of professional golfer Tom Kite. It contains three main steps: assessment, alignment, and attitude. In fact, I use it as a guideline, not only when playing golf, but also in other situations when I need to prepare myself. I believe you can do the same.

> The only thing that relieves pressure is preparation.

1. Assessment—Am I Evaluating Correctly?

Good preparation always begins with assessment. If you don't accurately evaluate where you need to go and what it will take to get there, then you're likely to get into trouble. In golf, good players typically ask themselves these questions to assist in the assessment process:

- *Where do I need to go?* The process begins with finding the right target. That target must be appropriate to your talent. You don't want to be like the Miss America contestant that Jay Leno quoted as saying, "My goal is to bring peace to the entire world—and to get my own apartment."

- *How far is my goal?* Next, a person needs to assess the distance. I enjoy telling my fellow golfers that I have a great short game—but unfortunately only off the tee! It may sound obvious, but you've got to know the distance to your goal to have a shot at making it there.

- *What are the conditions?* Good golfers always take the wind into account. The conditions make all the difference in the world. One of my personal highlights related to golf was the opportunity to play at St. Andrews in Scotland. And I shot really well that day—a 79. How did I do it? There was no wind! My caddie told me, "It's a whole different game with the wind."

- *What will it take to get there?* The final step in the assessment process is knowing what club to use. Gary Player says that bad club selection is the number one error of amateurs. They hit the ball short. It's important to know your skills and limitations when making your assessment.

How would I translate these questions for non-golfing situations? I'd say that you need to know *what* exactly you should be doing, what it will *cost* you in time, effort, and resources to get there, what *obstacles* you are likely to face, and what your *personal limitations* are. If you know these things, you will be well on your way to preparing yourself to achieve your goals.

2. Alignment—Am I Lined Up Correctly?

A good golfer can perform the assessment process flawlessly and still miss his or her target horribly. How? By lining up poorly. Psychologist James Dobson said, "What is the use of climbing the ladder of success only to find that it's leaning against the wrong building?"

When I first started playing golf, I tried to teach myself the game. I held the club with a baseball grip and lined up in a baseball stance, and more often than not, if I hit the ball any distance, I sent it into the woods. To improve my game, I had to change the way I played golf. I had to relearn the game, and that meant getting help.

If you want to take your game to the next level—personally, professionally, relationally, or recreationally—you need to find someone who is better than you to help you with the preparation process. Be open and honest with that person, and he or she will be able to evaluate your "alignment" and help you get on course.

3. Attitude—Am I Visualizing Correctly?

The final step after assessment and alignment is attitude. In golf, after you select a target and line it up, it's really a mental game. You're not just training your body—you're training your mind. But that's true for any endeavor. You have to believe in yourself and what you're doing. You have to be able to see yourself doing it with your mind's eye. If you can't imagine it, you probably will not be able to achieve it.

Preparation is one of the most obvious choices you must make in order to maximize your talent and become a talent-plus person. Sometimes the preparation process is long and slow. It may require formal education. It may necessitate your finding wise mentors. It may mean getting out of your comfort zone. Or it could mean simply fine-tuning a skill you've nearly mastered. But whatever it requires, remember that you must be ready when your time comes. People don't get a second chance to seize a once-in-a-lifetime opportunity.

TALENT + PREPARATION
APPLICATION EXERCISES

1. What process are you currently using to assess where you should be going and what you should be doing? How has it been working?

2. Find a mentor to help you check your current "alignment." Here are some questions you can ask him or her to help you get started:

   • Am I looking at the right "target"?
   • Am I seeing the potential problems?
   • Is where I'm headed going to put me in the best place for my next step?
   • What strengths do you see in me?
   • What is the potential downside of where I'm headed?
   • What is the potential upside?
   • What is my most urgent need?

3. Trainer and consultant Dru Scott Becker says that one of the best ways that people can prepare is to make use of the "Grab 15" principle. Whether you want to improve your garden, learn a new language, or get ready to start a new business, find fifteen minutes a day and work at it. She says fifteen-minute blocks add up fast, keep your head continually in the game, and often lead to even more concentrated time working on your goals. But even if you don't go beyond the fifteen-minute blocks, stick with it six days a week for a year, and you'll devote seventy-eight hours to your goal.

   Where and when can you grab fifteen minutes every day? Identify a goal and lay out a plan to achieve it—fifteen minutes at a time.

6

PRACTICE SHARPENS
YOUR TALENT

I t is a fact: you play at the level at which you practice. Consistently good practice leads to consistently good play. It sharpens your talent. Successful people understand this. They value practice and develop the discipline to do it. If you want to sum up what lifts most successful individuals above the crowd, you could do it with four little words: *a little bit more*. Successful people pay their dues and do all that is expected of them—plus a little bit more.

LOOKING FOR SUCCESS

In London, England, a young man sought to find his way in life. Only fifteen years old in 1827, young Charles possessed intelligence, ambition, and—he hoped—talent enough within himself to make his dreams for success a reality.

The boy grew up in a lower-middle-class family that had always struggled financially. His parents tended to spend a little more money than his father earned. And they had many mouths to feed, since the couple had eight children. As a result, they were continually borrowing money, putting off creditors, and moving from one place to another. In 1824, when his father was sent to debtors' prison, twelve-year-old Charles was put to work gluing labels on bottles in a factory. He hated it.

Charles had gone to school for several years before his time in the factory, and when the family's financial situation became less dire, he attended school again. He was a good student, but at age fifteen, with the family facing more hard times, he knew his school days were over. He was sent off to work, this time as a law clerk. At first he was glad to be doing tasks much different from those of his previous experience. In the factory, he had been among poor, illiterate boys doing dirty and tedious work. But it didn't take long for his work in the law office to become tedious to him. After a year and a half apprenticing there, he switched legal firms, but it was not much better. After a few months, he resigned.

Unlike his parents, with whom he still lived, Charles had managed to save some money while working, so he decided to take his time figuring out what kind of work he wanted to do. He spent long hours in the reading room at the British Museum. A profession that interested him was journalism. Not only did it appeal to his love of literature, but it would require no further formal education or any kind of apprenticeship. His uncle was a reporter, and his father wrote occasional pieces as well. How could he achieve his goal? Through hard work and lots of practice. With the benefit of books from the museum and some coaching from his uncle, John Henry Barrow, Charles began teaching himself the Gurney system of shorthand writing. Because of his diligence, it didn't take him long. Having "tamed the savage stenographic mystery," he became a freelance court stenographer at age eighteen.[1]

FROM OBSCURITY TO EXCELLENCE

His choice surprised his family, and they did not believe he would be successful. "None of us guessed at it," his father said, "and when we heard that he had become a reporter . . . my brother-in-law Barrow . . . and other relations anticipated a failure."[2] But he didn't fail. He was so good that his uncle soon hired him as a staff member of the *Mirror of Parliament* and later gave him managerial duties. By the time he was twenty-one, he was considered to be "the most rapid, the most accurate, and the most trustworthy reporter then engaged on the London press."[3]

Charles felt good about his professional progress and he was earning money, but he desired more. He desired greater income and greater fulfillment. He decided to start doing another kind of writing—more creative works. He wanted to be more than just a reporter; he wanted to become an author. He began by writing "sketches" of people and places, drawing upon his experiences traveling throughout Britain as a reporter and upon his observations while taking long daily walks throughout London. When the first sketch, "A Dinner at Poplar Walk," was complete, Charles hoped to get it published, dropping it into "a dark letter box, in a dark office, up a dark court in Fleet Street . . . with fear and trembling."[4] He was ecstatic when in December of 1833, his piece appeared in the *Monthly Magazine*. He was paid nothing for his effort, nor was his name included with his work. But that didn't matter. He was developing his talent by practicing his craft. He was on his way to becoming a professional author.

PRACTICING HIS CRAFT

He wrote more sketches in his "spare" time. With the creation of each new piece, he sharpened his talent. For a year and a half, he wrote for no payment, receiving only recognition from editors and readers as his pieces were published. His work was gaining such attention that his employer, the *Evening Chronicle*, requested that he create sketches regularly for the magazine. He agreed to do it at no charge, but also suggested that he would welcome some extra money in addition to his regular pay. His employer raised his salary from five to seven guineas a week.

The first half dozen sketches he had written were published unsigned. Later, he used the pen name "Boz." Over the next three years, he published sixty sketches in various magazines. Much to his surprise and delight, he was approached in 1836 by a young publisher who wanted to collect his writings into a volume along with ten prints from a well-known illustrator. It would be called *Sketches by Boz*. It was such a success that it went through four printings in its first year. It also earned him enough respect and recognition to be hired for another writing job: a collection of stories to be offered in monthly installments with illustrations. His years of practicing his craft by writing sketches were finally about to pay off. He knew he wanted to call this new work *The Pickwick Papers*, and he decided he would use his real name: Charles Dickens.

From Excellence to Fame

When we hear the name Charles Dickens today, most people think of long, old-fashioned novels that are required reading in English literature classes. But in his day, Charles Dickens's works were as popular as today's biggest hit television shows or movies. And there was no author in the entire world more popular than Dickens.

Jane Smiley, a Pulitzer Prize–winning novelist and biographer of Dickens, suggests that Dickens was "the first true celebrity of the popular arts—that is, a man whose work made him rich and widely famous, as close to a household name as any movie star is today" and the "first person to become a 'name brand.'"[5]

Dickens is also considered by many to be the most talented author in England's history—after Shakespeare. But before his fame, many people didn't recognize his talent. Dickens biographer Fred Kaplan writes, "When he left his legal clerkship to attempt to be a reporter, his family thought he had aimed too high. When, in the next two years, he went from legal to parliamentary reporting, they expected a failure. Understandably, they were unprepared for the explosive release of energy and talent that transformed him in a three-year period into an internationally celebrated writer."[6] How did he transform that talent? He practiced his craft by writing those sketches. Kaplan says, "The sketches were a testing ground for an apprentice author whose talent enabled him to progress precociously."[7]

The idea for Dickens to write his first novel in installments was a good one. He went on to write all of them in that fashion. Most were published in monthly installments called monthly numbers. People bought and read each installment similar to the way we now tune in to our favorite television series. People who missed the novel as a series could buy a complete bound version once the series was finished—just as we can now purchase a complete season of a TV series on DVD.

The Pickwick Papers was Dickens's first novel written in this fashion. The first monthly number sold fewer than 500 copies in April of 1836. However, Dickens kept fine-tuning the story and characters, and by the fourth "number," sales were up to 4,000. That may not seem like much, but consider this. The novel as an art form was only 100 years old, and most novels sold an average of only 300 to 400 copies. And with each episode, Dickens's sales continued growing. As the last few numbers came out, each sold a remarkable 40,000 copies. Dickens's first novel was more successful than any other novel in history to that point. At age twenty-five, he achieved success as an author that was unmatched until the next century. Over the next twenty years, more than 1.6 million copies of *Pickwick* sold in one form or another.[8]

Jane Smiley believes that Dickens's first three major works—*Sketches by Boz, The Pickwick Papers,* and *Oliver Twist*—were examples of his practicing his craft to sharpen his talent. She writes,

> Every novelist seeks . . . to extend his range of expression . . . In his twenties, [Dickens] was not unlike other youthful authors. Even

though he was a genius, he had artistic ambitions that he was not yet technically equipped to fulfill, and he used his first three books to write his way toward fulfilling them.[9]

During his thirty-five-year career, Dickens wrote more than a dozen full-length novels (some of which are considered masterpieces), several travel books, and numerous Christmas stories. And all those years, he also edited various monthly magazines and traveled extensively giving readings of his work. He was probably the most popular author in Britain's history. But as talented as he was, he didn't start out at the top. Even a genius needs practice to sharpen his talent and reach his potential.

The Power of Practice

There's a myth about highly talented people—it's that they are simply born that way. But the truth is that no people reach their potential unless they are willing to practice their way there. Recently I was traveling with Tom Mullins, a former football coach who wrote *The Leadership Game*, which contains successful leadership principles he gleaned from interviewing eight college national champion football coaches. As I talked about the idea of practice with him, he nearly leaped out of his seat. When Tom talks

> Preparation positions talent and practice sharpens it.

about anything related to leadership, it's like he's back in the locker room talking to his team at halftime when they're losing. I mean he gets excited!

"Let me tell you, John," he said, "all the national champion coaches told me the key to going from good to great came in two areas: the preparation of the team and the practice of the players. They were forever upgrading their preparation and sharpening their practices."

That made sense to me because preparation positions talent and practice sharpens it.

Before we go any further, there are three things you need to know about practice:

1. Practice Enables Development

How do we grow and develop? Through practice. People refine old skills and acquire new ones through practice. That is where the tension between where we are and where we ought to be propels us forward.

Former pro basketball player and U.S. senator Bill Bradley says that he attended a summer basketball camp when he was fifteen years old. There former college and pro basketball star "Easy" Ed Macauley told him, "Just remember that if you're not working at your game to the utmost of your ability, there will be someone out there somewhere with equal ability who will be working to the utmost of his ability. And one day you'll play each other, and he'll have the advantage."

If you desire to improve and develop, then you must practice. It allows you to break your own records and outstrip what you did yesterday. Done correctly, practice keeps making you better than you were yesterday. If you don't practice, you shortchange your potential.

2. Practice Leads to Discovery

In one of Charles Schulz's *Peanuts* strips, Charlie Brown laments to his friend Linus, "Life is just too much for me. I've been confused from the day I was born. I think the whole trouble is that we're thrown into life too fast. We're not really prepared."

"What did you want," Linus responds, "a chance to warm up first?"

> "A good leader understands that anything that has been done in a particular way for a given amount of time is being done wrong. Every single performance can be improved."
>
> —Harvey Mackay

We may not get a chance to warm up before entering childhood, but we *can* warm up by practicing the many activities we pursue once life has begun. And it is often during these "warm-ups" that we learn valuable things about ourselves. If you commit yourself to practice, here are a few things you are likely to learn:

Practice both shows and builds commitment. The true test of commitment is action. If you say, for example, that you are committed to becoming a great dancer but you never practice, that's not commitment. That's not dance. That's just talk. But when you follow through and practice, you show your commitment. And every time you follow through, your commitment becomes stronger.

Your performance can always be improved. Consultant and author Harvey Mackay says, "A good leader understands that anything that has been done in a particular way for a given amount of time is being done wrong. Every single performance can be improved." Since there is always a better way, your job is to find it.

The "sharpening" process is better in the right environment. You can't discover your abilities and improve your skills in an environment where you are not allowed to make mistakes. Improvement always requires some degree of failure. You must seek a practice area where experimentation and exploration are allowed.

You must be willing to start with small things. Human relations expert Dale Carnegie advised, "Don't be afraid to give your best to what seemingly are small jobs. Every time you conquer one it makes you that much stronger. If you do little things well, the big ones tend to take care of themselves." As you first start to practice, the gains you make may be small. But they will grow. They compound like interest. Swimming coach Daniel F. Chambliss says

> "Don't be afraid to give your best to what seemingly are small jobs. Every time you conquer one it makes you that much stronger."
>
> —Dale Carnegie

that great athletes pay attention to small details and practice them consistently. He observes, "Swimming is swimming, we can say—in practice, or in meets, it's all the same. If you swim sloppily for 364 days a year, nothing great is going to happen on the day of that big meet, no matter how excited you get."

Very small differences, consistently practiced, will produce results. A curious thing happens when you practice. At first the gains are small, as I said. Then they begin to grow. But there comes a time, if you persevere, when the gains become small again. However, at this season these small gains make big differences. In the Olympics, for example, the difference between the gold medalist and the athletes who finish without a medal is often just hundredths of a second.

There is a price to pay to reach the next level. One of the things you often learn in practice is what it will cost to reach a goal or go to the next level. As you get ready to practice, I recommend that you abide by the Taxicab Principle, which is something I learned traveling overseas: Before you get into the cab, find out how much the ride is

> "One half of knowing what you want is knowing what you must give up before you get it."
>
> —Sidney Howard

going to cost. If you don't, you may end up paying much more than the ride is worth! As you practice, keep in mind the words of screenwriter Sidney Howard, who remarked, "One half of knowing what you want is knowing what you must give up before you get it."

Many people regard practice as an essentially negative experience. It doesn't have to be that way. The best way to make practice exciting is to think of it in terms of discovery and development.

3. Practice Demands Discipline

One reason some people see practice as a grind is that it requires discipline. Even activities with intense physical demands also require lots of mental discipline. Bill McCartney, former national championship head football coach of the Colorado Buffaloes, used to tell me, "Mental preparation to physical preparation is four to one."

Developing discipline always begins with a struggle. There is no easy way to become a disciplined person. It has nothing to do with talent or ability. It is a matter not of conditions, but of choice. But once the choice is made and practice becomes a habit, two things become obvious. The first is a separation between the person who practices and the one who doesn't. Cyclist Lance Armstrong emphasizes that "success comes from training harder and digging deeper than others." He would know, having won a record seven Tour de France championships. The second thing that emerges is a winning spirit. The harder you work, the harder it becomes to surrender.

Greek philosopher Aristotle observed, "Excellence is an art won by training and habituation. We do not act rightly because we have virtue or excellence, but we rather have those because we have acted rightly. We are what we repeatedly do. Excellence, then, is not an act, but a habit." That habit is developed during practice.

THE FIVE PILLARS OF PRACTICE

I talked to a lot of leaders and coaches about practice while I was working on this chapter. And each one of them had a little different take on how to approach practice effectively. Warren Bottke is a PGA master professional who has helped thousands of amateurs and professionals improve their golf game. As Warren and I talked, we settled on five elements upon which great practice rests.

Pillar #1: An Excellent Teacher or Coach

One of my core beliefs is that everything rises and falls on leadership. I teach that truth to businesspeople all the time, but it also applies in other areas of life, including practice. People who perform at their peak practice effectively, and they practice effectively under the leadership of a great teacher.

Howard Hendricks, professor and chairman of the Center for Christian Leadership in Dallas, says, "Teaching is causing people to learn." How do good coaches do that? In part, they inspire. But good teachers do more than that. They tailor their instruction to their students. A good teacher or coach, like all good leaders, knows the strengths and weaknesses of each person. He knows whether a person is a right-brain creative/intuitive type or a left-brain analytical type. He knows whether a person learns visually, verbally, or kinesthetically. And he can tell when someone needs a pat on the back or a kick in the pants.

When Dickens started in his career, his uncle coached him as a reporter. With practice, he became the best in England. As he began writing creative pieces, a few key editors gave him feedback and, more important in his case, encouraged him to keep doing that kind of writing. Because his talent was so great, Dickens quickly outpaced the ability of those who would coach him. But throughout his life, he remained connected with other professional writers from whom he could receive advice and feedback, people such as Thomas Carlyle, Wilkie Collins, William Makepeace Thackeray, Edward Bulwer-Lytton, and John Forster.

Pillar #2: Your Best Effort

Industrialist and philanthropist Andrew Carnegie declared, "There is no use whatever trying to help people who do not help themselves. You cannot push anyone up a ladder unless he is willing to climb himself." People don't improve and reach their potential without putting forth great effort. That's why composer and orchestra leader Duke Ellington used to make a simple but demanding request of the musicians who played for him. "Just give me your best," he asked. Ellington worked hard and expected the same from others, knowing that hard work would not kill anybody (although it does seem to scare some people half to death).

Joe Theismann, who currently works as an announcer for ESPN, quarterbacked the Washington Redskins to two Super Bowl appearances in 1983 and 1984. The team won the first time and lost the second time. Today he wears his Super Bowl winner's ring and his "loser's" ring as reminders of the importance of effort. Why? Because his two experiences couldn't have been more different. During their championship season, Theismann was thrilled to be in the Super Bowl and gave his very best to win. But not the next year. About the next year, Theismann explained, "I was griping about the weather, my shoes, practice times, everything." He clearly wasn't giving his best effort. "The difference in those two rings," said Theismann, "lies in applying oneself and not accepting anything but the best."[10]

> "There is no use whatever trying to help people who do not help themselves. You cannot push anyone up a ladder unless he is willing to climb himself."
>
> —Andrew Carnegie

Pillar #3: A Clear Purpose

PGA Golfer Warren Bottke says that when he works with a new client, the first thing he does is to establish the purpose of practice. That usually means identifying a specific goal for each practice session. But the overarching purpose of practice is always improvement leading to excellence.

Pepperdine University sociology professor Jon Johnston makes a distinction between excellence and mere success:

> Success bases our worth on a comparison with others. Excellence gauges our value by measuring us against our own potential. Success grants its rewards to the few but is the dream of the multitudes.

Excellence is available to all living beings but is accepted by the . . . few. Success focuses its attention on the external—becoming the tastemaker for the insatiable appetites of the . . . consumer. Excellence beams its spotlight on the internal spirit . . . Excellence cultivates principles and consistency.[11]

As you practice, make excellence your target, and give your best to achieve it. Willow Creek founder Bill Hybels says, "Most people feel best about themselves when they have given their very best." If excellence is your goal and you arrive at it, you will be satisfied even though you never achieve success.

Pillar #4: The Greatest Potential

Have you ever noticed that two people on the same team with the same coach can practice with equal focus, effort, and purpose and have very different results? It's a fact that equal practice does not mean equal progress. I learned this fact when I was nine. By then I had been taking piano lessons for a couple of years. As I played, I thought to myself, *I'm pretty good at this.* But then one day I

> "Most people feel best about themselves when they have given their very best."
> —Bill Hybels

played at a piano recital, and it turned out to be a reality check. Elaine, a girl who had been taking piano lessons for only six months, played a more difficult piece than mine. How could she be so much better than I was so quickly? The answer is simple: her potential was much greater than mine. It didn't matter how much focused effort I put into practicing the piano. I was never going to go as far as Elaine could. Music wasn't one of my best gifts. I enjoyed playing, but I wasn't going to achieve excellence in it.

A few years ago after I spoke on leadership for Chick-fil-A, someone asked me during a Q&A session how to develop future leaders. I believe that when I quickly answered, "Find potential leaders," people thought I was being flippant. But my point was that it's much easier to train people in the area of their greatest potential. When I evaluate people's potential, I ask two questions: (1) Can they? and (2) Will they? The answers to these questions reveal something about their ability and their attitude. If both are right, the potential for excellence is high.

When Charles Dickens began thinking about writing fiction, he was already the best reporter in England. He could have remained where he was and been at the top of his profession. But something inside him must have known that as good as he was, he was not in the area of his most remarkable strength. So he took the risk of shifting his focus in search of his greatest potential.

You need to do the same. And once you figure out where your greatest potential lies, then start to practice there. If you don't, not only will you fail to increase your ability, but you'll eventually lose some of the ability you started with. You see, having potential works exactly opposite from the way a savings account does. When you put your money in a savings account, as time goes by, your money compounds and grows. The longer you leave it untouched, the more it *increases*. But when it comes to potential, the longer you leave it untouched, the more it *decreases*. If you don't tap into your talent, it wastes away.

One way that you can get the best from yourself is to set high standards for your greatest potential. Dianne Snedaker, cofounder and general partner of Wingspring, advises,

> If you are interested in success, it's easy to set your standards in terms of other people's accomplishments and then let other people measure you by those standards. But the standards you set for yourself are always more important. They should be higher than the standards anyone else would set for you, because in the end you have to live with

yourself, and judge yourself, and feel good about yourself. And the best way to do that is to live up to your highest potential. So set your standards high and keep them high, even if you think no one else is looking. Somebody out there will always notice, even if it's just you.

You can tell that you're not making the most of your potential when the standards set for you by others are higher than the ones you set for yourself. Anytime you require less of yourself than your boss, spouse, coach, or other involved person does, your potential will go untapped.

Pillar #5: The Right Resources

Even if you do many things right, including finding a good coach or mentor, focusing in your area of greatest potential, giving your best, and doing so with purpose, you can still fall short without the right resources. During World War II, General George Patton was one of the most talented and accomplished commanders for the Allied forces. He was innovative, focused, and fearless. He was a good strategist and tactician. And he possessed the tanks and men to strike boldly against the Nazis to help bring an end to the war. But one thing he often lacked: gasoline. Without fuel, his tanks were useless.

Resources are nothing more than tools you need to accomplish your purpose. Every human endeavor requires resources of some kind. To practice well, you need to be properly equipped.

TALENT + *PRACTICE* = A TALENT-PLUS PERSON
PUTTING THE TALENT-PLUS FORMULA INTO ACTION

There is one more secret to successful practice that will help you to sharpen your talent, and I believe it elevates top achievers above everyone else. Dickens displayed it. So did Joe Namath, Rueben Martinez, Meriwether Lewis, and the other highly talented people whose stories I recount in this book. It's summed up by the phrase "a little extra." Here's what I believe it takes for someone to become a talent-plus person in the area of practice:

1. A Little Extra Effort

Historian Charles Kendall Adams, who was president of Cornell University and later the University of Wisconsin, observed, "No one ever attains very eminent success by simply doing what is required of him; it is the amount of excellence of what is over and above the required that determines greatness." All accomplishments begin with the willingness to try—and then some. The difference between the ordinary and the extraordinary is the *extra!*

> "No one ever attains very eminent success by simply doing what is required of him; it is the amount of excellence of what is over and above the required that determines greatness."
>
> —Charles Kendall Adams

A little extra effort always gives a person an edge. Art Williams, the founder of Primerica Financial Services, once told me, "You beat fifty percent of the people in America by working hard; you beat forty percent by being a person of honesty and integrity and standing for something; and the last ten percent is a dogfight in the free enterprise system." If you want to win that dogfight, then do a little extra.

2. A Little Extra Time

Successful people practice harder and practice longer than unsuccessful people do. Success expert Peter Lowe, who has gleaned success secrets from hundreds of people who are at the top of their profession, says, "The most common trait I have found in all successful people is that they have conquered the temptation to give up."

Giving a little extra time requires more than just perseverance. It requires patience. The Law of Process in my book *The 21 Irrefutable*

Laws of Leadership says, "Leadership develops daily, not in a day." That can be said of any talent we try to cultivate and improve.

As you work to give a little extra time to your efforts, it is wise to maintain a longer view of the process of improvement. Such a perspective really helps. Gutzon Borglum, the sculptor who created the memorial to the American presidents at Mount Rushmore, was asked if he considered his work to be perfect. It's said he replied, "Not today. The nose of Washington is an inch too long. It's better that way, though. It will erode to be exactly right in 10,000 years." Now that's patience!

> "The most common trait I have found in all successful people is that they have conquered the temptation to give up."
>
> —Peter Lowe

3. A Little Extra Help

Anybody who succeeds at anything does so with the help of others. Alex Haley, the author of *Roots*, used to keep a reminder of that in his office. It said, "If you see a turtle on top of a fence post, you know he had help getting there."

I know that in my professional pursuits, I've always needed help. And I've been fortunate that others were willing to give it to me. Early in my career in the 1970s, I contacted the top ten leaders in my field and offered them $100 to meet with me for thirty minutes so that I could ask them questions. Many granted my request, and (fortunately for my thin wallet at the time) most declined to accept the $100. And today, I still make it a point to meet with excellent leaders from whom I desire to learn.

When I think about the ways that people have helped me in all aspects of my life, I am humbled and grateful. Some have given me advice. Others have presented me with opportunities. And a few, like my wife, Margaret, have lavished unconditional love on me. I know I am a very fortunate man.

4. A Little Extra Change

A letter was returned to the post office. Handwritten on the envelope were the words, "He's dead." Through an oversight, the letter was inadvertently sent again to the same address. It was again returned to the post office with another handwritten message: "He's still dead!"

> "We cannot become what we need to be by remaining what we are."
> —Max DePree

Let's face it. Most people are resistant to change. They desire improvement, but they resist changing their everyday routine. That's a problem because, as leadership expert Max DePree says, "We cannot become what we need to be by remaining what we are." To sharpen your talent through practice, you need to do more than just be *open* to change. You need to *pursue* change—and you need to do it a little bit more than other achievers. Here's what to look for and how to focus your energy to get the kinds of changes that will change you for the better:

- Don't change just enough to *get away* from your problems—change enough to *solve* them.

- Don't change your *circumstances* to improve your life—change *yourself* to improve your circumstances.

- Don't do *the same old things* expecting to get different results—get different results by doing *something new*.

- Don't wait to *see the light* to change—start changing as soon as you *feel the heat*.

- Don't see change as something *hurtful* that *must* be done—see it as something *helpful* that *can* be done.

- Don't avoid paying the *immediate* price of change—if you do, you will pay the *ultimate* price of never improving.

Poet and philosopher Johann von Schiller wrote, "He who has done his best for his own time has lived for all times." You can do your best only if you are continually seeking to embrace positive change.

When you have worked hard in practice to sharpen your talent and you begin to see results, please don't think that it's time to stop practicing. You never arrive at your potential—you can only continue to strive toward it. And that means continual practice.

Charles Swindoll's friend William Johnson, who owns the Ritz-Carlton hotels, was pleased when the organization won the Malcolm Baldridge National Quality Award. When Swindoll congratulated him, Johnson quickly gave others the credit for the achievement. But he also said that it made him and others in the organization work even harder to earn the respect that came with the award. Johnson summed up his attitude: "Quality is a race with no finish line." If you don't strive for excellence, then you are soon settling for acceptable. The next step is mediocrity, and nobody pays for mediocre! If you want to reach your potential and remain a talent-plus person, you have to keep practicing with excellence.

> "He who has done his best for his own time has lived for all times."
> —Johann von Schiller

TALENT + PRACTICE
APPLICATION EXERCISES

1. If you want to practice well, then you need to make sure you are incorporating the Five Pillars of Practice into your routine. Think about each one:

   - *An excellent teacher or coach.* Have you sought out someone who can help you learn your craft, sharpen your skills, or practice well? If you already have a coach, is he or she the best person to help you during this season? Do you need to find a specialist to help you improve in a specific area? You can't maximize your potential on your own.

   - *Your best effort.* Are you practicing in a way that allows you to give your best effort? Are you practicing at the right time? Are you in the best place? Are you giving yourself incentives to give your best? Do what you must to give your best.

   - *A clear purpose.* Every time you practice, do you know what you are trying to accomplish? Do you have the larger goal in mind as well as the specific improvement you are trying to make?

   - *The greatest potential.* Are you focused on developing your greatest talent? Are you staying in your strength zone? Your greatest progress and your greatest contributions will come from your areas of greatest talent.

   - *The right resources.* Do you have everything you need to practice well? What could you invest in that would facilitate your going to the next level?

2. Where are you on the practice continuum? Are you just starting out and facing a big learning curve? Are you at the phase of rapid progress? Have you already made the greatest gains of this season of your practice life and are now working on fine-tuning? Knowing where you are helps you tailor your practice routine to get the most out of it.

3. How disciplined are you when it comes to practice? Track yourself. Use a practice journal to record your practice sessions for thirty days. Write down not only when you practice and for what duration, but also make notes of what you worked on and how it went. At the end of that period, review your progress.

4. Elmer G. Letterman asserted, "The average human being in any line of work could double his productive capacity overnight if he began right now to do all the things he knows he should do, and to stop doing all the things he knows he should not do." How can you apply this piece of wisdom to your practice routine? What currently wastes your time? What task do you perform as a matter of habit that could be replaced by something that would sharpen your talent? "Audit" yourself and reinvent your practice routine.

5. Talent-plus people are always striving to do a little bit more. Upon which of the four areas outlined in the chapter do you currently need to focus more: effort, time, help, or change? What will you do to create that little extra that can take you from ordinary to *extra*ordinary?

7

PERSEVERANCE SUSTAINS YOUR TALENT

P erseverance is not an issue of talent. It is not an issue of time. It is about finishing. Talent provides hope for accomplishment, but perseverance guarantees it. Playwright Noel Coward commented, "Thousands of people have talent. I might as well congratulate you for having eyes in your head. The one and only thing that counts is: Do you have staying power?"

DARING TO DREAM

In July 2000, Vonetta Flowers landed in Sacramento, California, ready to compete in the U.S. Olympic trials for a place on the American team that would travel to Sydney, Australia, for the summer games. She had been training for it her whole life.

Vonetta had dreamed about being in the Olympics since she was a small child. She ran everywhere as a kid, and at age nine, when she had a chance to try out with an inner-city track club called the Alabama Striders in Birmingham, she gladly seized it. When the coach later looked over the list of times children ran in the 50-yard dash and saw that V. Jeffrey had the fastest time of all the kids in Jonesboro Elementary School, he assumed the time had come from one of the older boys. He was shocked to find out that it belonged to Vonetta—a third grade girl! Vonetta quickly became a star among the club's runners.

An excellent athlete, Vonetta lettered in track, volleyball, and basketball in high school and was named MVP of her track team three seasons. In college she focused exclusively on track, competing in the 200- and 400-meter sprints, long jump, triple jump, heptathlon, and relays. She was named all-American seven times.

At age twenty-six, Vonetta was competing as an elite athlete, and she was on course to make the Sydney team. She had tried out for the 1996 team at age twenty-two, competing in the 100-meter dash and long jump, but she hadn't made it. That had been tough for her. But she had dreamed of competing in the Olympics since she was nine, so she decided to put in four more years of grueling training, delayed starting a family, and gave it one more try. "In the years after college, while I worked as an assistant track coach," writes Flowers, "I continued my own training. I devoted countless hours to lifting weights, eating right, and staying mentally tough. I knew that my time as an athlete was coming to an end, and I'd hoped that the 2000 Olympic trials would prove to be my year to finally find out what it's like to be an Olympian."[1] But despite all her hopes, all her efforts, all her talent, Vonetta's best effort at the 2000 trials wasn't good enough. She did not finish with a good enough jump to make the team. Seventeen years of training had ended in failure. Her Olympic dream was over.

GIVE UP OR GO ON?

But a funny thing happened while she was in Sacramento. Her husband, Johnny, saw a flyer posted in a hallway. It read,

Continue Your Olympic Dream
by Trying Out for the Bobsled Team

Ideal candidates should be able to perform the following:

30 meters
60 meters
100 meters
Five Consecutive Hops

Vertical Jump
Shot Put Toss

Please call Bonny at [number] or come to
Davidson High School track on [date] for tryouts.

Johnny was very excited about it, but Vonetta wasn't. She knew nothing about bobsleds, she had never lived anywhere that it snowed, and she was still crestfallen about failing in the summer games trials.

Vonetta was at a crossroads. Her talent had seemed almost limitless, yet it hadn't carried her to her dream. Now here was another opportunity. But it wasn't in *her* sport. It wasn't even in her Olympics—the summer games. And even if she succeeded in passing the "audition," it would mean starting over again in a new sport on unfamiliar ground—ice. It would require a degree of perseverance beyond what she had already displayed.

Reluctantly Vonetta agreed to attend the tryouts. She discovered that her experience as a sprinter and triple jumper and her training with weights had prepared her well to become a bobsled brakewoman (the person who pushes the bobsled and rides with the driver). It took her two years of learning, training, and competing—along with the ability to survive the soap opera of drivers changing brakewomen multiple times—but she finally fulfilled her dream of making it to the Olympics, not as a track athlete in the summer games, but as a bobsledder in the winter Olympics. And in 2002, her perseverance paid off beyond her wildest dreams. Much to everyone's surprise, Vonetta and her driver, Jill Bakken, won the gold medal! And with that, Vonetta went into the record books as the first African-American to win a gold medal in a winter Olympics.

Principles of Perseverance

No matter how talented people are, there is no success without perseverance. World War I flying ace Eddie Rickenbacker said, "I can give you a six-word formula for success: Think things through—then follow through." Many people like to think things through; few follow through.

If you desire to become a talent-plus person, you need to understand some things about perseverance:

1. Perseverance Means Succeeding Because You Are Determined to, Not Destined To

Green Bay Packers coach Vince Lombardi said, "The difference between a successful person and others is not lack of strength, not a lack of knowledge, but rather a lack of determination." The greatest achievers don't sit back and wait for success because they think they deserve it. They keep moving forward and persevering because they are determined to achieve it.

> "We will either find a way or make one."
>
> —Hannibal

You can see this determination in successful people in every walk of life and in every age. Hannibal, the Carthaginian general who fought the Romans during the Second Punic War, asserted, "We will either find a way or make one." He lived out that attitude of perseverance when he led an unexpected campaign that took him over the Alps to defeat the Romans.

Talented people who succeed show similar determination. Joseph Lanier, one-time chairman and CEO of West Point-Pepperell, Inc., stated, "We are determined to win the battle. We will fight them until hell freezes over, and then, if we have to, we'll fight them on the ice." That kind of determination serves people well whether they are running an organization or pursuing a profession.

Actor Tom Hanks has been in some incredible movies of seemingly every type: comedy, suspense, action, romantic comedy, fantasy, and mystery. From *Sleepless in Seattle*, *Forrest Gump*, and *Toy Story* to *Apollo 13*, *Saving Private Ryan*, and *Philadelphia*, his movies have received popular and critical acclaim. He has been called a modern-day Jimmy Stewart. As of early 2006, the movies he's appeared in have made more than $3 billion at the box office.[2] He has also expanded his efforts into writing, directing, and producing. What actor wouldn't want a career like his?

Looking back, one might be tempted to assume that he was so talented that he was destined to succeed. Yet it didn't appear that way early on. When he started in his career, he couldn't seem to get any steady work. He tried to act in commercials but couldn't break in. He auditioned repeatedly for television shows but was constantly rejected. Finally in 1980, he landed a steady job on a sitcom called *Bosom Buddies*. It lasted two years and paid Hanks only $5,000 per episode. But it also earned him the opportunity to guest star on other TV shows. That exposure eventually led to his first big break, a starring role in the movie *Splash*.

What made the difference for Hanks? Perseverance! He never let rejection dissuade him from persevering in his career. He kept going—when he couldn't get a part, when he couldn't land a regular job, when the parts he was offered were mediocre. Ten years into his career, Hanks is reported to have said, "I've made over twenty movies and five of them are good." Today he has made nearly fifty movies, many of them first-rate. He has won two Academy Awards. And he earns $25 million per film now![3] His success has nothing to do with destiny—it has to do with determination.

2. Perseverance Recognizes Life Is Not a Long Race, but Many Short Ones in Succession

Have you heard the saying, "Life is a marathon"? Whoever first said it was almost certainly trying to encourage people to keep trying when things get tough and to have a patient yet tenacious approach to life. But I think whoever said it didn't quite get it right. Life isn't one very long race. It's actually a long series of shorter races, one after another. Each task has its own challenges. Each day is its own event. True, you have to get out of bed the next day and race again, but it's never exactly the same race as before. To be successful, you just need to keep plugging away. Talk show host Rush Limbaugh observed, "In life or in football, touchdowns rarely take place in seventy-yard increments. Usually it's three yards and a cloud of dust."

I've read that explorer Christopher Columbus faced incredible difficulties while sailing west in search of a passage to Asia. He and his crews encountered storms, experienced hunger and deprivation, and dealt with extreme discouragement. The crews of the three ships were near mutiny. But Columbus persevered. The account of the journey written by Columbus said the same thing, day after day: "Today we sailed on." And his perseverance paid off. He didn't discover a fast route to the spice-rich Indies; instead he found new continents. But as he sailed, his focus was clear—making it through the day. Winning each short race. And that's key. Management consultant Laddie F. Hutar affirmed that "success consists of a series of little daily victories."

> "Success consists of a series of little daily victories."
>
> —Laddie F. Hutar

3. Perseverance Is Needed to Release Most of Life's Rewards

At a sales convention, the corporate sales manager got up in front of all two thousand of his firm's salespeople and asked, "Did the Wright brothers ever quit?"

"No!" the sales force shouted.

"Did Charles Lindbergh ever quit?" he asked.

"No!" the salespeople shouted again.

"Did Lance Armstrong ever quit?"

"No!"

He bellowed for a fourth time, "Did Thorndike McKester ever quit?" There was a confused silence for a long moment.

Then a salesperson stood up and asked, "Who in the world is Thorndike McKester? Nobody's ever heard of him."

The sales manager snapped back, "Of course you never heard of him—because he quit!"[4]

How many highly successful people do you know who gave up? How many do you know who have been richly rewarded for quitting? I don't know any, and I bet you don't either. It's said that Walt Disney's request for a loan was rejected by 301 banks before he finally got a yes. The loan he received allowed him to build Disneyland, the first and most famous theme park in history.

Inventor Thomas Edison asserted, "Many of life's failures are people who did not realize how close they were to success when they gave up." It's the

> "Many of life's failures are people who did not realize how close they were to success when they gave up."
>
> —Thomas Edison

last step in the race that counts the most. That is where the winner is determined. That is where the rewards come. If you run every step of the race well *except* the last one and you stop before the finish line, then the end result will be the same as if you never ran a step.

4. Perseverance Draws Sweetness Out of Adversity

The trials and pressures of life—and how we face them—often define us. Confronted by adversity, many people give up while others rise up. How do those who succeed do it? They persevere. They find the benefit to them personally that comes from any trial. And they recognize that the best thing about adversity is coming out on the other side of it. There is a sweetness to overcoming your troubles and finding something good in the process, however small it may be.

I came across a poem by Howard Goodman called "I Don't Regret a Mile" that expresses this idea well. It says, in part:

> I've dreamed many a dream that's never come true,
> I've seen them vanish at dawn,
> But enough of my dreams have come true
> To make me keep dreaming on
>
> I've prayed many a prayer that seemed no answer would come,
> Though I'd waited so patient and long;
> But enough answers have come to my prayers
> To make me keep praying on
>
> I've sown many a seed that's fallen by the wayside,
> For the birds to feed upon
> But I've held enough golden sheaves in my hands
> To make me keep sowing on
>
> I've trusted many a friend that's failed me
> And left me to weep alone
> But enough of my friends have been true-blue
> To make me keep trusting on
>
> I've drained the cup of disappointment and pain,
> And gone many a day without song
> But I've sipped enough nectar from the roses of life
> To make me want to live on[5]

Giving up when adversity threatens can make a person bitter. Persevering through adversity makes one better.

5. Perseverance Has a Compounding Effect on Life

Author Napoleon Hill says, "Every successful person finds that great success lies just beyond the point when they're convinced their idea is not going to work." How do you get beyond that point? How do you go beyond what you believe is your limit? How do you achieve *lasting* success? Do the right thing, day after day. There are no shortcuts to anything worthwhile.

Every day that you do the right things—work hard, treat others with respect, learn, and grow—you invest in yourself. To do these things every day takes relentless perseverance, but if you do them, your success compounds over time. Weight-loss expert and author Judy Wardell Halliday supported this idea: "Dreams become reality when we keep our commitment to them."

6. Perseverance Means Stopping Not Because You're Tired but Because the Task Is Done

Former diplomat and recipient of the Presidential Medal of Freedom Robert Strauss commented, "Success is a little like wrestling a gorilla. You don't quit when you're tired—you quit when the gorilla is tired." If you think about it, perseverance doesn't really come into play until you *are* tired. When you're fresh, excited, and energetic, you approach a task with vigor. Work is fun. Only when you become tired do you need perseverance.

> "Success is a little like wrestling a gorilla. You don't quit when you're tired—you quit when the gorilla is tired."
>
> —Robert Strauss

To successful people, fatigue and discouragement are not signs to quit. They perceive them as signals to draw on their reserves, rely on their character, and keep going. One problem of many people is that they underestimate what it will take to succeed. Enlightenment political philosopher Montesquieu declared, "In most things success depends on knowing how long it takes to succeed." When we haven't counted the cost of success, we approach challenges with mere interest; what is really required is total commitment. And that makes all the difference.

7. **Perseverance Doesn't Demand More Than We Have but All That We Have**

Author Frank Tyger observed, "In every triumph there is a lot of try." But perseverance means more than trying. It means more than working hard. Perseverance is an investment. It is a willingness to bind oneself emotionally, intellectually, physically, and spiritually to an idea or task until it has been completed. Perseverance demands a lot, but here's the good news: everything you give is an investment in yourself.

THE FIVE ENEMIES OF PERSEVERANCE

French scientist Louis Pasteur said, "Let me tell you the secret that has led me to my goal. My strength lives solely in my tenacity." Perseverance begins with the right attitude—an attitude of tenacity. But the desire to persevere alone isn't enough to keep most people going when they are tired or discouraged. Perseverance is a trait that can be cultivated. And the initial step to developing it is to eliminate its five greatest enemies:

1. A Lifestyle of Giving Up

A little boy had been promised an ice-cream cone if he was good while accompanying his grandfather on some errands. The longer they were gone, the more difficult the boy was finding it to be good. "How much longer will it be?" the boy asked.

"Not too long," replied the grandfather. "We've got just one more stop before we get ice cream."

"I don't know if I can make it, Grandpa," the little boy responded. "I can be good. I just can't be good enough long enough."

When we were kids and we didn't follow through on a task, people often gave us a break. That's to be expected. Children tend to jump from one activity to another and to bounce from idea to idea. Adults can't do that and expect to be successful. Scientist L. G.

Elliott advised, "Vacillating people seldom succeed. They seldom win the solid respect of their fellows. Successful men and women are very careful in reaching decisions and very persistent and determined in action thereafter."

If you desire to be successful and to maximize your talent, you need to be consistent and persistent. Talent without perseverance never comes to full fruition. Opportunities without persistence will be lost. There is a direct correlation between perseverance and potential. If you have a habit of giving up, you need to overcome it to be successful.

2. A Wrong Belief That Life Should Be Easy

Debra K. Johnson tells about an incident with her seven-year-old daughter who wanted to take violin lessons. When they went to a music store together to rent an instrument, Debra began lecturing her about the expense of lessons and the commitment that would be required of her if she got her the violin. "There will be times you'll feel like giving up," Debra said, "but I want you to hang in there and keep on trying."

Her daughter nodded and, in her most serious voice, responded, "It will be just like marriage, right, Mom?" Having the right expectations going into anything is half the battle. John C. Norcross, a clinical psychologist and professor at the University of Scranton, has studied people and their goals, and he has found a characteristic that distinguishes those who reach their goals from those who don't: expectations. Both types of people experience the same amount of failure during the first month they strive for their goals. But members of the successful group don't expect to succeed right away, and they view their failures as a reason to recommit and a reminder to refocus on their goals with more determination. Norcross says, "Those who are unsuccessful say a relapse is evidence that they can't do it."[6]

3. A Wrong Belief That Success Is a Destination

The NBA's Pat Riley has won many championships as a basketball coach. In his book *The Winner Within*, he writes, "Complacency is the last hurdle any winner, any team must overcome before attaining poten-tial greatness. Complacency is the success disease: it takes root when you're feeling good about who you are and what you've achieved." It's ironic, but past success can be the fiercest enemy to future success.

In February 2006, I was invited to join some friends who were going to the Super Bowl on a private plane. I sat next to Lester Woerner, the owner of the plane and a very successful entrepreneur and businessman. He started investing in real estate when he was a teenager, helped build one of the finest turf grass companies in the country in his twenties and thirties, and now in his forties is the chairman of Woerner Holdings with investments in agriculture, real estate, and financial securities. Within minutes we were engaged in conversation, and one of the questions I asked him was how he maintained success after having achieved it.

Lester described a day when he came to the realization that he had "made it," and he started to wonder what was next for him. "I started to change," Lester explained. "I went from thinking *why not* about every opportunity that approached me to thinking *but why* when an opportu-nity arose. I lost the hunger."

When Lester stopped seizing opportunities, the opportunities began drying up. And he hit a plateau.

"How did you break out of it?" I asked.

"The first thing was to recognize that I was on a plateau; the second was to close the door on yesterday's success," he answered. "Once I did that, I was able to take steps to change, to begin going after opportuni-ties again."

I told Lester that I found that people tend to celebrate and then to relax when they see success as a destination.

"It's good to celebrate and even take a rest," Lester responded, "but not for long. We must close the door on yesterday's success."

If you think you have arrived, then you're in trouble. As soon as you think you no longer need to work to make progress, you'll begin to lose ground.

4. A Lack of Resiliency

Harvard professor of psychiatry George E. Vaillant, in his book *Aging Well*, identifies resiliency as a significant characteristic of people who navigate the many transitions of life from birth to old age. He writes, "Resilience reflects individuals who metaphorically resemble a twig with a fresh, green living core. When twisted out of shape, such a twig bends, but it does not break; instead it springs back and continues growing."[7]

That's an excellent description of how we must be if we desire to persevere through adversity and make the most of the talent we have. We must not become dry, brittle, and inflexible. And we must endeavor to bounce back, no matter how we may feel. We would be wise to remember the words of former NBA player, coach, and executive Jerry West: "You can't get much done in life if you only work on the days you feel good."

> "You can't get much done in life if you only work on the days you feel good."
>
> —Jerry West

5. A Lack of Vision

Everything that is created is actually created twice. First it is created mentally; then it is created physically. Where does that mental creation come from? The answer is vision.

People who display perseverance keep a larger vision in mind as they toil away at their craft or profession. They see in their mind's eye what they want to create or to do, and they keep working toward it as they labor. For example, years ago I read an account of an amateur golfer who played a round with Sam Snead, member of the World Golf Hall of Fame, recipient of the PGA Tour Lifetime Achievement Award, and three-time captain of the U.S. Ryder Cup team. On the first hole, Snead shot a seven—three over par, an unusually poor score for a golfer of his caliber. As the pair exited the green, Snead didn't seem to be bothered by his triple bogey. When his amateur companion asked Snead about it, he responded, "That's why we play eighteen holes." Snead's vision of the big picture helped him to maintain perspective, remain resilient, and persevere. By the end of the round, Snead finished four strokes under par.

TALENT + PERSEVERANCE = A TALENT-PLUS PERSON
PUTTING THE TALENT-PLUS FORMULA INTO ACTION

Clearing away the five enemies of perseverance is a preliminary step to becoming a talent-plus person in the area of perseverance. Right thinking always precedes right action. If you want to be able to sustain your talent, then take the following steps:

Purpose: Find One

Rich De Voss, owner of the NBA's Orlando Magic, remarked, "Persistence is stubbornness with a purpose." It is very difficult for people to develop perseverance when they lack a sense of purpose. Conversely, when one has a passionate sense of purpose, energy rises, obstacles become incidental, and perseverance wins out.

> "Persistence is stubbornness with a purpose."
>
> —Rich De Voss

Perhaps you've seen *America's Most Wanted*, the television program that re-creates the crime stories and encourages viewers to help authorities locate and capture the criminals who are wanted for these often violent crimes. The program's host is John Walsh. Many people think he is an actor or journalist—a television professional hired to host the show. But he isn't, and his story is quite remarkable.

Walsh owned his own company, and along with three partners, he built deluxe hotels. But one day his six-year-old son, Adam, disappeared. The child had been abducted, but because there was no evidence of a crime, the authorities were slow to help Walsh and his wife find their only child. They searched for sixteen days. Tragically, by the time he was found, it was too late. He was dead.

Walsh's life was thrown into chaos. He lost thirty pounds. His house went into foreclosure. And he lost his business—he just couldn't bring himself to return to his work. He had lost all hope. Then one day Dr. Ronald Wright, the county coroner, looked at Walsh and asked, "You're thinking about suicide, aren't you?"

"What do I have to live for?" Walsh replied. "I have nothing. My only child has been murdered. I can't even talk to my wife. I have no job, my house is in foreclosure, my whole life is over."

"No, it isn't," Wright responded. "You are articulate. You mounted the greatest campaign for a missing child in the history of Florida. Go out and try to change things."

Walsh says that it was the best advice he'd gotten from anyone. It gave him purpose. And that sense of purpose did more than give him a reason not to kill himself. It energized him to serve and help others. In 1988, he began hosting *America's Most Wanted,* which he continues to do as I write this. The show has been responsible for the capture of hundreds of fugitives, including fourteen who were on the FBI's Ten Most Wanted lists.

If you want to maximize your talent as a talent-plus person, you need to find your purpose. That is the only way you will be able to persevere, as John Walsh did, even when facing the most difficult circumstances.

Excuses: Eliminate Them

One of the most striking things that separates people who sustain their success from those who are only briefly or never successful is their strong sense of responsibility for their own actions. It is easier to move from failure to success than it is from excuses to success.

According to Bruce Nash, author of a series of "Hall of Shame" books on sports figures, one notorious person for making excuses was Rafael

> It is easier to move from failure to success than it is from excuses to success.

Septien, former placekicker for the NFL's Dallas Cowboys. Nash writes, "We're all guilty of using excuses. When we do, we place ourselves in the company of great sports heroes. Take Rafael Septien, for example. Rafael Septien has no peers—when it comes to making up lamebrained excuses for missed field goals." Among the excuses, perhaps tongue-in-cheek, that Septien offered:

- "I was too busy reading my stats on the scoreboard."

- "The grass was too tall." (Texas Stadium doesn't even have grass; its surface is artificial turf.)

- "The 30-second clock distracted me."

- "My helmet was too tight and it was squeezing my brain. I couldn't think."

- "No wonder [I missed]. You placed the ball upside down" (said to his holder).[8]

If you want to maximize and sustain your talent, don't allow yourself to offer excuses when you don't perform at the best of your ability. Instead, take complete responsibility for yourself and your actions. And keep in mind the words of George Washington Carver, who said, "Ninety-nine percent of failures come from people who have the habit of making excuses."

Stamina: Develop Some

Former world heavyweight champion boxer Muhammad Ali, called "The Greatest," asserted, "Champions aren't made in the gyms. Champions are made from something they have deep inside them—a desire, a dream, a vision. They have to have last-minute stamina, they have to be a little faster, they have to have the skill, and the will. But the will must be stronger than the skill." All people who achieve and maintain success possess stamina. Truly, stamina is a key to perseverance, and perseverance is a key to becoming a talent-plus person.

In February 2006, I accompanied a group of leaders from two organizations, EQUIP and Lidere, on a trip to Central and South America. We traveled together by private plane. Our mission was to launch a leadership training initiative in seven countries.

The first leg of our journey was to Honduras. We were scheduled to train a group of leaders there at a conference, and part of our plan was to have leadership books available for anyone who might want to buy them. Abraham Diaz, who works with Marcos Witt at Lidere, took charge of working out the details of getting the books through customs in Guatemala and then on to Honduras, which we needed to happen in one day in order for them to make it to the conference on time the next day. Little did we know that getting those books to the conference was going to be an exercise in perseverance. Here, in Abraham's own words, is what happened after he landed in Guatemala:

> Before I left Atlanta, where we were to meet with the rest of the group, I spent two days in Houston receiving all the instructions I needed. The books were coming down in another plane, and the plan was to keep the books in the plane so that when we arrived we wouldn't have to go through the process of importing all the material. But the company in Guatemala that we hired to bring the books in didn't follow instructions. They said that they had turned all the books over to Customs officials. It took two and a half hours to find this out. Now they didn't have any control of those boxes, and I had to go directly to Customs to see where they were located.
>
> 2:30 p.m.—I went to Customs' main office to find the boxes. But they couldn't search for them. They needed me to go back to the company

which brought in the books and get the documents they received when they turned over the boxes. I went back to get them, but was told I would have to wait for the person in charge of this matter.

3:00 p.m.—The person in charge arrived. He informed me that I needed to pay a fee at another location so that he could release these documents. I went to the other location and made the payment.

3:30 p.m.—I went back to the handling company and received the papers which included the airway bill number and invoice that Customs required.

4:00 p.m.—I arrived back at Customs and they started searching for the hundreds of boxes. As they reviewed their information, they realized the number of boxes that arrived was one less than the number reported in the documents, so they said they could not release them to me. To get them, I needed to provide a letter, stamped and approved by another Customs official, stating that I relinquished my right to the missing box.

4:30 p.m.—I walked to this office. I saw a man there who appeared to be important. When I started to explain my problem, he invited me into his office. It turned out he was the administrative director of Customs for all of Guatemala. He started typing the letter I needed himself. Then he got all of the signatures and stamps I needed to get the boxes out. I finally felt like I might succeed.

5:15 p.m.—I went back to the warehouse where international shipments are held. They kept me waiting for forty-five minutes while they processed other orders.

6:00 p.m.—The warehouse official said that in order for them to release the boxes, I had to make two different payments for storage and other charges. I went to the other location to make the payment, but I had only U.S. dollars with me, which they wouldn't take. So I jumped into a cab and went to a nearby bank to exchange money.

6:30 p.m.—I returned to make the payment and waited in line for more than twenty minutes before I could pay the fees.

7:00 p.m.—I returned to the warehouse and waited for the person who would take the receipts showing I made the proper payments. After waiting forty-five minutes, he finally arrived. He looked over the papers. He couldn't believe I had been able to do all the procedures in a few hours. He made some phone calls and looked over the papers again.

8:00 p.m.—He finally gave the okay and called the people who would operate the machinery to move the boxes to the front of the warehouse.

9:00 p.m.—I found out the workers who move the boxes in the warehouse were not the same people who would move them to the plane, so I started searching for someone who could perform this service. I waited for nearly an hour for the person in charge to show up so that I could find out how much it was going to cost and whether he had workers to do it.

10:00 p.m.—After coming to an agreement, workers started loading boxes and moving them to where the plane was. I then realized that the FBO [fixed base of operations] at this airport had no place to store the boxes overnight, so I worked it out for the people who moved them to stay with the boxes until 5:00 a.m. the next morning.

11:00 p.m.—The captain of our plane called me to let me know that his aircraft could not take all the boxes we had because of the weight. As the boxes arrived from the warehouse, I began contacting other pilots with small planes near ours to find one who was willing to take the remaining boxes to Honduras. I finally found one who was willing to do it.

The next morning, we departed and flew to Honduras—where we had to start a similar process all over again!

A lot of leaders in Honduras were very grateful for the perseverance of Abraham Diaz. Because of him, they were able to get the books they needed.

Earlier in this chapter I stated that life is not one long race but a series of many short ones in succession. Abraham Diaz's experience is a perfect illustration of this truth. On that day in Guatemala, he ran race after race for eight and a half hours—and the official who finally gave the okay to him was amazed that he had been able to do it. The next day he ran another race. And the day after that.

Abraham is a talented leader. He demonstrates the number one characteristic of good leaders: the ability to make things happen. That takes perseverance. That's true no matter what your talent is or what skills you possess. Without perseverance, a talented person is little more than a flash in the pan.

TALENT + PERSEVERANCE
APPLICATION EXERCISES

1. Purpose gives passion, and passion feeds perseverance. What is your purpose? If you haven't defined it and written it out, do so now.

2. How often do you think you make excuses when you fail to accomplish something you set out to do? Is it 20 percent of the time? Perhaps 60 percent of the time? Define it as a percentage. Now do this: ask three people who know you well (and who see you at your worst) to define how often you make excuses.

   If the figure they give you averages more than 10 percent, then you need to work on this area. First, ask those people to hold you accountable for not making excuses. Second, train yourself to ask, *What can I learn from this?* rather than, *What went wrong?*

3. What is your attitude toward life's challenges? Do you expect obstacles and failures? What do you do if you don't succeed right away? Do you give up and try something else, or do you keep working at it?

   Stamina comes from expecting life to be difficult, from developing the habit of overcoming adversity, and from taking one more step when you think you have nothing left. What recent obstacle, failure, or setback that stopped you can you revisit and attack again with renewed energy? Take it on again. And when you feel like quitting again, push yourself to take one more step. *Then* reevaluate it and see if you need to take *one more step* again.

4. How can you personally apply the concept of life as a series of short races? Where will this idea most benefit you? How will it change your approach to a task, responsibility, or opportunity?

5. What are you willing to give to realize your potential and maximize your talent as a talent-plus person? Give it some think time and create two lists: things you are willing to give up to go to the next level, and things you are unwilling to compromise.

8

COURAGE TESTS
YOUR TALENT

People think of courage as a quality required only in times of extreme danger or stress, such as during war or disaster. But it is much larger than that—and more ordinary than we think. Courage is an everyday virtue. Professor, writer, and apologist C. S. Lewis wrote, "Courage is not simply one of the virtues, but the form of every virtue at its testing point." You can do nothing worthwhile without courage. The person who exhibits courage is often able to live without regrets.

BRITISH BULLDOG

When I think about people whose talent was elevated—and tested—by their courage, one individual who immediately comes to mind is Winston Churchill. As a young man, Churchill anticipated greatness for himself. While he was in school at Harrow at age sixteen, Churchill's response to a classmate's queries about his future were bold. "I can see vast changes coming over a now peaceful world," said the teenage Churchill, "great upheavals, terrible struggles, wars such as one cannot imagine; and I tell you London will be in danger, London will be attacked and I shall be very prominent in the defence [sic] of London . . . In the high position I shall occupy, it will fall to me to save the Capital, to save the Empire."[1] The vision Churchill had of his role was remarkably on target.

After Europe fell to the Nazis, Great Britain stood alone against them for two years with Churchill as their leader. He defied Hitler and continually rallied the people of the nation while they suffered under repeated German bombings and faced the threat of a possible German invasion. In the 1930s prior to war, Britain's strategy had been to appease Hitler. All during that time, Churchill vocally expressed his opposition to such actions. In 1940, when Prime Minister Neville Chamberlain was forced from office, Britain looked for a strong leader to replace him. The natural successor to Chamberlain would have been Lord Halifax, the foreign secretary. But Halifax knew that he didn't possess the qualities needed to lead Britain in war, and he declined the potential appointment. That's when Churchill, then age sixty-six, was called to step into the gap.[2]

Why would Churchill be chosen as prime minister? He had been out of favor for many years. Why would anyone believe Churchill had the courage to lead the nation in what appeared to be a cause for which many believed there was little hope? The answer is that his courage had been tested time and time again, and it had proven his talent.

A Desire to Distinguish Himself

Growing up, Churchill was a merely average student. He was clumsy and accident prone. As a teenager in boarding school at Harrow, he didn't really begin to shine until he prepared for a career in the army. He excelled at history, was an excellent rider, and won the school's fencing championship. After Harrow, he completed his military officer's training at Sandhurst, and in 1895, at twenty years old, he was commissioned into the 4th Hussars, a cavalry unit that was destined for India.

His long-term goal was to enter politics, as his father had. But first he wanted to make a name for himself in the military. While waiting to ship out to India, he was eager for action, and he managed to join with Spanish forces, which were in combat in Cuba, as an observer to test his mettle. He later wrote, "I thought it might be as well to have a private rehearsal, a secluded trial trip in order to make sure that the ordeal was not unsuited to my temperament."[3] He proved himself courageous under fire and was even recommended for the Cross of the Order of Military Merit.

Once stationed in quiet Madras, India, he quickly grew bored, and once again, he sought action. He managed to get attached as a correspondent to the Malakand Field Force on the northwest frontier of India more than two thousand miles from Madras, but soon he ended up joining the commanding general's staff. "I mean to play this game out and if I lose, it is obvious that I could never have won any other," he wrote to his family. "I am more ambitious for a reputation for personal courage than anything else in the world."[4]

A HISTORY OF COURAGE

He didn't have to wait long to begin proving himself. He saw battle twice. The first time the unit was attacked, Churchill was under fire for thirteen hours. He was clearheaded in battle and even assisted another officer in carrying a wounded soldier to safety. He later wrote, "Bullets are not worth considering . . . I do not believe the gods would create so potent a being as myself for so prosaic an ending."[5] He described his second experience as the hardest fighting on the northwest frontier for forty years. During the five-hour battle, the unit suffered fifty wounded and seventeen killed, including the regimental commander.

When things quieted down, Churchill again looked for action. His mother's influence helped him get into the 21st Lancers in Cairo. With them, he participated in what's been called the last great cavalry charge in the history of the British Army. His unit was on reconnaissance that day near Khartoum and spotted 150 enemy spearmen. The British charged them, only to find that they had ridden into a trap. They ended up in fierce hand-to-hand combat. Within two minutes, 119 of the British army's horses were wounded, 21 of their force were killed, and 50 more were wounded. Churchill fought valiantly, and his unit was victorious

In 1899, Churchill was ready to start his political career. He resigned from the army and ran for a seat in Parliament. He lost. Later that year, when war broke out in South Africa, Churchill went there to cover it as a correspondent for the *Morning Post*. Two weeks later, as he traveled with troops on an armored train, rebels attacked and derailed it. Churchill calmly took charge and rallied the troops. He helped to clear the rails, allowing the locomotive and tender to escape with the wounded. Then he went back to try to help the troops commander, only to be captured. He was taken to a temporary prison in Pretoria.

But Churchill refused to give in to defeat. After a month of captivity, he made a daring escape from the prison. He climbed over the prison wall and hopped a freight train. The Boer rebels posted a reward for his capture—dead or alive—but Churchill managed to make it to Durban. When he arrived there, he found that he had become a national hero and an international celebrity. After a six-month stint in the South African Light Horse, an irregular cavalry regiment, he returned to England where he once again ran for Parliament. This time he won. He was twenty-six years old.

Churchill's grandson, Winston S. Churchill, wrote,

When one considers the number of occasions on which he hazarded his life, even after he resigned his commission and entered Parliament at the age of 26 in 1900, walking out of the wreck of a crashed airplane in the earliest days of aviation, serving in the trenches of Flanders where he commanded the 6th Battalion of the Royal Scots Fusiliers in the line in 1917, and again when he was knocked down by a New York taxi in 1930 one cannot help but reflect that his preservation through all these hazards was nothing short of miraculous.[6]

So when Winston Churchill was chosen to be prime minister in 1940, people who knew him understood what the country was getting. His courage, toughness, and talent had been well tested. His entire life had prepared him for what he would face during those five war years. And his performance didn't disappoint.

Why Does Talent Need Courage?

The stakes were high for Churchill as he carried out his duties as prime minister. He was doing more than just defending London and the empire, though those responsibilities were obviously monumental. Freedom and democracy were hanging in the balance. But his first tests didn't come when the stakes were so high. They came early. If he hadn't possessed the courage to step up when he was young and untested, he never would have discovered the depth of his talent, nor would he have been ready when he had to perform on the world stage.

English writer and clergyman Sydney Smith asserted, "A great deal of talent is lost to the world for want of a little courage." To develop and discover our talent, we need courage. The English word *courage* comes from the French word *coeur*, which means "heart." And we need to recognize that if we display courage, our hearts will be tested continually. Here's what I mean:

> "A great deal of talent is lost to the world for want of a little courage."
>
> —Sydney Smith

Our Courage Will Be Tested . . .
As We Seek a Truth That We Know May Be Painful

Before he joined the army, Winston Churchill had a desire to create a reputation for bravery, but he didn't know whether he had the talent for it. To make that discovery, he went to Cuba. His goal was to test his courage in a relatively controlled and somewhat safer environment than he thought he would face in India, what he called "a private rehearsal."

> "The truth that makes men free is for the most part the truth which men prefer not to hear."
>
> —Herbert Agar

He understood that a person doesn't know what he's really made of until tested. If we fear the test, then we will never get a chance to develop the talent.

Most of us will never be asked to face flying bullets in a physical battle. Often our tests are much more private and involve an internal battle, and many people find that painful. Pulitzer Prize–winning columnist Herbert Agar said, "The truth that makes men free is for the most part the truth which men prefer not to hear."

In order to grow, we need to face truths about ourselves, and that is often a difficult process. It usually looks something like this:

- *The issue*. Often it is something we do not want to hear about.
- *The temptation*. We want to ignore it, rationalize it, spin it, or package it.
- *The decision*. To grow, we must face the truth and make personal changes.
- *The challenge*. Change is not easy; our decision to change will be tested daily.
- *The response*. Others will be slow to acknowledge it; they will wait to see if our behavior changes.
- *The respect*. Respect is always gained on difficult ground, and it comes from others only when our behavior and words match.

Winston Churchill said, "Courage is what it takes to stand up and speak; courage is also what it takes to sit down and listen." It takes a brave person to listen to unpleasant truths. I have to admit that this has been a challenging area for me. I find it much easier to cast vision, motivate people, and lead the charge than to sit, listen to others speak truth, humble myself, and respond appropriately, but I'm continuing to work on it.

Our Courage Will Be Tested . . . When Change Is Needed but Inactivity Is More Comfortable

Being inactive and never leaving what is familiar may mean that you are comfortable, but having the willingness to continually let go of the familiar means that you are courageous. American historian James Harvey Robinson asserted, "Greatness, in the last analysis, is largely due to bravery—courage in escaping from old ideas and old standards and respectable ways of doing things."

Our situation doesn't make us; we make our situation. Our circumstances don't have to define us; we can redefine our circumstances by our actions. At any given time, we must be willing to give up all we have in order to become all we can be. If we do that, if we are willing to leave our comfort zone and bravely keep striving, we can reach heights we thought were beyond us. We can go farther than others who possess greater talent than we do. Italian actress Sophia Loren observed, "Getting ahead in a difficult profession requires avid faith in yourself. That is why some people with mediocre talent, but with the inner drive, go much farther than people with vastly superior talent."

> "Getting ahead in a difficult profession requires avid faith in yourself. That is why some people with mediocre talent, but with the inner drive, go much farther than people with vastly superior talent."
>
> —Sophia Loren

Our Courage Will Be Tested . . . When Our Convictions, Once Expressed, Are Challenged

Anytime you are willing to stand up for something, someone else will be willing to take a shot at you. People who express their convictions and attempt to live them out will experience conflict from others with opposing views. Ralph Waldo Emerson wrote, "Whatever you do, you need courage. Whatever course you decide upon, there is always someone to tell you you are wrong. There are always difficulties arising which tempt you to believe that your critics are right. To map out a course of action and follow it to an end, requires some of the same courage which a soldier needs. Peace has its victories, but it takes brave men to win them." So should we simply keep a low profile, swallow our convictions, and keep the peace? Of course not! The opposite of courage isn't cowardice; it is conformity. It's not enough just to believe in something. We need to live for something. Howard Hendricks said, "A belief is something you will argue about. A conviction is something you will die for." You cannot really live unless there are things in your life for which you are willing to die.

Our Courage Will Be Tested . . . When Learning and Growing Will Display Our Weakness

Learning and growing always require action, and action takes courage—especially in the weak areas of our lives. That is where fear most often comes into play. It's easy to be brave in an area of strength; it's much more difficult in an area of weakness. That is why we need courage most. General Omar Bradley remarked, "Bravery is the capacity to perform properly even when scared half to death."

When I am striving to learn and grow in an area of weakness and I am afraid of failing or looking foolish, I encourage myself with these quotations:

- "Courage is fear holding on a minute longer."
  —George S. Patton

- "The difference between a hero and a coward is one step sideways."—Gene Hackman
- "Courage is fear that has said its prayers."—Karl Barth
- "Courage is doing what you're afraid to do. There can be no courage unless you're scared."—Eddie Rickenbacker
- "Courage is being scared to death but saddling up anyway." —John Wayne

We often mistakenly believe that learning is passive, that we learn by reading a book or listening to a lecture. But to learn, we must take action. As Coach Don Shula and management expert Ken Blanchard state, "Learning is defined as a change in behavior. You haven't learned a thing until you can take action and use it." And that is where fear often comes into play. The learning process can be summarized in the following five steps:

1. Observe.
2. Act.
3. Evaluate.
4. Readjust.
5. Go back to step 2.

Every time you prepare to take action, fear will to some degree come into play. It is at those times that you must rely on courage.

David Ben-Gurion, the first prime minister of Israel, observed, "Courage is a special kind of knowledge; the knowledge of how to fear what ought to be feared, and how not to fear what ought not to be feared. From this knowledge comes an inner

> "Learning is defined as a change in behavior. You haven't learned a thing until you can take action and use it."
>
> —Don Shula and Ken Blanchard

strength that subconsciously inspires us to push on in the face of great difficulty. What can seem impossible is often possible, with courage." Courage is a releasing force for learning and growth.

Our Courage Will Be Tested . . . When We Take the High Road Even as Others Treat Us Badly

In 2004 I wrote a book called *Winning with People: Discover the People Principles That Work for You Every Time.* In it is the High Road Principle, which says, "We go to a higher level when we treat others better than they treat us." When it comes to dealing with others, there are really only three routes we can take:

The low road—where we treat others worse than they treat us

The middle road—where we treat others the same as they treat us

The high road—where we treat others better than they treat us[7]

The low road damages relationships and alienates others from us. The middle road may not drive people away, but it doesn't attract them either. But the high road creates positive relationships with others and attracts people to us—even in the midst of conflict.

Taking the high road requires two things. The first is courage. It certainly isn't one's immediate inclination to turn the other cheek and treat people well while they treat you badly. How does one find the courage to do that? By relying on the second thing, about which clergyman Dr. James B. Mooneyhan writes:

There is a great cancer working at the integrity of our society. It gets in the way of our efficiency and hampers our success. It robs us of the promotions we seek and the prestige we desire. The great tragedy is that none of us are immune to it automatically. Each of us must work to overcome it.

This malignancy is the lack of the ability to forgive. When some-one wrongs us we make mental notes to remember what was done or we think of ways to "get back at them." Someone gets the promotion we wanted so badly and resentment toward that person begins to build. Our spouse makes a mistake or does something offensive to us and we see what we can do to get even or at least make sure they never forget the hurt they have caused us.

When we keep score of wrongs committed against us, we reveal a lack of maturity. Theodore Roosevelt once said, "The most important single ingredient in the formula of success is knowing how to get along with people." Those who do not forgive are persons who have not yet learned this truth and they are usually unsuccessful people.

If you wish to improve this area of your life, here are some things that should help. First, practice forgiving . . . Secondly, think good thoughts of those persons . . . It is difficult to have hostile feelings toward one in whom you see good. Finally, let people know through your actions that you are one who can forgive and forget. This will gain respect for you.

Remember this: Committing an injury puts you below your enemy; taking revenge only makes you even with him, but forgiving him sets you above.

No one makes the most of his talent in isolation. Becoming your best will require the participation of other people. When you take the high road with others, you make yourself the kind of person others want to work with—and you put yourself in the best position to help others at the same time.

Our Courage Will Be Tested . . . When Being "Out Front" Makes Us an Easy Target

Many people admire leaders and innovators. Organizations give them honors; historians write books about them; sculptors chisel their images on the face of mountains. However, while many people lift leaders up, others want to knock them down. C. V. White describes this tension well:

> The man who makes a success of an important venture never waits for the crowd. He strikes out for himself. It takes nerve, it takes a lot of grit; but the man that succeeds has both. Anyone can fail. The public admires the man who has enough confidence in himself to take the chance. These chances are the main things after all. The man who tries to succeed must expect to be criticized. Nothing important was ever done but the greater number consulted previously doubted the possibility. Success is the accomplishment of that which people think can't be done.

If you are a leader or even an innovative thinker, you will often be ahead of the crowd, and that will at times make you an easy target. That requires courage.

For many years, I hosted an event in Atlanta called Exchange. It was a weekend leadership experience for executives. I usually did some leadership teaching, brought in some high-profile leaders to answer questions, and arranged a unique leadership experience. One year we took the group to the King Center so that they could be impacted by the life and legacy of a great leader, Martin Luther King Jr. We then took them over to Ebenezer Baptist Church. And as a surprise we had arranged for King's widow, Coretta Scott King, and daughter Bernice to be there so that everyone could meet them.

One question asked of Mrs. King was what it was like being with Dr. King during the civil rights movement, and she talked about the loneliness of being a pioneer and taking new territory. She said that her husband was often misunderstood, and she pointed out how much courage it took to stand alone.

We will almost certainly never have to face the hatred and violence that Martin Luther King Jr. did, but that doesn't mean that we don't need courage to lead. Often leaders are misunderstood, their motives are misconstrued, and their actions are criticized. That, too, can be a test—one that makes us stronger and sharpens our talent if only we have the courage to endure it.

Our Courage Will Be Tested . . . Whenever We Face Obstacles to Our Progress

Advice columnist Ann Landers wrote, "If I were asked to give what I consider the single most useful bit of advice for all humanity, it would be this: Expect trouble as an inevitable part of life and when it comes, hold your head high, look it squarely in the eye and say, 'I will be bigger than you. You cannot defeat me."

Adversity is always the partner of progress. Anytime we want to move forward, obstacles, difficulties, problems, and predicaments are going to get in the way. We should expect nothing less. And we should even welcome such things. Novelist H. G. Wells asked, "What on earth would a man do with himself if something didn't stand in his way?" Why would he make such a comment? Because he recognized that adversity is our friend, even though it doesn't feel that

> Adversity is always the partner of progress. Anytime we want to move forward, obstacles, difficulties, problems, and predicaments are going to get in the way.

way. Every obstacle we overcome teaches us about ourselves, about our strengths and weaknesses. Every obstacle shapes us. When we succeed in the midst of difficulty, we become stronger, wiser, and more confident. The greatest people in history are those who faced the most difficult challenges with courage and rose to the occasion. That was certainly true of Winston Churchill.

Pat Williams, in his book *American Scandal*, writes about Churchill's last months. He says in 1964, former president and World War II general Dwight D. Eisenhower went to visit the former prime minister.

Eisenhower sat by the bold-spirited leader's bed for a long period of time, neither speaking. After about ten minutes, Churchill slowly raised his hand and painstakingly made the "V" for victory sign, which he had so often flashed to the British public during the war. Eisenhower, fighting back tears, pulled his chair back, stood up, saluted him, and left the room. To his aide out in the hallway, Eisenhower said, "I just said good-bye to Winston, but you never say farewell to courage."[8]

TALENT + COURAGE = A TALENT-PLUS PERSON
PUTTING THE TALENT-PLUS FORMULA INTO ACTION

It's tempting to learn about the life of someone like Churchill or Eisenhower and believe that certain people are born with courage and are destined for greatness while others must sit on the sidelines and simply admire them. But I don't think that is true. I believe that anyone can develop courage. If you desire to become a more courageous person, then do the following:

1. Look for Courage Inside, Not Outside, Yourself

During the Great Depression, Thomas Edison delivered his last public message. In it he said, "My message to you is: Be courageous! I have lived a long time. I have seen history repeat itself again and again. I have seen many depressions in business. Always America has come out stronger and more prosperous. Be as brave as your fathers before you. Have faith! Go forward!" Edison knew that when we experience fear, we must be willing to move forward. That is an individual decision. Courage starts internally before it is displayed externally. We must first win the battle within ourselves.

I love the story about the shortest letter to the editor written to England's newspaper the *Daily Mail*. When the editor invited readers to send in their answers to the question, "What's wrong with the world?" writer G. K. Chesterton is reputed to have sent the following:

Dear Sir,

I am.

Yours sincerely,

G. K. Chesterton

The old saying goes, "If we could kick the person responsible for most of our troubles, we wouldn't be able to sit down for a week." Courage, like all other character qualities, comes from within. It begins as a decision we make and grows as we make the choice to follow through. So the first step toward becoming a talent-plus person in the area of courage is to decide to be courageous.

2. Grow in Courage by Doing the Right Thing Instead of the Expedient Thing

Florence Nightingale observed, "Courage is . . . the universal virtue of all those who choose to do the right thing over the expedient thing. It is the common currency of all those who do what they are supposed to do in a time of conflict, crisis, and confusion." The acquisition of courage can often be an internal battle. We often desire to do what is most expedient. The problem is that what is easy and expedient is frequently not what is right. Thus the battle. But psychotherapist and author Sheldon Kopp stated, "All the significant battles are waged within self."

As you strive to do what you know to be right, you must know yourself and make sure you are acting in integrity with your core values. There's a saying that inside every individual there are six people. They are . . .

Who You Are Reputed to Be
Who You Are Expected to Be
Who You Were
Who You Wish to Be
Who You Think You Are
Who You Really Are

You must strive to be true to who you really are. If you do and you do the right thing, then you will increase in courage.

3. Take Small Steps of Courage to Prepare You for Greater Ones

Most of us want to grow quickly and be done with it. The reality is that genuine growth is slow, and to be successful, we should start with small things and do them every day. St. Francis de Sales advised, "Have patience with all things, but chiefly have patience with yourself. Do not lose courage in considering your own imperfections, but instantly start remedying them—every day begin the task anew."

People's lives change when they change something they do every day. That's how they change the "who they wish to be" into "who they really are." What kinds of things can you do every day? You can have the courage to be positive as you get up in the morning to face the day. You can have the courage to be gracious in defeat. You can have the courage to apologize when you hurt someone or make a mistake. You can have the courage to try something new—any small thing. Each time you display bravery of any kind, you make an investment in your courage. Do that long enough, and you will begin to live a *lifestyle* of courage. And when the bigger risks come, they will seem much smaller to you because you will have become much larger.

> People's lives change when they change something they do every day.

4. Recognize That a Leadership Position Won't Give You Courage, but Courage Can Make You a Leader

In my years of teaching leadership, I have found many people who believed that if only they could receive a title or be given a position, that would make them a leader. But life doesn't work that way. Former British prime minister Margaret Thatcher remarked, "Being a leader is a lot like being a lady. If you have to tell people you are one, you aren't." The position doesn't make the leader; the leader makes the position.

In similar fashion, people should not expect the acquisition of a leadership position to give them courage. However, anytime people continually display courage, they will likely become leaders because others will look up to them, emulate them, and follow them. Jim Mellado, president of the Willow Creek Association, described leadership as "the expression of courage that compels people to do the right thing."

> Leadership is "the expression of courage that compels people to do the right thing."
>
> —Jim Mellado

5. Watch Your Horizons Expand with Each Courageous Act

The life you live will expand or shrink in proportion to the measure of courage you display. Those who are willing to take risks, explore their limits, face their shortcomings, and sometimes experience defeat will go farther than people who timidly follow the safe and predictable path. Founder of *Success* magazine, Orison Swett Marden, stated it this way:

> The moment you resolve to take hold of life with all your might and make the most of yourself at any cost, to sacrifice all lesser ambitions to your one great aim, to cut loose from everything that interferes with this aim, to stand alone, firm in your purpose, whatever happens, you set in motion the divine inner forces the Creator has implanted in you for your own development. Live up to your resolve, work at what the Creator meant you to work for the perfecting of His plan, and you will be invincible. No power on earth can hold you back from success.

If you want to become a talent-plus person, you must show courage. There is no other way to reach your potential.

When I began my leadership career, I was very ineffective as a leader. I believed I had talent. I had been able to influence and lead others at every phase of my school career. But when I got out into the real world, I fell far short of my expectations. My talent was being tested, and I was falling short. My problem was that I wanted to please everybody. Making people happy was the most important thing to me. The bottom line was that I lacked the courage to make right but unpopular decisions. How did I turn things around? By making small decisions that were difficult. With each one, I gained more confidence and more courage, and I began to change. The process took me four years.

At the end of that time, I felt I had learned many valuable lessons, and I wrote the following to help me cement what I had learned:

Courageous Leadership Simply Means I've Developed:

1. Convictions that are stronger than my fears.
2. Vision that is clearer than my doubts.
3. Spiritual sensitivity that is louder than popular opinion.
4. Self-esteem that is deeper than self-protection.
5. Appreciation for discipline that is greater than my desire for leisure.
6. Dissatisfaction that is more forceful than the status quo.
7. Poise that is more unshakeable than panic.
8. Risk taking that is stronger than safety seeking.
9. Right actions that are more robust than rationalization.
10. A desire to see potential reached more than to see people appeased.

You don't have to be great to become a person of courage. You just need to want to reach your potential and to be willing to trade what seems good in the moment for what's best for your potential. That's something you can do regardless of your level of natural talent.

TALENT + COURAGE
APPLICATION EXERCISES

1. How often do you fail? The frequency is a sure indication of your inclination to take risks. Successful people understand that failure is a natural part of the process of making progress. For seven days, make it a point to record every failure in a journal or planner. At the end of the week, evaluate your willingness to take risks.

2. Talk to your spouse or a trusted friend and ask where you most need to change and grow. Promise this individual that if he or she will confide in you, you will hold your peace and not defend yourself or make excuses for a week. Then keep your promise and use those seven days to reflect on the person's assessment of you. Remember, it takes courage to seek a truth that may be painful to you.

3. Which do you value more highly, pleasure or progress? One of the ways to assess the honesty of your answers is to examine your goals. Do your goals involve comfort or accomplishment? If pleasure and comfort are higher on your priority list, you may not be taking enough chances to maximize your talent and reach your potential.

4. Plan to develop your courage by doing something uncomfortable or scary once or twice a week for two months. Put them on your calendar and to-do list. These actions can be small. You don't have to sky-dive or bungee jump, although you can do those kinds of things if you are inclined to. The more actions requiring courage that you take, the braver you will become. Your goal is to develop a lifestyle of courage.

5. When others treat you poorly, how do you respond? Do you respond in kind, giving tit for tat? It's often not easy to take the high road. However, if you can, you will find that your life has less conflict, you will experience less stress, and others will be attracted to you. Begin by forgiving others for past hurts. Make a list of any grudges you are currently holding or ill feelings you are carrying toward others. Then work through them on your own. If you need to go to anyone on the list to forgive him, do so. Then make it a point to treat others better than they treat you, not only for their sake, but also for your own.

9

TEACHABILITY EXPANDS YOUR TALENT

If you are a highly talented person, you may have a tough time with teachability. Why? Because talented people often think they know it all. And that makes it difficult for them to continually expand their talent. Teachability is not so much about competence and mental capacity as it is about *attitude*. It is the desire to listen, learn, and apply. It is the hunger to discover and grow. It is the willingness to learn, unlearn, and relearn. I love the way Hall of Fame basketball coach John Wooden states it: "It's what you learn after you know it all that counts."

When I teach and mentor leaders, I remind them that if they stop learning, they stop leading. But if they remain teachable and keep learning, they will be able to keep making an impact as leaders. Whatever your talent happens to be—whether it's leadership, craftsmanship, entrepreneurship, or something else—you will expand it if you keep expecting and striving to learn. Talented individuals with teachable attitudes become talent-plus people.

More Than Enough Talent

Who is the most talented person who ever lived? There's really no way for us to make that determination. How would you even pick your criteria? What talent would you value? Intelligence? Creativity? Athletic prowess? Musical ability? Business acumen? Artistic mastery? Charisma? People skills? Professional influence? You could perhaps make a strong argument for any of these criteria. But what if you used *all* of these characteristics to judge who was most talented? If you did, Leonardo da Vinci would certainly be a strong candidate.

Leonardo has been called *Homo Universalis*, a "universal man," for his incredible ability to master diverse disciplines. The term *Renaissance man* was coined for him because he embodied the rebirth movement and displayed so many talents. He was admired by his peers, by his protégés, and by the artists, scientists, and historians who have studied his life. Giorgio Vasari, author of the classic work *The Lives of the Artists*, captured the common opinion of da Vinci when he wrote:

> The greatest gifts often rain down upon human bodies through celestial influences as a natural process, and sometimes in a supernatural fashion a single body is lavishly supplied with such beauty, grace, and ability that wherever the individual turns, each of his actions is so divine that he leaves behind all other men and clearly makes himself known as a genius endowed by God (which he is) rather than created by human artifice. Men saw this in Leonardo da Vinci, who displayed great physical beauty (which has never been sufficiently praised), a more than infinite grace in every action, and an ability so fit and so vast that wherever his mind turned to difficult tasks, he resolved them completely with ease. His great personal strength was joined to dexterity, and his spirit and courage were always regal and magnanimous. And the fame of his name spread so widely that not only was he held in high esteem in his own times, but his fame increased even more after his death.[1]

If Leonardo had only sculpted, he would have been famous as a sculptor. If he had only painted, he still would have been revered as a master. If he had only studied anatomy, hydraulics, and optics, he would have been viewed as a groundbreaking scientist. If he had only engineered fortifications, designed buildings, and manufactured heavy weapons—for which he was employed much of his professional life—he would have been held in high regard. He was a good athlete, a fine musician, and an excellent singer. He assisted the Italian mathematician Luca Pacioli in creating the *Divina Proportione*. He seemed able to do anything.

HUNGER TO LEARN

What set Leonardo apart? Was it a simple case, as Vasari says, of all talents coming together in a single person? I believe it was more than that. Da Vinci's talent was extraordinary—but so was his teachability. And the evidence for it can be found in his notebooks. They are a physical record of a mind that never stopped discovering and never ceased learning.

Many artists create notebooks to record their ideas and to make practice sketches. For example, Picasso produced 178 sketchbooks during his life, often using them to explore themes and make compositional studies before creating a painting. But Leonardo's notebooks go far beyond an artist's sketches. They display a highly teachable mind at work, and they show the breadth of his learning and the depth of his thinking.

Microsoft founder Bill Gates purchased one of those notebooks in 1994. The notebook is called the Codex Leicester and was created by da Vinci between 1506 and 1510. Its seventy-two pages contain sketches and text on water, light, and several other subjects. Sometimes his writings were motivated by his desire to discover more about art, such as his observations about how light is reflected off paint. Other times, like the great scientists who lived before and after him, he made acute observations and rendered scientific explanations. For example, da Vinci noted that sometimes when viewing the crescent moon in the twilight sky, the entire circular outline of the moon was faintly visible. He deduced that sunlight reflected from the earth's oceans to create the effect, which was confirmed more than a hundred years later.[2]

Gates says, "I've been fascinated by da Vinci's work since I was 10. Leonardo was one of the most amazing people who ever lived. He was a genius in more fields than any scientist of any age, and he was an astonishing painter and sculptor. His notebooks were hundreds of years ahead of their time. They anticipated submarines, helicopters and other modern inventions.

"His scientific 'notebooks' are awe inspiring," continues Gates, "not simply as repositories of his remarkable ideas but as records of a great mind at work. In the pages of the Codex Leicester, he frames important questions, tests concepts, confronts challenges, and strives for answers."[3]

In one notebook, da Vinci wrote, "Iron rusts from disuse; stagnant water loses its purity and in cold weather becomes frozen; even so does inaction sap the vigor of the mind."[4] That distaste for inaction drove his intellectual curiosity his entire life. Leonardo da Vinci's love for learning never stopped. He was learning and writing his discoveries in his notebooks until the very end of his life. And it is the main reason we remember him.

TEACHABILITY TRUTHS

The good news is that we don't have to have the talent of a Leonardo da Vinci to be teachable. We just need to have the right attitude about learning. To do that, consider the following truths about teaching:

1. Nothing Is Interesting If You Are Not Interested

Management guru Philip B. Crosby writes in his book *Quality Is Free*:

> There is a theory of human behavior that says people subconsciously retard their own intellectual growth. They come to rely on clichés and habits. Once they reach the age of their own personal comfort with the world, they stop learning and their mind runs on idle for the rest of their days. They may progress organizationally, they may be ambitious and eager, and they may even work night and day. But they learn no more.[5]

It's a shame when people allow themselves to get in a rut and never climb out. They often miss the best that life has to offer. In contrast, teachable people are fully engaged in life. They get excited about things. They are interested in discovery, discussion, application, and growth. There is a definite relationship between passion and potential.

German philosopher Goethe advised, "Never let a day pass without looking at some perfect work of art, hearing some great piece of music and reading, in part, some great book." The more engaged you are, the more interesting life will be. The more interested you are in exploring and learning, the greater your potential for growth.

> "Never let a day pass without looking at some perfect work of art, hearing some great piece of music and reading, in part, some great book."
>
> —Goethe

2. Successful People View Learning Differently from Those Who Are Unsuccessful

After more than thirty-five years of teaching and training people, I've come to realize that successful people think differently from unsuccessful ones. That doesn't mean that unsuccessful people are unable to think the way successful people do. (In fact, I believe that just about anyone can retrain himself to think differently. That's why I wrote *Thinking for a Change*—to help people learn the thinking skills capable of making them more successful.) Those successful thinking patterns pertain to learning as well.

Teachable people are always open to new ideas and are willing to learn from anyone who has something to offer. American journalist Sydney J. Harris wrote, "A winner knows how much he still has to learn, even when

> "A winner knows
> how much he still has to learn,
> even when he is considered
> an expert by others.
> A loser wants to be considered an
> expert by others,
> before he has learned enough
> to know how little he knows."
>
> —Sydney J. Harris

he is considered an expert by others. A loser wants to be considered an expert by others, before he has learned enough to know how little he knows." It's all a matter of attitude.

It's truly remarkable how much a person has to learn before he realizes how little he knows. Back in 1992, I wrote a book called *Developing the Leader Within You*. At the time, I thought, *I've had some success at leadership. I'll write this book, and it will be my contribution to others on this important subject.* I then put *everything* I knew about leadership in that book. But that book was only the beginning. Writing it made me want to learn more about leadership, and my drive to learn went to another level. I searched out more books, lectures, people, and experiences to help me learn. Today, I've written a total of *eight* books on leadership. Am I finished with that topic? No. There are still things to learn—and to teach. My leadership world is expanding, and so am I. The world is vast, and we are so limited. There is much for us to learn—as long as we remain teachable.

3. Learning Is Meant to Be a Lifelong Pursuit

It's said that the Roman scholar Cato started to study Greek when he was more than eighty years old. When asked why he was tackling such a difficult task at his age, he replied, "It is the earliest age I have left." Unlike Cato, too many people regard learning as an event instead of a process. Someone told me that only one-third of all adults read an entire book after their last graduation. Why would that be? Because they view education as a period of life, not a way of life!

Learning is an activity that is not restricted by age. It doesn't matter if you're past eighty, like Cato, or haven't yet entered your teens. Author Julio Melara was only eleven years old when he began to acquire major life lessons that he has been able to carry with him into adulthood and to teach others. Here are some of the things he's learned, taken from his book *It Only Takes Everything You've Got!: Lessons for a Life of Success*:

> Here is a list of all the jobs you will not find on my resume but lessons that have lasted a lifetime:
>
> - Started cutting grass for profit at age 11
>
>   *Lesson learned*: It is important to give things a clean, professional look.
>
> - Stock clerk at a local food store
>
>   *Lesson learned*: Making sure that if I am going to sell something, the merchandise needs to be in stock.
>
> - Dishwasher at local restaurant
>
>   *Lesson learned*: Somebody always has to do the job no one else wants to do. Also, most people have a lot of food on their plates. (They do not finish what they start.)
>
> - A janitor at an office building
>
>   *Lesson learned*: The importance of cleanliness as it related to image.

- Fry and prep cook at a steak house

  Lesson learned: The importance of preparation and the impact of the right presentation.

- Construction helping hand (lug wood and supplies from one place to another)

  Lesson learned: I do not want to do this for the rest of my life.

- Sold newspaper subscription for daily paper

  Lesson learned: The job of rejection—had to knock on at least 30 doors before I ever sold one subscription.

- Shipping clerk at a plumbing supply house

  Lesson learned: Delivering your project or service on time is just as important as selling it.

- Breakfast cook at a 24-hour restaurant stop

  Lesson learned: How to do 15 things at once. Also learned about the weird things people like to eat on their eggs.

- Cleaned cars at detailing shop

  Lesson learned: The importance of details (washing vs. detailing). You can pay $15 just to wash the outside of the car or $150 to clean the car inside and out and cover all the details. Details are a pain, but details are valuable.

- Shoe salesman at a retail store

  Lesson learned: To sell customers what they want and like. Also, learned to compliment people and be sincere.

- Busboy at a local diner

  Lesson learned: People enjoy being served with a smile and they love a clean table.

Every stage of life presents lessons to be learned. We can choose to be teachable and continue to learn them, or we can be closed-minded and stop growing. The decision is ours.

4. Talented People Can Be the Toughest to Teach

The other day I was having lunch with my friend Sam Chand, and we were talking about talent and teachability. Sam mentioned that he had a lot of musical talent. "I can play any type of keyboard, accordion, drums, guitar, saxophone, fiddle," he said. "I can basically play anything. If I hear a tune once, I can play it."

That sounds like a wonderful gift. But Sam said that when he decided to raise his saxophone playing to a new level by taking jazz lessons, he quickly became frustrated. Because he had played by ear and music had always come so easily to him, he didn't possess the patience and perseverance he needed to succeed. Eventually he gave up.

> One of the paradoxes of life is that the things that initially *make* you successful are rarely the things that *keep* you successful.

One of the paradoxes of life is that the things that initially *make* you successful are rarely the things that *keep* you successful. You have to remain open to new ideas and be willing to learn new skills. J. Konrad Hole advises,

If you cannot be teachable, having talent won't help you.
If you cannot be flexible, having a goal won't help you.
If you cannot be grateful, having abundance won't help you.
If you cannot be mentorable, having a future won't help you.
If you cannot be durable, having a plan won't help you.
If you cannot be reachable, having success won't help you.[6]

This may sound strange, but don't let your talent get in the way of your success. Remain teachable.

5. Pride Is the Number One Hindrance to Teachability

Author, trainer, and speaker Dave Anderson believes that the number one cause of management failure is pride. He writes,

> There are many reasons managers fail. For some, the organization out-grows them. Others don't change with the times. . . A few make poor character choices. They look good for a while but eventually discover they can't get out of their own way. Increasingly more keep the wrong people too long because they don't want to admit they made a mistake or have high turnover become a negative reflection on them. Some failures had brilliant past track records but start using their success as a license to build a fence around what they had rather than continue to risk and stretch to build it to even higher levels. But all these causes for management failure have their root in one common cause: pride. In simplest terms, pride is devastating . . . the pride that inflates your sense of self-worth and distorts your perspective of reality.

While envy is the deadly sin that comes from feelings of *inferiority*, the deadly sin of pride comes from feelings of *superiority*. It creates an arrogance of success, an inflated sense of self-worth accompanied by a distorted perspective of reality. Such an attitude leads to a loss of desire to learn and an unwillingness to change. It makes a person unteachable.

THE PROBLEMS WITH PRIDE

Pride is such a huge barrier to success and the development of talent that we need to examine it in greater detail. Here are just a few of the negative effects of pride as they relate to teachability:

Pride Closes Our Minds to New Ideas

I've yet to meet a conceited, arrogant, or prideful person who possessed a teachable spirit. How about you? The writer of Proverbs observed,

"Do you see a man who is wise in his own eyes? There is more hope for a fool than for him."[7] Teachability in its most fundamental form is a willingness to open our minds to new ideas. Pride prevents that.

Pride Closes Our Minds to Feedback

Stephen Covey comments, "It takes humility to seek feedback. It takes wisdom to understand it, analyze it, and appropriately act on it." I've already confessed to you that I have not always been a good listener. But I've learned over the years that I cannot do anything of real value alone. Achievement requires teamwork, and none of us is as smart as all of us. Having learned that lesson, I am continually asking members of my team to give me input on my ideas. I find this most valuable before team members or I take action, but I also solicit feedback throughout the process. The communication process looks something like this:

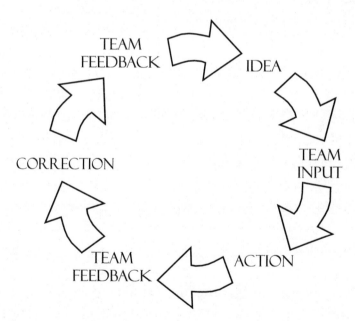

The process begins with an idea, which becomes improved through the interaction of the team. But what also happens is that because of the input and feedback I receive, my next idea improves. As long as I am willing to listen to and embrace feedback, it not only improves whatever task we're working on; it also improves me!

Pride Prevents Us from Admitting Mistakes

The commanding admiral ordered a group of navy pilots on maneuvers to maintain radio silence. But one young pilot mistakenly turned on his radio and was heard to mutter, "Man, am I fouled up!"

When the admiral heard it, he grabbed the microphone from the radio operator and barked into it, "Will the pilot who broke radio silence identify himself immediately!"

After a long pause, a voice on the radio was heard to say, "I may be fouled up, but I'm not *that* fouled up!"

> "The most important thing in life is not to capitalize on our gains. Any fool can do that. The really important thing is to profit from our losses. That requires intelligence; and makes the difference between a man of sense and a fool."
>
> —William Bolitho

Fear may keep some people from admitting mistakes, but pride is just as often the cause. The problem is that one of the best ways we grow is by admitting mistakes and learning from them. Writer William Bolitho observed, "The most important thing in life is not to capitalize on our gains. Any fool can do that. The really important thing is to profit from our losses. That requires intelligence; and makes the difference between a man of sense and a fool."

Pride Keeps Us from Making Needed Changes

Anytime we do a job and think we did it well, we become reluctant to make changes to our work. We become dedicated to the status quo instead of progress. Why? Because we have an emotional investment in it. For example, anytime in the past when I've taken a leadership position in which I inherited a staff, I had little reluctance to make changes for the good of the organization. If someone wasn't doing the job and would not or could not grow and improve, I would replace him or her. However, if someone I selected was falling short, I was much slower to make the needed change. Pride caused me to defend what sometimes should not have been defended. When it comes to changing others, we want to do it immediately. But changing ourselves? Not so fast! That's a problem.

HOW TO OVERCOME A PRIDE PROBLEM

If pride is an obstacle to your growth, then you need to take some deliberate and strategic steps to overcome it. That may not be easy. Founding Father Benjamin Franklin observed, "There is perhaps not one of our natural passions so hard to subdue as pride. Beat it down, stifle it, mortify it as much as one pleases, it is still alive. Even if I could conceive that I had completely overcome it, I should probably be proud of my humility." To start the process, here is what I suggest:

1. Recognize and Admit Your Pride

The first and most difficult step in overcoming pride is recognizing that it's a problem since those who are bound by it are often unaware of it. To defeat pride, we need to embrace humility, and few desire that. Writer and apologist C. S. Lewis remarked, "If anyone would like to acquire humility, I can, I think, tell him the first step. The first step is to realize that one is proud. And a biggish step, too. At least, nothing whatever can be done before it. If you think you are not conceited, you are very conceited indeed."

To try to maintain perspective, I have carried a poem by Saxon White Kessinger with me. And when I'm starting to think that I'm really important, I pull it out and read it. The poem is called "Indispensable Man."

Sometime when you're feeling important;
 Sometime when your ego's in bloom
Sometime when you take it for granted
 You're the best qualified in the room,

Sometime when you feel that your going
 Would leave an unfillable hole,
Just follow these simple instructions
 And see how they humble your soul;
Take a bucket and fill it with water,
 Put your hand in it up to the wrist,
Pull it out and the hole that's remaining
 Is a measure of how you'll be missed.

You can splash all you wish when you enter,
 You may stir up the water galore,
But stop and you'll find that in no time
 It looks quite the same as before.

The moral of this quaint example
 Is do just the best that you can,
Be proud of yourself but remember,
 There's no indispensable man.

People have a natural tendency to believe—or to hope—that they are indispensable, that the world will stop and take notice if anything happens to them. But I have to tell you, as someone who has presided over many funerals, life goes on. When someone dies, the family and friends closest to him grieve. But the rest of the people who attend the reception after the funeral are more worried about the potato salad than the dearly departed. So Kessinger's advice is really good: do your best but remember that no one is indispensable.

2. Express Gratitude Often

Once when I was chatting with Zig Ziglar, he told me that he thought the least expressed of all virtues is gratitude. I think that is true. I also think that it is the most appreciated expression by recipients. I think Oprah Winfrey's suggestion for cultivating gratitude is excellent. She says,

Keep a grateful journal. Every night, list five things that happened this day that you are grateful for. What it will begin to do is change your perspective of your day and your life. If you can learn to focus on what you have, you will always see that the universe is abundant; you will have more. If you concentrate on what you don't have, you will never have enough.

Therein lies the problem of people filled with selfish pride. They are not grateful because they never think they get as much as they deserve. Expressing gratitude continually helps to break this kind of pride.

3. Laugh at Yourself

I love the Chinese proverb that says, "Blessed are they that laugh at themselves, for they shall never cease to be entertained." People who have the problem of pride rarely laugh at themselves. But engaging in humor at your own expense shows that pride isn't a problem, and it is a way of breaking a pride problem.

> "Blessed are they that laugh at themselves, for they shall never cease to be entertained."
>
> —Chinese proverb

There's a story about a judge named Robert S. Gawthorp who had a distinguished career on the bench beginning in 1977 at age forty-four. But he refused to take himself too seriously and maintained his sense of humor. Gawthorp commented, "Just because people stand up when you walk into court and you wear a black dress to work and sit on an elevated chair . . . you have to remind yourself you're just another person who happens to be a lawyer elected to serve as a judge." To remind himself of this, he used to keep a small framed statement near his private courtroom door—a gift from relatives—that said, "To us, you'll always be just the same old jackass."[8]

TALENT + *TEACHABILITY* = A TALENT-PLUS PERSON PUTTING THE TALENT-PLUS FORMULA INTO ACTION

If you want to expand your talent, you must become teachable. That is the pathway to growth. Futurist and author John Naisbitt believes that "the most important skill to acquire is learning how to learn." Here is what I suggest as you pursue teachability and become a talent-plus person:

1. Learn to Listen

The first step in teachability is learning to listen. American writer and philosopher Henry David Thoreau wrote, "It takes two to speak the truth—one to speak and one to hear." Being a good listener helps us to know people better, to learn what they have learned, and to show them that we value them as individuals.

Abraham Lincoln was one of the most teachable presidents. When he began his career, he was not a great leader. But he grew into his presidency. He was always an avid listener, and as president, he opened the doors of the White House to anyone who wanted to express an opinion to him. He called these frequent sessions his "public opinion baths." He also asked nearly everyone he met to send him ideas and opinions. As a result, he received hundreds of letters every month—many more than other presidents had received in the past. From this practice, he learned much. And even if he didn't embrace the arguments, he learned more about how the letter writers thought, and he used that knowledge to help him craft his policies and persuade others to adopt them.

As you go through each day, remember that you can't learn if you're always talking. As the old saying goes, "There's a reason you have one mouth but two ears." Listen to others, remain humble, and you will begin to learn things every day that can help you to expand your talent.

2. Understand the Learning Process

Sometimes things are painfully obvious and need little explanation. For example, read the following humorous warnings and pieces of advice collected from the military:

- "Aim towards enemy."—Instruction printed on U.S. rocket launcher
- "When the pin is pulled, Mr. Grenade is not our friend." —U.S. Army
- "If the enemy is in range, so are you."—Infantry Journal
- "It is generally inadvisable to eject directly over the area you just bombed."—U.S. Air Force Manual
- "If your attack is going too well, you're probably walking into an ambush."—Infantry Journal
- "Never tell the platoon sergeant you have nothing to do." —Unknown army recruit
- "Don't draw fire; it irritates the people around you."—Your buddies
- "If you see a bomb technician running, try to keep up with him."—U.S. Ammo Troop[9]

When things aren't so obvious, it is helpful to understand the learning process in order to learn and grow. Here is how it typically works:

STEP 1: Act.
STEP 2: Look for your mistakes and evaluate.
STEP 3: Search for a way to do it better.
STEP 4: Go back to step 1.

> The greatest enemy of learning is knowing.

Remember, the greatest enemy of learning is knowing, and the goal of all learning is action, not knowledge. If what you are doing does not in some way contribute to what you or others are doing in life, then question its value and be prepared to make changes.

3. Look for and Plan Teachable Moments

I recently read a book called *The Laws of Lifetime Growth* that presents an excellent perspective on this idea. The second law states, "Always make your learning greater than your experience." Authors Dan Sullivan and Catherine Nomura go on to explain,

> Continual learning is essential for lifetime growth. You can have a great deal of experience and be no smarter for all the things you've done, seen, and heard. Experience alone is no guarantee of lifetime growth. But if you regularly transform your experience into new lessons, you will make each day of your life a source of growth. The smartest people are those who can transform even the smallest events or situations into breakthroughs in thinking and action. Look at all of life as a school and every experience as a lesson, and your learning will always be greater than your experience.[10]

The authors are describing a lifestyle of teachability. If you look for opportunities to learn in every situation, you will become a talent-plus person and expand your talent to its potential. But you can also take another step beyond that and actively seek out and plan teachable moments. You can do that by reading books, visiting places that will inspire you, attending events that will prompt you to pursue change, listening to lessons, and spending time with people who will stretch you and expose you to new experiences.

I've had the privilege to spend time with many remarkable people, and the natural reward has been the opportunity to learn. In my personal relationships, I've also gravitated toward people from whom I can learn. My closest friends are people who challenge my thinking—and often change it. They lift me up in many ways. And I've found that I often live out something

> "Make your friends your teachers and mingle the pleasures of conversation with the advantages of instruction."
>
> —Baltasar Gracian

stated by Spanish philosopher and writer Baltasar Gracian: "Make your friends your teachers and mingle the pleasures of conversation with the advantages of instruction." You can do the same. Cultivate friendships with people who challenge and add value to you, and try to do the same for them. It will change your life.

4. Make Your Teachable Moments Count

Years ago I saw a *Peanuts* cartoon by Charles Schulz that showed Charlie Brown at the beach building a magnificent sand castle. With it completed, he stood back to admire his work, at which point he and his work were engulfed by a downpour that leveled his beautiful castle. In the last frame, he says, "There must be a lesson here, but I don't know what it is."

Unfortunately that's the way many people feel after a potentially valuable experience. Even people who are strategic about seeking teachable moments can miss the whole point of the experience. I say this because for thirty years I've been a speaker at conferences and workshops—events that are designed to help people learn. But I've found that many people walk away from an event and do very little with what they heard after closing their notebooks. It would be like a jewelry designer going to a gem merchant to buy fine gems, placing them carefully into a case, and then putting that case on the shelf to collect dust. What's the value of acquiring the gems if they're never going to be used?

We tend to focus on learning events instead of the learning process. Because of this, I try to help people take action steps that will help them implement what they learn. I suggest that in their notes, they use a code to mark things that jump out at them:

T indicates you need to spend some time thinking on that point.

C indicates something you need to change.

☺ A smiley face means you are doing that thing particularly well.

A indicates something you need to apply.

S means you need to share that information with someone else.

After the conference I recommend that they create to-do lists based on what they marked, then schedule time to follow through.

5. Ask Yourself, Am I Really Teachable?

Someone sent me a list of statements that are reported to have come from actual employee performance evaluations. They display the lack of teachability at its most humorous:

- Since my last report, this employee has reached rock bottom and has started to dig.
- Works well when under constant supervision and when cornered like a rat.
- When she opens her mouth, it seems that it is only to change feet.
- He would be out of his depth in a parking lot puddle.
- This young lady had delusions of adequacy.

- He sets low personal standards and consistently fails to achieve them.

- This employee should go far, and the sooner he starts, the better.

- He doesn't have ulcers, but he is a carrier.

- He's been working with glue too much.

- He brings a lot of joy whenever he leaves the room.

- If you see two people talking and one looks bored, he's the other one.

- Gates are down, the lights are flashing, but the train isn't coming.

- If you give him a penny for his thoughts, he'd give you change.

- Takes him two hours to watch 60 *Minutes*.

- The wheel is turning but the hamster is dead.

- Some drink from the fountain of knowledge; he only gargled.[11]

I've said it before, but it bears repeating: all the good advice in the world won't help if you don't have a teachable spirit.

To know whether you are *really* open to new ideas and new ways of doing things, answer the following questions:

1. Am I open to other people's ideas?

2. Do I listen more than I talk?

3. Am I open to changing my opinion based on new information?

4. Do I readily admit when I am wrong?

5. Do I observe before acting on a situation?

6. Do I ask questions?

7. Am I willing to ask a question that will expose my ignorance?

8. Am I open to doing things in a way I haven't done before?

9. Am I willing to ask for directions?

10. Do I act defensive when criticized, or do I listen openly for the truth?

If you answered no to one or more of these questions, then you have room to grow in the area of teachability. You need to soften your attitude and learn humility, and remember the words of John Wooden: "Everything we know we learned from someone else!"

> "Everything we know we learned from someone else!"
>
> —John Wooden

Thomas Edison was the guest of the governor of North Carolina when the politician complimented him on his creative genius.

"I am not a great inventor," countered Edison.

"But you have over a thousand patents to your credit," the governor stated.

"Yes, but about the only invention I can really claim as absolutely original is the phonograph," Edison replied.

"I'm afraid I don't understand what you mean," the governor remarked.

"Well," explained Edison, "I guess I'm an awfully good sponge. I absorb ideas from every course I can, and put them to practical use. Then I improve them until they become of some value. The ideas which I use are mostly the ideas of other people who don't develop them themselves."

What a remarkable description of someone who used teachability to expand his talent! That is what a talent-plus person does. That is what all of us should strive to do.

TALENT + TEACHABILITY APPLICATION EXERCISES

1. How would you describe your attitude toward teachability? To get a realistic view, name all the things within the last twelve months that you initiated and followed through with in order to learn. (If your list is short, your attitude is probably not as good as you think.)

2. On a scale from 1 to 10 (with 10 the highest), how talented do you think you are in general? How talented in your area of greatest expertise? If you rate yourself above a 7 in either area, you may be prone to resist learning because of either pride or a belief that you already know "enough." These attitudes can be a major hindrance to your teachability. To combat them, employ gratitude and laughter to help you change. For a month, keep a gratitude journal similar to the one Oprah Winfrey describes. Or make it a point to find something funny in mistakes you made in the last fourteen days and tell others about it in a humorous way. (If they look shocked or don't laugh, it probably means you take yourself too seriously and you need to do this kind of thing often until you get different responses.)

3. For the next week, practice active listening. Make it a point to ask others for their advice and to withhold advice you would usually give. At the end of each day, write down something you learned by being attentive to others.

4. Seek out, plan, and schedule teachable moments for the next year. Select one conference to attend, one inspiring location to visit, a minimum of six books to read, another six lessons or books to listen to, and

at least two important people to meet. Don't forget to create an action plan to apply what you've learned after each of these events.

5. Take the advice of Ian Harvey, CEO of London-based BTG, who asks people in his inner circle to tell him:

> *Two things he should stop doing*
> *Two things he should keep doing*
> *Two things he should start doing*

10
CHARACTER PROTECTS YOUR TALENT

M any people with talent make it into the limelight, but the ones who have neglected to develop strong character rarely stay there long. Absence of strong character eventually topples talent. Why? Because people cannot climb beyond the limitations of their character. Talented people are sometimes tempted to take shortcuts. Character prevents that. Talented people may feel superior and expect special privileges. Character helps them to know better. Talented people are praised for what others see them build. Character builds what's inside them. Talented people have the potential to be difference makers. Character makes a difference in them. Talented people are often a gift to the world. Character protects that gift.

When it comes to talent, everything is not always as it seems to the casual observer. Sometimes what appears to be a huge success isn't. And in time, the truth comes out. That was the case for Dr. Hwang Woo Suk.

STRONG ON THE SURFACE

In 2004, *Time* published its annual list of "People Who Mattered" in a special issue of the magazine. Among those cited was Hwang Woo Suk. The brief article accompanying his picture stated,

A veterinarian by training, Hwang began to research cloning for a practical purpose: he wanted to create a better cow. But his work didn't stop in the barnyard. Hwang and his team at Seoul National University became the first to clone human embryos capable of yielding viable stem cells that might one day cure countless diseases. While such research raises troubling ethical questions, Hwang has already proved that human cloning is no longer science fiction, but a fact of life.[1]

The recognition by *Time* was just the latest in many honors and much adulation Hwang had received. His was an incredible success story. He grew up in a poor mountain town in South Korea. The son of a widow, he had worked his way through school, earning money by laboring on a farm. After receiving his bachelor's degree, he was advised to become a medical doctor. But he had another vision. He wanted to create a genetically superior cow for his nation. He earned his doctorate in veterinary medicine, and then after a couple of years practicing as a veterinarian, he entered the field of scientific research.

His talent was incredible—his drive remarkable. Both carried him all the way to a professorship at Seoul National University. It was there that he first gained attention in the scientific community. In 1999 he announced that he had succeeded in cloning a dairy cow. He became a national celebrity in South Korea. But he made a much greater impression in early 2004 when he announced that he had succeeded in creating human embryonic stem cells through cloning. Up to that time most experts around the world believed that cloning any kind of primate would be impossible because of the complexity of the genetic structure. Hwang followed his announcement to the media with an article in a prestigious scientific journal.

In 2005, Hwang announced additional breakthroughs and published them as well. He also announced that he had successfully cloned a dog—an Afghan hound that he named Snuppy. Hwang became an international celebrity among scientists and a national hero in Korea where he was a favorite of the nation's president. He was regarded as one of the top experts on stem cells in the world. He already held the prestigious POSCO (Pohang Iron and Steel Company) Chair as a professor at Seoul National University. To that were added an appointment to lead the World Stem Cell Hub, the title "Supreme Scientist" by Korea's Ministry of Science and Technology, and the creation of a postage stamp in his honor, depicting a man in a wheelchair getting up and walking as a result of his research. And he was receiving the equivalent of millions of dollars in financial support for his work. His talent and hard work had paid off, and he was at the pinnacle of his career and one of the most respected scientists in the world.

QUESTIONS

But later that year a shadow was cast over Hwang's work. An American scientist with whom he had published his stem cell research suddenly announced that he would no longer collaborate with Hwang. The other scientist said his reason was a concern about the way eggs had been collected from donors during Hwang's work. Soon afterward, another colleague of Hwang, Roh Sung-il, admitted that he had collected eggs from their junior researchers and had paid some donors, both ethical violations. Of great concern was the possibility that donors had been coerced. Hwang claimed that he hadn't been aware of Roh's actions until after the fact and that he later hadn't identified the researchers as egg donors to protect their privacy.

Despite these ethical concerns, support for Hwang remained high. In South Korea, people who criticized him were often deemed unpatriotic. There were large public rallies to support the scientist. And Korea's president, Roh Moo-hyun, had always supported Hwang. He stated, "It is not possible nor desirable to prohibit research, just because there are concerns that it may lead to a direction that is deemed unethical," and "Politicians have a responsibility to manage bioethical controversies, not to get in the way of this outstanding research and progress."[2] What mattered most to the people was that there had been a scientific breakthrough.

However, while most of his countrymen cheered, a group of young Korean scientists grew skeptical of his claims. And a Korean investigative television show, similar to 60 Minutes in the United States, criticized Hwang's research methods and questioned his work. In response, Hwang offered to resign from all of his official posts, but also defended himself. "I was blinded by work and my drive for achievement," he stated.[3] Even as late as December 2005, Hwang insisted that he had merely acted to protect the identity of the egg donors.[4] A month later, the truth came out.

THE REAL STORY

Things began to unravel when a journal that had published one of Hwang's articles issued a retraction and Seoul National University created a panel to investigate Hwang's work. On January 10, 2006, the panel announced an amazing conclusion: Hwang had fabricated all of his stem cell research.[5] Then other reports surfaced, saying Hwang had forced one female researcher to donate her own eggs after she accidentally knocked over petri dishes containing eggs from other donors.[6] Questions followed about how he had spent $2.6 million of the nearly $40 million in funding he had received.[7] On May 12, 2006, Hwang was indicted on embezzlement and bioethics law violations.

Had Hwang told the truth about anything? Was there any evidence that the scientist really did have talent? Or were all of his claims lies? No, as it turns out, he did tell the truth about one breakthrough— Snuppy the Afghan hound. Hwang and his team truly *had* been the first in the world to clone a dog. But the rest simply wasn't true.

What happened to Hwang Woo Suk? Had his talent let him down? No, he had enough talent. What failed him was his character. Because it was weak, it neglected to protect his talent. And now his talent—no matter how great—is irrelevant. His career is over.

THE COMPONENTS OF CHARACTER

People are like icebergs. There's much more to them than meets the eye. When you look at an iceberg, only about 15 percent is visible—that's talent. The rest—their character—is below the surface, hidden. It's what they think and never share with others. It's what they do when no one is watching them. It's how they react to terrible traffic and other everyday aggravations. It's how they handle failure—and success. The greater their

> People are like icebergs. There's much more to them than meets the eye.

talent is, the greater their need is for strong character "below the surface" to sustain them. If they are too "top heavy" with talent, then they are likely to get into trouble, as Dr. Hwang did.

Tim Elmore, who worked for me many years and is the founder and president of Growing Leaders, is the first person I heard compare character to an iceberg. When he speaks to college students, he often tells some little-known details about the infamous sinking of the *Titanic*:

> The huge and unsinkable ship received five iceberg warnings that fateful night of April 14, 1912, just before it went down. When the sixth message came in during the wee hours of the next morning, "Look out for icebergs," the operator wired back, "Shut up! I'm busy." Those were his last words over the wire before it all happened. Exactly thirty minutes later, the great vessel—the one whose captain said even God couldn't sink this ship—was sinking . . . They underestimated the power of the iceberg and overestimated their own strength. What an accurate description of so many people today.

196 ~~ Beyond Talent

No one can expect to succeed without strong character below the surface to protect his talent and sustain him during difficult times. Character holds us steady, no matter how rough the storm becomes. Or to put it another way, as David McLendon did when we spent time together recently, "Character is the pedestal that determines how much weight a person can sustain. If your character is the size of a tooth pick, you can only sustain a postage stamp. If your character is as thick as a column, you can sustain a roof."

So what exactly comprises character? Ask a dozen people and you'll get a dozen answers. I believe it boils down to four elements: (1) self-discipline, (2) core values, (3) a sense of identity, and (4) integrity. Let's consider each of them:

1. Self-Discipline

At the most basic level, self-discipline is the ability to do what is right even when you don't feel like doing it. Outstanding leaders and achievers throughout history understood this. Greek philosopher Plato asserted, "The first and best victory is to conquer self."

> Self-discipline is the ability to do what is right even when you don't feel like doing it.

The greatest victories are internal ones. Oswald Sanders, the author of the book on leadership that launched my personal journey as a leader, *Spiritual Leadership*, wrote that the future is with the disciplined. He said that without self-discipline, a leader's other gifts—however great—will never realize their maximum potential. That's true not only of leaders but also of anyone who wants to reach his or her potential. Talent alone is never enough. A person must have talent plus character. The battle for self-discipline is won within. The notable mountain climber Sir Edmund Hillary observed, "It's not the mountains we conquer, but ourselves."

One of the joys of my life is playing golf. I only wish my talent matched my passion! I have had the privilege of playing the East Lake course in Atlanta, home course of golf legend Bobby Jones, considered by some to be the greatest golfer who ever played the game. The club house is filled with pictures of him playing and with many of his championship trophies. Yet many people don't know that Jones's most significant victory was over himself.

Jones began playing golf at age five and won his first tournament at age six. By age twelve he was winning tournaments against adults. But Jones had a temper. His nickname was "Club Thrower." An older gentleman called Grandpa Bart, who had retired from golf but worked in the pro shop, recognized Jones's talent *and* his character issues. After Jones made it to the third round of the U.S. Amateur Championship, the older man advised, "Bobby, you are good enough to win that tournament, but you'll never win until you can control that temper of yours. You miss a shot—you get upset—and then you lose." Jones did master his temper and won his first U.S. Open when he was twenty-one. Grandpa Bart used to say, "Bobby was fourteen when he mastered the game of golf, but he was twenty-one when he mastered himself."

> "What we do on some great occasion will probably depend on what we already are; and what we are will be the result of previous years of self-discipline."
>
> —Henry Parry Liddon

English theologian and orator Henry Parry Liddon observed, "What we do on some great occasion will probably depend on what we already are; and what we are will be the result of previous years of self-discipline." The first step to strong character is conquering self.

2. Core Values

Our core values are the principles we live by every day. They define what we believe and how we live. Ideally we should write out our core values so that they become a clear beacon we can always use to guide us.

One person I most admire is John Wooden, the Hall of Fame former coach of UCLA's basketball team. When he graduated from grade school at twelve years old, his father gave him a seven-point creed. From that time, Wooden has carried a written copy of that creed with him every day. Here is what it says:

1. Be true to yourself.

2. Help others.

3. Make each day your masterpiece.

4. Drink deeply from good books, especially the Bible.

5. Make friendship a fine art.

6. Build a shelter against a rainy day.

7. Pray for guidance and give thanks for your blessings every day.

I had read about the creed, and when I got to meet Coach Wooden, I asked him about it. Sitting in a restaurant at breakfast, he pulled a copy out of his pocket and showed it to me. Of course, since he has it memorized, he doesn't need to carry a copy with him, but it has

> "The man who has no inner life is the slave of his surroundings."
>
> —Henri Frederic Amiel

been his lifelong practice. Most important, he has always carried it in his heart and sought to live it out every day.

Swiss philosopher Henri Frederic Amiel stated, "The man who has no inner life is the slave of his surroundings." Core values give order and structure to an individual's inner life, and when that inner life is in order, a person can navigate almost anything the world throws at him.

3. A Sense of Identity

When it comes to character, each of us must answer the critical question, "Who am I?" That answer often provides the motivation to practice self-discipline. It is fundamental for the identification of core values. And it helps to establish emotional security. Our sense of security—or lack of it—often drives what we do.

American novelist Nathaniel Hawthorne recognized this truth: "No man can for any considerable time wear one face to himself and another to the multitude without finally getting bewildered as to which is the true one." How do you identify yourself? Where does your personal value come from? What is your motivation as it relates to money and power?

> People are set up to fail if they envision what they want to do before they figure out what kind of person they should be.

If you live with a chip on your shoulder, believe deep down you have no intrinsic value, or see yourself as a victim, you will have a distorted view of yourself and your surroundings. That, in turn, will impact your character. No matter how hard you try, you cannot consistently behave in a way that is inconsistent with how you see yourself. Thus, a strong and accurate sense of identity is essential. To paraphrase author Ruth Barton, people are set up to fail if they envision what they want to do before they figure out what kind of person they should be.

4. Integrity

The final component in strong character is integrity, which is an alignment of values, thoughts, feelings, and actions. People who possess the consistency that comes with strong integrity can be very compelling. In his book *American Scandal*, Pat Williams tells the story of Mahatma Gandhi's trip to England to speak before Parliament. The British government had opposed Indian independence, and Gandhi, one of its most vocal proponents, had often been threatened, arrested, and jailed as a result. Gandhi spoke eloquently and passionately for nearly two hours, after which the packed hall gave him a standing ovation.

Afterward, a reporter asked Gandhi's assistant, Mahadev Desai, how the Indian statesman had been able to deliver such a speech without any notes.

"You don't understand Gandhi," Desai responded. "You see, what he thinks is what he feels. What he feels is what he says. What he says is what he does. What Gandhi feels, what he thinks, what he says, and what he does are all the same. He does not need notes."

When values, thoughts, feelings, and actions are in alignment, a person becomes focused and his character is strengthened. Visually it could be represented by this:

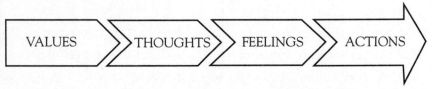

However, when these components aren't aligned, it creates confusion and internal conflict, which looks more like this:

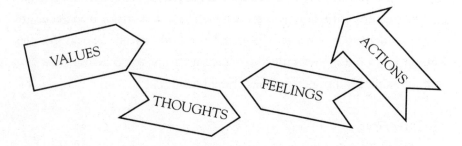

Developing talent without developing character is a dead end. It won't take people where they want to go. The lives of people who are long on talent but short on character always get out of balance.

A joint study conducted by Korn/Ferry International and the UCLA Graduate School of Management asked 1,300 senior executives to identify the top trait needed to enhance a business executive's effectiveness. Coming in first was integrity. In second place was concern for results, with responsibility third. What's true for the boardroom is also true in the classroom, living room, soup kitchen, or gym. If you want your talent to take you far, you need to protect that talent with integrity.

CHARACTER COMMUNICATES

The choice to develop strong character may not be the most important one to make the *most* of your talent. But it is certainly the most important to make sure you don't make the *least* of your talent. You can't really underestimate its impact. Entrepreneur Roger Babson, who founded Babson College and Webber International University, asserted, "A character standard is far more important than even a gold standard. The success of all economic systems is still dependent upon both righteous leaders and righteous people. In the last analysis, our national future depends upon our national character—that is, whether it is spiritually or materially minded."

As I hope I've already made clear, character creates a foundation upon which the structure of your talent and your life can build. If there are cracks in that foundation, you cannot build much. That's why you must first develop within before you can achieve much without. But once you build strong character, it does more than provide a platform for your personal success and the maximization of your talent. It also impacts others and allows you to build with them. It does that through what it communicates to people:

1. Character Communicates Consistency

Cultural anthropologist Margaret Mead stated, "What people say, what people do, and what people say they do are entirely different things." That is true of people who live without character, without integrity. Such people communicate confusion to others. They can say anything they like, but their actions determine the message we receive. It was philosopher-poet Ralph Waldo Emerson who said, "What you do thunders so loudly in my ears I cannot hear what you say."

Amazingly there are people who actually promote this inconsistency. Designer Ralph Lauren was quoted as saying, "The crux of a person's identity . . . resides in the trappings, not in the person himself . . . One needn't be well read, so long as one surrounds himself with books. One needn't play the piano, so long as one has a piano. In short, one can be whoever one wants to be. Or—more accurately—one can seem to be whoever one wants to be."[8] While one may be able to make an *impression* with "trappings," the real person always comes through in the end. Impressions are like shadows—they disappear when a strong enough light is shone on them. Character is the genuine article—and the more you shine light on it, the more of its details you can see. Character shows that who you are and who you appear to be are one and the same, and that, according to Greek philosopher Socrates, is the first key to greatness.

> Character shows that who you are and who you appear to be are one and the same, and that is the first key to greatness.

2. Character Communicates Choices

Earlier in this chapter, I mentioned that Bobby Jones needed to overcome a terrible temper to succeed at golf. Not only did Jones do that, but he actually became a model of sportsmanship and character. Both could be seen in his play. During the final play-off of a U.S. Open tournament, Jones's ball ended up in the rough just off the fairway. As he set up to play his shot, he accidentally caused his ball to move. He immediately turned to the marshals and announced the foul. The marshals discussed the situation among themselves. They hadn't seen the ball move. Neither did anyone in the gallery. They left it up to Jones whether to take the penalty stroke, which he did.

Later, when a marshal commended Jones on his high level of integrity, Jones replied, "Do you commend a bank robber for not robbing a bank? No, you don't. This is how the game of golf should be played at all times." Jones lost the match that day—by one stroke. But he didn't lose his integrity. His character was so well-known that the United States Golf Association's sportsmanship award came to be named the Bob Jones Award.[9]

It's an interesting paradox. Our character creates our choices, yet our choices create our character. Author and speaker Margaret Jensen observed, "Character is the sum total of all our everyday choices. Our character today is a result of our choices yesterday. Our character tomorrow will be a result of our choices today. To change your character, change your choices. Day by day, what you think, what you choose, and what you do is who you become." Once you get a handle on the character of a person, you can understand his choices and even predict what they will be.

> "Character is the sum total of all our everyday choices."
>
> —Margaret Jensen

3. Character Communicates Influence

Today, many people try to demand respect. They believe that influence should be granted to them simply because they have position, wealth, or recognition. However, respect and influence must be earned over time, and they are built and sustained by character. First and foremost, influence is based on character. U.S. Army General J. Lawton Collins asserted, "No matter how brilliant a man may be, he will never engender confidence in his subordinates and associates if he lacks simple honesty and moral courage."

I've taught leadership for three decades, and I've written many books on it. During that time, I've tried to help people develop skills that will benefit them as leaders. However, all the skills in the world won't assist someone whose character is hopelessly flawed. Experienced leaders understand this. Author Stephen Covey writes,

> If I try to use human influence strategies and tactics of how to get other people to do what I want, to work better, to be more motivated to like me and each other while my character is fundamentally flawed, marked by duplicity or insincerity then, in the long run, I cannot be successful. My duplicity will breed distrust, and everything I do—even using so-called good human relations techniques will be perceived as manipulative.

It simply makes no difference how good the rhetoric is or even how good the intentions are; if there is little or no trust, there is no foundation for permanent success.[10]

Character cannot be inherited. It cannot be bought. It is impossible to weigh, and it cannot be physically touched. It can be built, but only slowly. And without it, one cannot lead others.

4. Character Communicates Longevity

If you want to know how long it will take to get to the top, consult a calendar. If you want to know how long it can take to fall to the bottom, try a stopwatch. Character determines which will happen. Dreams become shattered, possibilities are lost, organizations crumble, and people are hurt when a person doesn't have character protecting his talent. Character provides the opportunity for longevity in any career, any relationship, and any worthwhile goal.

Author and pastor J. R. Miller wrote, "The only thing that walks back from the tomb with the mourners and refuses to be buried is the character of a man. This is true. What a man is, survives him. It can never be buried." If you want your talent to last, and you want to sleep well at night, depend upon good character. Asked about the secret of a long and happy life, Coach John Wooden remarked on his ninetieth birthday, "There is no pillow as soft as a clear conscience." Character protects your talent, and it also guards you from regret.

TALENT + CHARACTER = A TALENT-PLUS PERSON
PUTTING THE TALENT-PLUS FORMULA INTO ACTION

Never forget that talent is a gift—either you have it or you don't—but character is a choice. If you want it, you must develop it. Here's how to become a talent-plus person in the area of character:

1. Don't Give Up or Give In to Adversity

It takes character to weather life's storms. At the same time, adversity develops character. Author and activist Helen Keller, who could not hear or see, remarked, "Character cannot be developed in ease and quiet. Only through experience of trial and suffering can the soul be strengthened, vision cleared, ambition inspired, and success achieved."

Anyone who does what he must only when he is in the mood or when it is convenient isn't going to develop his talent or become successful. The core foundation of character is doing what you don't want to do to get what you want. It is paying a higher price than you wanted to for something worthwhile. It is standing up for your principles when you know someone is going to try to knock you down. Every time you face adversity and come through it with your core values affirmed and your integrity intact, your character becomes stronger.

In his first novel, *One Day in the Life of Ivan Denisovich*, Russian dissident author Alexander Solzhenitsyn wrote about Ivan Denisovich Shukhov, a political prisoner in a Siberian labor camp. In one part of the novel, Shukhov is forced to build a wall in weather that is twenty degrees below zero. As it gets dark and even colder, the foreman gives the order to hurry the job by throwing leftover mortar over the wall, instead of using it, so that they can be finished for the day. "But Shukhov wasn't made that way," wrote Solzhenitsyn, telling how the man resists the order, determined to finish the job right. "Eight years in a camp couldn't change his nature. He worried about anything he could make use of, about every scrap of work he could do—nothing must be wasted without good reason."

The foreman yells at him and then hurries away. "But Shukhov— and if the guards had put the dogs on him it would have made no difference—ran to the back and looked about," writes the author. "Not bad. Then he ran and gave the wall a good look over, to the left, to the right. His eye as accurate as a carpenter's level. Straight and even." Only *then* does Shukhov stop working.[11]

German philosopher-poet Johann Wolfgang von Goethe observed, "Talent can be cultivated in tranquility; character only in the rushing stream of life." The irony is that if you have never experienced the resistance of the rushing stream, then whatever talent you have cultivated in tranquility may not survive. If you want your talent to take you far, then don't quit under duress. Don't give up in the midst of a storm. Don't bail out in the middle of conflict. Wait until the trouble is behind you before assessing whether it's time to change course or stop. Do that, and you may have additional opportunities to develop your talent.

2. Do the Right Thing

Doing the right thing doesn't come naturally to any of us. As America's first president, George Washington, said, "Few men have virtue enough to withstand the highest bidder." Yet that is what we must do to develop the kind of character that will sustain us.

It's not easy to do the right thing when the wrong thing is expedient. Molière commented, "Men are alike in their promises. It is only in their deeds that they differ. The difference in their deeds is simple: People of character do what is right regardless of the situation." It's not easy to do the right thing when it will cost you. It's not easy to do the right thing when no one but you will know. But it's in those moments that a person's character becomes strong. Civil rights leader Martin Luther King Jr. asserted this:

> *Cowardice asks the question:* Is it safe?
> *Consensus asks the question:* Is it popular?
> *Character asks:* Is it right?

That is the bottom line. Are you going to do what's right?

One way that I've tried to control my natural bent to do wrong is to ask myself some questions (adapted from questions written by business ethicist Dr. Laura Nash):[12]

1. Am I hiding something?

2. Am I hurting anyone?

3. How does it look from the other person's point of view?

4. Have I discussed this face-to-face?

5. What would I tell my child to do?

If you do the right thing—and keep doing it—even if it doesn't help you move ahead with your talent in the short term, it will protect you and serve you well in the long term. Character builds—

> "Men are alike in their promises. It is only in their deeds that they differ."
>
> —Molière

and it builds you. Or as Dr. Dale Bronner, a board member of my nonprofit organization EQUIP, puts it, "Honesty is not something you do; honesty is who you are."

3. Take Control of Your Life

I have observed that the people with the weakest character tend to place the blame on their circumstances. They often claim that poor upbringing, financial difficulties, the unkindness of others, or other circumstances have made them victims. It's true that in life we must face many things outside our control. But know this: while your circumstances *are* beyond your control, your character *is not*. Your character is always your choice.

People can no sooner blame their character on their circumstances than they can blame their looks on a mirror. Developing character is

> While your circumstances *are* beyond your control, your character *is not*.

your personal responsibility. It cannot be given to you; you must earn it. Commit yourself to its development because it will protect your talent. Every time you make a character-based decision, you take another step toward becoming a talent-plus person. The process begins with deciding to make good character your goal and to stop making excuses. French writer François La Rochefoucauld asserted, "Almost all our faults are more pardonable than the methods we think up to hide them." The process continues with the determination to manage that decision every day.

You have God-given talent; develop it. You have opportunity before you; pursue it. You have a future that is bright; look forward to it. But above all else, you have the potential to become a person of character; follow through with it. Character, more than anything else, will make you a talent-plus person. It will protect everything in your life that you hold dear.

TALENT + CHARACTER
APPLICATION EXERCISES

1. Have you ever taken time to identify and write down your core values? If you haven't, you need to. There is no substitute for taking what may be some vague, general notions and making them specific and tangible by putting them in writing. Taking the time to do it can change your life.

2. Most people think of integrity as being the same thing as honesty. However, if you think of integrity as *consistency*—where your values, thoughts, feelings, and actions all line up—would you still consider yourself to have high integrity? If you completed the previous exercise, you've already written your core values. How do your thoughts match up to those values? Think about the various intellectual, moral, political, or religious issues that are important to you. How about your feelings? Are they consistent with your values and thinking? What about your actions? If you need help judging your consistency, enlist the assistance of people close to you and ask them to weigh in. And if you discover inconsistencies, try to discover where the breakdowns lie.

3. How would you rate yourself on a scale of 1 to 10 when it comes to self-discipline (with 10 being perfect)? Is yours what you would consider to be an acceptable score? How can you improve in this area? Identify specific goals that will help you. Remember that self-discipline is a lifestyle to be achieved. The more disciplined you are in one area, the more it helps you become disciplined in others. Each victory makes you stronger.

4. Jot down the times in your life when you faced great adversity. Try to remember at least ten. Put them in chronological order. Now next to each, note your response: paralysis, escape, avoidance, endurance, perseverance, or victory. What pattern do you see? If your responses don't tend to become stronger over time and lean more toward perseverance and victory, then this is probably a problem area for you. How will you learn to better handle adversity? Through teamwork? Better health and fitness? Stronger relationships? Professional counseling? Explore the options.

5. Write down the incidents, circumstances, choices, and habits that have helped to create your character until now. Try to list everything you can think of. How many of the things on the list are beyond your control, and how many are the result of actions you took or choices you made? If many of the things you list are due to circumstances and other things beyond your control, then you need to take greater control of your life. Start by making a choice every day that will strengthen your character. (Note: these kinds of choices usually involve doing things you would rather not do.)

11
RELATIONSHIPS INFLUENCE YOUR TALENT

In his book *My Personal Best*, John Wooden writes, "There is a choice you have to make in everything you do, so keep in mind that in the end, the choice you make makes you." Nowhere is this more evident than in your relationships. Nothing will influence your talent as much as the important relationships in your life. Surround yourself with people who add value to you and encourage you, and your talent will go in a positive direction. Spend time with people who constantly drain you, pull you in the wrong direction, or try to knock you down, and it will be almost impossible for your talent to take flight. People can trace the successes and failures in their lives to their most significant relationships.

MUSIC LEGEND

In 2005, Margaret and I went to see the movie *Walk the Line*. I have to admit, I didn't know very much about Johnny Cash before I saw the movie, but I was fascinated by his relationship with June Carter. And that got me reading about them.

During his career, Johnny Cash recorded more than 1,500 songs, had 14 number one hit songs, was awarded 11 Grammys, and sold 50 million albums.[1] He was inducted into the Rock and Roll Hall of Fame, the Songwriters Hall of Fame, and the Country Music Hall of Fame. He was a huge star. In 1959, he made a quarter of a million dollars by playing concerts.[2] In 1961, he performed at 290 concerts attended by nearly a million people.[3] He was a major influence on performers such as Elvis and Bob Dylan. And he was as much of a mess as the movie depicted him to be.

LEGENDARY MESS

Cash took his first pill—an amphetamine tablet called Benzedrine—in 1957. He was instantly hooked.

"It increased my energy, it sharpened my wit, it banished my shyness, it improved my timing, it turned me on like electricity flowing through a light bulb," Cash recalled. For the next ten years, Cash was addicted to pills. "Every pill I took was an attempt to regain the wonderful, natural feeling of euphoria I experienced the first time. Not a single one of them, not even one among many thousands that slowly tore me away from my family and my God and myself, ever worked. It was never as great as the first time, no matter how hard I tried to make it so."[4] And Cash tried hard to make it so.

The damage that it did him was all that the movie *Walk the Line* showed and even more. At one point, Cash decided that he couldn't stand to live with it anymore. In his autobiography, Cash explained what happened:

> I just went on and on. I was taking amphetamines by the handful, literally, and barbiturates by the handful too, not to sleep but just to stop the shaking from the amphetamines. I was canceling shows and

recording dates, and when I did manage to show up, I couldn't sing because my throat was too dried out from the pills. My weight was down to 155 pounds on a six-foot, one-and-a-half-inch frame. I was in and out of jails, hospitals, car wrecks. I was a walking vision of death, and that's exactly how I felt. I was scraping the filthy bottom of the barrel of life.[5]

Having lost all hope, Cash traveled to Tennessee to Nickajack Cave, a series of deep caves he had visited before, where spelunkers and explorers had sometimes lost their way and died failing to find a way out. Cash intended to share their fate. He parked his Jeep, went in, and crawled for hours—until the batteries in his flashlight gave out. Then he lay down in the dark to die.

Cash said in the dark he experienced an encounter with God, and he realized his life was not his own to throw away. With newfound hope, he decided to start crawling in the dark. Miraculously he found his way out. And when he emerged blinking in the sunlight, he was dumbfounded and confused to find his mother and June Carter waiting for him. "I knew there was something wrong. I had to come and find you," his mother told him.[6] She had traveled all the way from California.

RECOVERY

During the next few weeks and months, June Carter and her mother cared for him, shielded him from negative influences, and nursed him back to health, similar to the way it was depicted in the movie. In the past June had tried to help Cash, encouraging him to give up the drugs, and often getting rid of them. Now Cash readily accepted her help. A few months later, they were married. For the next thirty-five years, they were inseparable. And in the 1980s when Cash got addicted to painkillers due to a stomach problem, she helped him recover again. The battle was so hard-fought that when Cash later underwent heart bypass surgery, he refused any painkillers.

Walk the Line depicted June Carter as a positive influence on Johnny Cash, but even as good a job as it did, it couldn't capture her true character. Perhaps the best description came from Rosanne Cash, Johnny's daughter from his first marriage. At June's funeral, Rosanne said:

> In her eyes, there were two kinds of people in the world: those she knew and loved, and those she didn't know and loved. She looked for the best in everyone; it was a way of life for her. If you pointed out that a particular person was perhaps not totally deserving of her love, and might in fact be somewhat of a lout, she would say, "Well, honey, we just have to lift him up." She was forever lifting people up. It took me a long time to understand that what she did when she lifted you up was to mirror the very best parts of you back to yourself. She was like a spiritual detective: she saw into all your dark corners and deep recesses, saw your potential and your possible future, and the gifts you didn't even know you possessed, and she "lifted them up" for you to see. She did it for all of us, daily, continuously. But her great mission and passion were lifting up my dad. If being a wife were a corporation, June would have been the CEO. It was her most treasured role. She began every day by saying, "What can I do for *you*, John?" Her love filled up every room he was in, lightened every path he walked, and her devotion created a sacred, exhilarating place for them to live out their married life. My daddy has lost his dearest companion, his musical counterpart, his soul mate and best friend.[7]

The bottom line is that June Carter made Johnny Cash a better man. He reached his potential as an artist and as a human being in large part because of her influence. Cash put her impact on him in perspective a few years before they died:

The publicity in the 1960s was that June saved my life, and I sometimes still hear it said that she's the reason I'm alive today. That may be true, but knowing what I do about addiction and survival, I'm fully aware that the only human being who can save you is yourself. What June did for me was post signs along the way, lift me up when I was weak, encourage me when I was discouraged, and love me when I felt alone and unlovable. She's the greatest woman I have ever known.[8]

THE IMPACT OF RELATIONSHIPS

I think many people mistakenly minimize the impact that other people can have on their lives. My parents understood the influence of relationships. Today as I look back on my formative years, I see how intentional they were about who we spent time with and who we selected as our friends. My parents made our house the place to be in the neighborhood. We had a pool table, a Ping-Pong table, and a chemistry set in our basement. We had a shuffleboard court, a basketball court, and a Wiffle ball diamond in our yard. Everybody wanted to come to our house. And that was the strategy. My parents wanted to be able to

> Almost all our sorrows can be traced to relationships with the wrong people and our joys to relationships with the right people.

know the kids we played with. Typical of the times (it was the 1950s and 1960s), my mom didn't work outside the home, so she was always there to keep an eye on us.

Mom was always on the periphery of our play, fixing us lunch or a cold drink, putting Band-Aids on cuts, and observing the interaction and behavior of each person. Every now and then, she would ask my brother, Larry, my sister, Trish, or me about a particular friend. As children, we had no idea of the importance of associating with good kids rather than bad ones, but our parents did. They made sure the influences on our lives were positive.

Years later when I was an adult and I spent several hours a week counseling people, I learned through daily observation what my parents knew. Almost all our sorrows can be traced to relationships with the wrong people and our joys to relationships with the right people.

The Direction Relationships Take Us

The relationships in our lives really do make or break us. They either lift us up or take us down. They add, or they subtract. They help to give us energy, or they take it away. Here's what I mean:

Some Relationships Take from Us

There are a couple of good ways to tell whether a relationship is positive or negative. The first is to note whether a person makes you feel better or worse about yourself. The second relates to how much energy the relationship requires. Let's face it, some relationships feel as if they could suck the life out of you. In his book *High Maintenance Relationships*, Les Parrott identifies the types of people who are likely to hurt us and take energy from us. Here are some of them:

Critics constantly complain or give unwanted advice.
Martyrs are forever the victim and wracked with self-pity.
Wet blankets are pessimistic and habitually negative.
Steamrollers are blindly insensitive to others.
Gossips spread rumors and leak secrets.
Control freaks are unable to let go and let things be.
Backstabbers are irrepressively two-faced.
Green-eyed monsters seethe with envy.
Volcanoes build steam and are always ready to erupt.

Sponges are always in need but never give anything back.

Competitors always keep track of tit for tat.

Les also offers a straightforward quiz that can help you tell whether someone in your life is a negative person who takes energy from you. Answer yes or no to each of the following questions:

_____ Do you feel especially anxious when a particular person has called and left a message for you to return the call?

_____ Have you recently been dealing with a relationship that drains you of enthusiasm and energy?

_____ Do you sometimes dread having to see or talk to a particular person at work or in a social situation?

_____ Do you have a relationship in which you give more than you get in return?

_____ Do you find yourself second-guessing your own performance as a result of an interaction with this person?

_____ Do you become more self-critical in the presence of this person?

_____ Is your creativity blocked, or is your clarity of mind hampered somewhat, by the lingering discomfort of having to deal with a difficult person?

_____ Do you try to calm yourself after being with this person by eating more, biting your nails, or engaging in some other unhealthy habit?

_____ Do you ever have imaginary conversations with this person or mental arguments in which you defend yourself or try to explain your side of a conflict?

_____ Have you become more susceptible to colds, stomach problems, or muscle tension since having to deal with this difficult person?

_____ Do you feel resentful that this person seems to treat other people better than she or he treats you?

_____ Do you find yourself wondering why this person singles you out for criticism but rarely acknowledges things you do well?

_____ Have you thought about quitting your job as a result of having to interact with this difficult person?

_____ Have you noticed that you are more irritable or impatient with people you care about because of leftover frustrations from your interaction with this difficult person?

_____ Are you feeling discouraged that this person has continued to drain you of energy despite your efforts to improve the relationship?

Les says that if you answered yes to ten or more of the questions, then you are certainly in a high-maintenance relationship.[9]

I don't mean to imply that only negative relationships require you to put energy into them. All relationships require you to give *some* energy. Relationships don't cultivate and sustain themselves. The question is, how much energy do they require? And do they give anything in return? For example, some of the positive relationships that require a tremendous amount of energy in my life include:

- My *family*—every family has ups and down, but that's okay; that's what it means to be in a family.

- My *inner circle of friends*—these people get everything I've got, and they give their all, too; that's what friendship is all about.

- My *team*—leadership begins with a serving attitude; I always try to give more than I receive.

- *Those less fortunate than I am*—every year I travel to developing countries to train leaders and add value to people through EQUIP, my nonprofit organization.

If a relationship requires you to expend energy some of the time, that's normal. If a relationship saps your energy all the time, then that relationship has a negative effect on you. You may be able to see its effects in many areas of your life. It dilutes your talent because it robs you of energy that you could be using toward your best gifts and skills. It distracts you from your purpose. And it detracts from your best efforts. In the long run, a negative relationship cannot influence your talent in a positive direction.

Some Relationships Add to Us

Some relationships clearly make us better. They energize, inspire, and validate us. They lift us up and give us joy. We should consider the people in these relationships friends and value them highly. Helen Keller remarked, "My friends have made the story of my life. In a thousand ways they have turned my limitations into beautiful privileges, and enabled me to walk serene and happy in the shadow cast by my deprivation."

In my book *The Treasure of a Friend*, I reflect on the nature of friendship. Who else but a friend is there . . .

to believe in your dreams,
to share your joys,
to dry your tears,
to give you hope,
to comfort your hurts,
to listen,
to laugh with you,
to show you a better way,

to tell you the truth,
to encourage you.
Who else can do that for you?
That's what friends are for.

Not long ago, I sat down and listed the types of people who add value to my life and give me energy. Here is what I wrote:

1. *My family*—the best moments with my family are *my* best moments.

2. *Creative people*—they unleash creativity within me like no others.

3. *Successful people*—I love to hear their stories.

4. *Encouraging people*—encouragement is like oxygen to my soul.

5. *Fun people*—laughter always lifts my spirit.

6. *Good thinkers*—conversations with them are my favorite things.

7. *My team*—they always add value to me.

8. *Learners*—interested people are interesting people.

Positive relationships take us to a higher level. They encourage us and bring out the best in us. They make us better than we otherwise would be without them. They are some of life's greatest gifts!

Some Relationships Are Pivotal to Our Lives

Throughout a lifetime, people are in contact with thousands of people in varying levels of relationships. Most have a very limited impact on us. But a few relationships have such a tremendous impact that they change the course of our lives. They are pivotal to who we are and what we do.

Relationships commonly go through four stages:

1. *Surface relationships.* These require no commitment from either person. Examples include the clerk who helps you at the post office, acquaintances at church or the gym, and your favorite waiter at the neighborhood restaurant. You recognize these people and they recognize you. You may even know their names, but you don't know much beyond what you can observe from a distance.

2. *Structured relationships.* The next level is a little more involved than surface relationships. Structured relationships occur around routine encounters, usually at a particular place at a particular time. They often develop around a common interest or activity. The people you know from school or work, the parents at your kid's activities, and people who share your hobbies fall into this category.

3. *Secure relationships.* When a surface or structured relationship grows, trust develops, and the people involved begin to want to spend time together, it starts to develop into a genuine personal relationship. This is the level where you develop friendships.

4. *Solid relationships.* When people in a secure relationship build on their friendship and develop complete trust and absolute confidentiality, it can go to the solid relationship level. These relationships are long term and are characterized by a mutual desire to give and serve one another. Your desire should be to cultivate the most important relationships in your life: your spouse, your best friends, and your inner circle.

As the level of relationship increases, so does the influence of people on one another. And each time people try to take the relationship higher, it creates a period of testing. During that time, the relationship can go one way or another, positive or negative. If the dynamic becomes lose-lose or win-lose, the relationship is negative. Positive relationships are *always* overall win-win.

Every now and then, a relationship goes beyond *solid* to become *significant*, a relationship that is pivotal to your life. I don't think anyone can try to create one of these relationships. I call them simply God's gift to me. I don't deserve them—but I do need them. People with whom I have enjoyed this kind of relationship give beyond reason and lift me up to a level I *could not* achieve without them.

Tom Phillippe is one such friend. Tom and I have been friends for more than thirty years. We have traveled the world together, yet we also enjoy just sitting at home talking with no other agenda. Not long ago a group of Tom's friends got together with him to celebrate his seventieth birthday. Each of us had the chance to tell the others how Tom has affected our lives. I wrote what I wanted to say and read it to the group:

> Tom has loved me unconditionally. Victor Hugo said, "The supreme happiness of life is being loved in spite of yourself." Tom has also loved me continually. In 1980, he encouraged me to join the Wesleyan denomination. In 1981, he began assisting me in starting leadership conferences. He gave me an opportunity to enter the business world. He managed my personal development organization when time would not allow me to do it. He financially kept my nonprofit organization alive in its beginning days. Today it trains millions of leaders internationally. One of God's gifts to me was Tom's friendship.

I then closed with a poem called "Your Name Is Written . . . at the Top of My List."[10] Tom has changed my life forever. He has been a lifter in so many areas of my life. If you ever encounter someone who has that impact on you, fight to preserve that relationship, show your gratitude often, and give whatever you can in return.

FIVE SIGNS OF A SOLID RELATIONSHIP

Relationships at the secure level validate us and help us to become more comfortable with who we are and to discover our gifts and talents. Solid relationships add value to us so that our talent is actually enhanced. Our solid friends tell us the truth in a supportive way. They keep us grounded. If we start to get off course, they help keep us on track. They encourage us when we're down and inspire us to go higher. A few solid relationships can make all the difference in where a talented person ends up in life.

As you engage in relationships, try to find people with whom you can build solid relationships that are mutually beneficial. Here are the signs that a relationship is headed toward that level:

1. Mutual Enjoyment

In solid relationships, people spend time together just for the enjoyment of being together. What they do is not of significance. For example, my wife, Margaret, and I often run errands together. What's enjoyable about dropping off the dry cleaning, buying groceries, or picking up items at a neighborhood shop? Nothing—except spending time with her.

I think when many of us were kids, we intuitively understood the value of spending time with someone special. Do you remember how it felt to sit on the lap of your mother or father when you were small? Or how excited you got when a favorite uncle or a grandparent came to visit? Or how it felt when you first started dating? Unfortunately the busyness and pressures of life often cause us to forget what a joy this can be. I've always valued time with Margaret. Now that she and I are grandparents, time with people I love means even more to me. Try not to let the stresses of life make you lose track of that.

2. Respect

When you value someone on the front end of a relationship, you earn respect on the back end. And that's foundational to all solid relationships.

> Respect
> is almost always
> built on
> difficult ground.

When do people respect you? When you don't let obstacles or circumstances become more important to you than the relationship. When the pressure is on and you still treat them with patience and respect. When the relationship is struggling and you are willing to work hard to protect and preserve it. That's when you have proven worthy of others' respect. Respect is almost always built on difficult ground.

Proverbs, the book of wisdom, teaches about the strength of relationships:

- Friends are scarce (18:24).
- Friends will not jump ship when the going gets rough (17:17).
- Friends will be available for counsel (27:9).
- Friends will speak the truth to you (27:6).
- Friends will sharpen you (27:17).
- Friends will be sensitive to your feelings (26:18–19).
- Friends will stick with you (16:28; 18:24).

People who respect each other and build a solid relationship enjoy all of these benefits of friendship.

3. Shared Experiences

Going through a significant experience with another person creates a mutual bond. The experience can be positive or negative. Families come together and enjoy reminiscing about vacations they took years before (often the more disastrous, the more fondly remembered!). Colleagues build relationships as they work together on high-pressure projects. Soldiers talk about the bond that occurs as they train together and how it only increases if they go to war together. We all need others to lean on and to celebrate with. Shared experiences give us those opportunities.

I still remember vividly my father taking me out of school when I was ten years old so that I could accompany him on a business trip. At the time, he was a district superintendent in our denomination, which meant that he was a pastor and leader to many pastors of local churches in our region. Dad and I packed for the trip and traveled from town to town by car. As we rode along, we talked. As he met with the various pastors, I watched him encouraging them. It not only created a special bond between us, but it modeled the kind of work with people that I would one day be doing myself. It was an experience I will treasure until the day I die.

> "The glory of friendship is not in the outstretched hand, nor the kindly smile, nor the joy of companionship; it is in the spiritual inspiration that comes to one when he discovers that someone else believes in him and is willing to trust him."
>
> —Ralph Waldo Emerson

4. Trust

Ralph Waldo Emerson wrote, "The glory of friendship is not in the outstretched hand, nor the kindly smile, nor the joy of companionship; it is in the spiritual inspiration that comes to one when he discovers that someone else believes in him and is willing to trust him." Trust is both a joy of relationships and a necessary component. In my book *Winning with People*, I described the Bedrock Principle, which says, "Trust is the foundation of any relationship." Nothing is more important in relationships. If you don't have trust, you don't have much of a relationship.

5. Reciprocity

All relationships experience ebb and flow. Sometimes one person is the primary giver. Sometimes the other person is. But relationships that continue to be one-sided will not remain solid. When they continue to be out of balance, they become unstable and often unhealthy. If you want the relationship to continue, you will need to make changes. Here's how it works:

- When you are getting the better of the relationship, changes must be made.
- When the other person is getting the better part, changes must be made.
- When you're both getting an equally good deal, continue as before.

> Relationships that continue to be one-sided will not remain solid.

Friendships are like bank accounts. You cannot continue to draw on them without making deposits. If either of you becomes overdrawn and it stays that way, then the relationship won't last.

Solid relationships must be beneficial to both parties. Each person has to put the other first, and both have to benefit. Hall of Fame football coach Vince Lombardi described this when he was asked what made a winning team. He observed,

> There are a lot of coaches with good ball clubs who know the fundamentals and have plenty of discipline but still don't win the game. Then you come to the third ingredient: if you're going to play together as a team, you've got to care for one another. You've got to *love* each other. Each player has to be thinking about the next guy and saying to himself, "If I don't block that man, Paul is going to get his legs broken. I have to do my job in order that he can do his." The difference between mediocrity and greatness is the feeling these guys have for each other.

Solid relationships are always win-win. If both people aren't winning, then the relationship isn't solid, and it won't last.

TALENT + *RELATIONSHIPS* = A TALENT-PLUS PERSON
PUTTING THE TALENT-PLUS FORMULA INTO ACTION

If you desire to become a talent-plus person in the area of relationships—a person whose relationships influence him or her in a positive direction—then here is what I suggest you do:

1. Identify the Most Important People in Your Life

Who are the significant people in your life, the people you spend the most time with, the people whose opinions mean the most to you? These people are your greatest influencers. You need to identify who they are before you can assess how they are influencing your talent.

2. Assess Whether They Are Influencing You in the Right Direction

Once you have identified the people who are influencing you, you would be wise to discern *how* they are influencing you. The easiest way to do that is to ask the following questions about each person:

What does he think of me? People tend to become what the most important person in their lives believes they can be. Think about small children. If their parents tell them they are losers, stupid, or worthless, they believe they are. If their parents tell them they are smart, attractive, and valuable, they believe they are. We embrace the opinions of people we respect.

Ralph Waldo Emerson asserted, "Every man is entitled to be valued by his best moments." If you want to be influenced in a positive direction, you need to spend time with people who think positively about you. They need to believe in you.

What does he think of my future? Novelist Mark Twain advised, "Keep away from people who try to belittle your ambitions. Do the most important people in your life envision a positive future for you? Do they see great things ahead of you?

Margaret, my wife, has given me many wonderful gifts during the course of our relationship. One that I cherish is the ministry log book she gave me the year before we were married, knowing that a pastoral career was ahead of me. In it, I could record my activities such as sermon topics, weddings, and funerals. It is a record of my life leading local churches. But I value it most for something she wrote in it in 1968. It said simply,

> John,
> You're going to accomplish great things.
> Love,
> Margaret

Her few words weren't poetic or profound, but they communicated her confidence in me and her belief in my future. And she has demonstrated that belief in me every day of our marriage.

How does he or she behave toward me in difficult times? There's an old saying: "In prosperity our friends know us. In adversity we know our friends." Haven't you found that to be true? When times are tough and you're having difficulties, a friend who is influencing you in the right direction is . . .

Slow to	but	Quick to
Suspect		Trust
Condemn		Justify
Offend		Defend
Expose		Shield
Reprimand		Forbear
Belittle		Appreciate
Demand		Give
Provoke		Help
Resent		Forgive

When you get knocked down, good friends don't kick you while you're down or say, "I told you so." They pick you up and help you keep going.

What does he bring out of me? British prime minister Benjamin Disraeli observed, "The greatest good you can do for another is not just to share your riches but to reveal to him his own." That is really the essence of positive relationships that influence people to rise up and reach their potential. They see the best in you and encourage you to strive for it, as June Carter did for Johnny Cash.

Author William Allen Ward remarked, "A true friend knows your weaknesses but shows you

> "In prosperity our friends know us. In adversity we know our friends."

your strengths; feels your fears but fortifies your faith; sees your anxieties but frees your spirit; recognizes your disabilities but emphasizes your possibilities." That's what positive relationships should do.

3. If Your Friends Aren't Friends, Then Make New Friends

A friend sent me a hilarious story that he said was called "Bob's Last Letter." Here's what it said:

Dear Friends:

It is important for men to remember that as women grow older it becomes harder for them to maintain the same quality of housekeeping as they did when they were younger. When men notice this, they should try not to yell.

Let me relate how I handle the situation.

When I got laid off from my consulting job and took "early retirement" in April, it became necessary for Nancy to get a full-time job, both for extra income and for health benefits that we need. It was shortly after she started working that I noticed that she was beginning to show her age.

I usually get home from fishing or hunting about the same time she gets home from work. Although she knows how hungry I am, she almost always says that she has to rest for half an hour or so before she starts supper. I try not to yell, instead I tell her to take her time and just wake me when she finally does get supper on the table. She used to do the dishes as soon as we finished eating. It is now not unusual for them to sit on the table for several hours after supper.

I do what I can by reminding her several times each evening that they aren't cleaning themselves. I know she appreciates this, as it does seem to help her get them done before she goes to bed.

Now that she is older she seems to get tired so much more quickly. Our washer and dryer are in the basement. Sometimes she says she just can't make another trip down those steps. I don't make a big issue of this. As long as she finishes up the laundry the next evening I am willing to overlook it.

Not only that, but unless I need something ironed to wear to the Monday lodge meeting or to Wednesday's or Saturday's poker club or to Tuesday's or Thursday's bowling or something like that, I will tell her to wait until the next evening to do the ironing. This gives her a little more time to do some of those odds and ends things like shampooing the dog, vacuuming or dusting.

Also, if I have had a really good day fishing, this allows her to gut and scale the fish at a more leisurely pace.

Nancy is starting to complain a little occasionally. For example, she will say that it is difficult for her to find time to pay the monthly bills during her lunch hour. In spite of her complaining, I continue to try to offer encouragement. I tell her to stretch it out over two or even three days. That way she won't have to rush so much. I also remind her that missing lunch completely now and then wouldn't hurt her any, if you know what I mean.

When doing simple jobs she seems to think she needs more rest periods.

She had to take a break when she was only half finished mowing the yard. I try not to embarrass her when she needs these little extra rest breaks. I tell her to fix herself a nice, big, cold glass of freshly squeezed lemonade and just sit for a while. I tell her that as long as she is making one for herself, she may as well make one for me and take her break by the hammock so she can talk with me until I fall asleep.

I know that I probably look like a saint in the way I support Nancy on a daily basis. I'm not saying that the ability to show this much consideration is easy. Many men will find it difficult. Some will find it impossible. No one knows better than I do how frustrating women can become as they get older. However, guys, even if you just yell at your wife a little less often because of this article, I will consider that writing it was worthwhile.

Signed, Bob

P.S. Bob's funeral was on Saturday, January 25th.
P.P.S. Nancy was acquitted Monday, January 27th[11]

If the people close to you are dragging you down, then it may be time to make some changes. Speaker Joe Larson remarked, "My friends didn't believe that I could become a successful speaker. So I did something about it. I went out and found me some new friends!"

When you really think about it, the things that matter most in life are the relationships we develop. Remember:

You may build a beautiful house, but eventually it will crumble.
You may develop a fine career, but one day it will be over.
You may save a great sum of money, but you can't take it with you.
You may be in superb health today, but in time it will decline.
You may take pride in your accomplishments, but someone will
     surpass you.

Discouraged? Don't be, for the one thing that really matters, lasts
forever—your friendships.

Life is too long to spend it with people who pull you in the wrong
direction. And it's too short not to invest in others. Your relationships
will define you. And they will influence your talent—one way or the
other. Choose wisely.

TALENT + RELATIONSHIPS
APPLICATION EXERCISES

1. Make a list of the important people in your life. Next to each person's name, write a plus sign if the person adds value to you and a minus sign if that individual primarily takes from you. Use the questions in the chapter as criteria:

    - What does he think of me?
    - What does he think of my future?
    - How does he behave toward me in difficult times?
    - What does he bring out of me?

    For people on the list who are subtractors, you will need to develop a strategy to deal with them.

    If you work with some of the negative people, you will have to try to find a way to distance yourself. If that isn't possible, consider changing jobs.

    If the negative people are friends or acquaintances, it's time to find new ones. Separate yourself from the people who are having a negative influence on your life, and start looking for friends who will lift you up.

    If the negative people are family members, you may have to limit the amount of time you spend with them and counteract their impact by spending more time with positive people. (It's said that it takes at least five positive remarks to counteract the effects of one negative one.)

    If one of the negative people is your spouse, seek professional help. It is highly unlikely that you will be able to turn around the relationship without assistance.

2. Pick the relationship that matters most to you, and evaluate it. Write two columns: "What I Give" and "What I Get." Under each column, write all the benefits you receive from your relationship and all the benefits the other person receives.

   If the relationship is healthy, the two columns should balance each other. That doesn't necessarily mean they will have the same number of entries. Not all benefits are equal in value. Take that into account. But if the two columns are out of balance, you will need to make adjustments to preserve the relationship.

   If you are the primary giver, then first ask yourself *why*. Second, make plans to step back and give less. Sometimes the other person has just been waiting to step up and contribute more. If the other person is the primary giver, consider how you can add more value to the relationship and take action.

3. Write a thank-you note to a pivotal person in your life, expressing your gratitude and explaining what the person has done for you and what it has meant.

12

RESPONSIBILITY STRENGTHENS YOUR TALENT

Nothing adds "muscle" to talent like responsibility. It lifts talent to a new level and increases its stamina. However, as I consider the thirteen choices that help to create a talent-plus person, I realize that responsibility is often the last choice people desire to make. The result is "flabby" talent that fails to perform and never realizes its potential. How sad for the person who fails to take responsibility. How sad for others. Author and editor Michael Korda said, "Success on any major scale requires you to accept responsibility . . . In the final analysis, the one quality that all successful people have . . . is the ability to take on responsibility." If you desire success, make responsibility your choice.

EXTREME TALENT

One day when I was flipping through television channels, I came across a program on PBS about rock climbers. What amazed me were their Spiderman-like qualities. The program focused on Dan Osman, a man in his midthirties who scrambled up a rock face in record time without the benefit of safety ropes. At one point in his climb, he literally jumped in order to reach a handhold and was momentarily airborne. If he had missed the hold he was reaching for, the fall would have killed him.

Intrigued, I did some research. I discovered that this particular climb was in California at a place called Lover's Leap. The route he took is called Bear's Reach. Evidently specific routes are named and rated by the first climber to successfully navigate them. Bear's Reach is considered a 5.7 in difficulty on the Yosemite Decimal System. I didn't know what that meant, so I looked it up. Any climb that begins with a 5 involves "climbing involving technical moves and protective hardware in case of a fall" or "thin, exposed climbing, requiring skill (the holds are not obvious to a novice—this is where weird moves such as laybacks, underclings, and evangelical hammerlocks come into play) . . . where serious injury or death is very likely if you take an unprotected fall."[1]

In other words, it was very difficult. One rock climbing guide estimated that the average time it would take to climb the 400-foot-tall cliff face of Bear's Reach was three hours.[2] That would typically be done using safety ropes. On camera, Osman did what's called a free solo climb—with no help and no ropes—just him against the rock face. He accomplished the feat in 4 minutes, 25 seconds! (Go to the Internet, type in his name on a search engine, and you will find a video of him in action.)

DEVELOPING HIS SKILLS

Osman started rock climbing when he was twelve years old. The son of a police officer father and a champion barrel racer mother, he is the descendant of samurai warriors. As a kid, he studied kung fu and aikido, a Japanese martial art that places high value on balance, control, and economy of motion. It took Osman eight years to become an expert climber, slow in his opinion, but he developed into a world-class climber and an expert rope rigger.

After more than a decade of climbing, Osman began experimenting with free falling. That's where a person jumps bungee-fashion from a high place, such as a bridge or cliff, but instead of being connected to a springy bungee cord, he is connected to a climber's rope. The rope has some stretch, but the fall is much more dramatic. It requires expert rigging and iron nerves. Osman began setting and breaking records for free falls. He became a legend among climbers and BASE jumpers (people who parachute from fixed objects). His fame grew, and soon creators of TV commercials and print ads started calling him.

UNLIMITED TALENT—LIMITED RESPONSIBILITY

But there was another side to Dan Osman. He had a difficult time functioning in the real world. His friends joked about Dano time—showing up to appointments hours late or sometimes not at all. His mother's childhood nickname for him was "Danny I Forgot." He continually received tickets for speeding and driving with a suspended license or unregistered vehicle—which he neglected to pay. He regularly depended on others to rescue him. Andrew Todhunter, who was so intrigued with Osman that he spent time with him over the course of three years and wrote a book about the experience, writes about Osman's arrest for unpaid traffic violations. As Osman was being led away, he asked the writer to call friends, a retired couple who had "adopted" him. They were used to bailing him out. The woman, a retired executive, remarked, "I do worry a lot for him . . . What scares me is his jumping. He continues to want to jump farther and farther. I told him, 'You're not getting any younger, Dan. You're going to have to think about your future a little more.'" Her concern was not for just him. Osman had a twelve-year-old daughter named Emma. He also had a live-in fiancée with a daughter.

Todhunter was amazed that Osman had such intense attention to detail and a strong sense of responsibility when climbing but so little for the rest of life. And he asked Osman about his responsibility to his daughter.

"If I fell while soloing I'd go against everything I represent, which is not pushing it, which is having the route 'in hand.' By dying I would let everybody down—my family, my friends," said Osman. "I'd be robbing her if I fell. She knows her dad's rad. Other dads don't do this. She's afraid, but she's proud of what I'm doing. It's like my father: I worry about him, getting shot, but then I hear what a good cop he is. And there's a plaque on the wall: Officer of the Year."[3]

RECORD BREAKER

On November 23, 1998, Dan Osman attempted his longest free fall— 1,000 feet. He had originally intended to set the new record on October 26. He had prepared his rigging at Yosemite's Leaning Tower and did some intermediate-distance jumps all the way up to 900 feet. Then he got a call from Emma. She was crying; she was worried about him. He dropped everything and went to see her. Two days later he was back at Yosemite and ready to resume his jumps, but he was arrested for the kinds of things he never took responsibility for: parking tickets and a suspended license. He spent fourteen days in jail.

His friend filmmaker Eric Perlman, who had offered his house against Osman's bail, talked to him after he got out of jail. Perlman recalls, "I told him, 'You've gone far enough, pushed it probably farther than it should be pushed. Nobody's going to touch this one [record] for a long time. Take the rig down, show the judge you're serious, that you're playing by the rules here.' And he agreed absolutely. He said, 'You know, you're right. It's what I should do. And my guardian angels need a break anyway. They've been working overtime for me.'"[4]

But when Osman went back with a friend on November 22 to take down his rigging and pack up all his equipment, he couldn't resist the urge to go for another record. First, he jumped at 925 feet. The next day, he talked his friend into jumping. Then Osman hastily rerigged everything for his own longer jump. By then it was late in the day, the sun was going down, and he couldn't see well. He jumped anyway. When the sound of the rope going taut didn't sound right, his friend knew something had gone wrong. He went to the base of the cliff where he found Osman dead.[5] His rope had snapped.

CHANGE IN PERSPECTIVE

While Todhunter was researching his book and spending time with Osman, he at first admired the climber and made allowances for his frequent displays of irresponsibility. He compared Osman's behavior to "Picasso's philandering" and "Faulkner's drunkenness," saying that great artists and athletic geniuses had an "inability or refusal to live within ordinary parameters."[6] But as Todhunter witnessed one reckless act after another, his point of view changed. He writes, "There are those professionals and volunteers who consciously and repetitively risk their lives in public service—and not infrequently lose them—for a worthy cause. Many of them, like Osman, have families to support. Watching the bridge jumping, I am struck for the first time by its profound pointlessness, by the immeasurable *gratuity* of the risk."[7]

Dan Osman's talent was off the charts. Few people in the world can do what he did. His physical gifts, like those of Michael Jordan, Tiger Woods, or Lance Armstrong, were phenomenal. But his lack of responsibility limited his life, and it eventually killed him. What a tragedy.

THE STRENGTH OF RESPONSIBILITY

We live in a culture that overvalues talent and undervalues responsibility. If you doubt that, then examine the way we treat our athletes. When

> We live in a culture that overvalues talent and undervalues responsibility.

athletes are in high school and college, their reckless or irresponsible acts are often overlooked in proportion to the talent they display on the court or playing field. What a disservice to them. Responsibility actually strengthens talent and increases the opportunity for long-term success. Here is how it helps:

1. Responsibility Provides the Foundation of Success

Sociology professor Tony Campolo points out the importance of having a strong sense of responsibility, especially in a culture like ours that values freedom. Of the American system, he writes,

> While I think it lays down the principles that make for the best political system ever devised, the Constitution has one basic flaw. It clearly delineates the Bill of Rights, but it nowhere states a Bill of Responsibilities . . . Government that ensures people of their rights but fails to clearly spell out their responsibilities, fails to call them to be the kind of people God wants them to be.[8]

I agree wholeheartedly with Campolo's call for responsibility. In fact, for years I've taught leaders that as they move up the ladder and take on greater responsibility, their rights actually *decrease*. Leadership requires sacrifice. And while taking on responsibility is also a sacrifice, it is one that brings tremendous rewards.

Recently I had the opportunity to spend time on the aircraft carrier USS *Enterprise*. I received a tour of the ship and listened to many officers explain the various tasks and functions of the 5,500 people aboard the ship. What struck me was that the officers' messages had a common theme. They talked about the importance of their area to the overall mission of the ship and how the responsibility for those functions was shouldered by a bunch of nineteen-year-old sailors. The officers made these statements with pride.

One officer told me about leading a former gang member under his command. The young man had been given the choice of jail or the navy. The troubled youth became an effective part of the team and was then the leader of his squad. His proudest moments in the military, this officer said, came from helping troubled kids to succeed.

What turned kids into productive citizens and troublemakers into leaders? Responsibility! When they entered the service, they became immersed in a culture of responsibility. That culture demanded that they act accordingly, that they become responsible and productive. When people respond to a call for responsibility by giving their best, good things happen.

The young men and women I met had made the choice to embrace responsibility, and it was creating success for them in the military. It will continue to provide a foundation for their success in the coming years, no matter what they do.

2. Responsibility, Handled Correctly, Leads to More Responsibility

Years ago the editor of the *Bellefontaine (Ohio) Examiner*, Gene Marine, sent a new sports reporter to cover a big game. The reporter returned to the paper with no report.

"Where's the story?" asked Marine.

"No report," replied the reporter.

"What?" growled Marine. "And why not?"

"No game."

"No game? What happened?" quizzed the editor.

"The stadium collapsed."

"Then where's the report on the collapse of the stadium?" demanded Marine.

"That wasn't my assignment, sir."

People who handle their responsibilities well get the opportunity to handle additional responsibilities. Those who don't, don't.

3. Responsibility Maximizes Ability and Opportunity

During the major-league baseball players' strike of 1994, many trading card manufacturers found themselves in a tough spot. Pinnacle Brands, however, was determined not to lay off any of its employees. Yet the company had to make some changes to be able to pay everyone until business picked up again. So what did management do? Placed the responsibility on the workers for finding ways to replace the $40 million in lost revenue. CEO Jerry Meyer told his employees, "I'm not going to save your jobs. You're going to save your jobs. You know what you can change and what you can do differently."

The people did not let themselves down. A custodian reported that the company spent $50,000 on sodas for conference rooms, an expense that was cut. A finance department worker found a way to streamline trademark searches that saved the company $100,000. A PR manager signed a deal to distribute pins at the Olympics, generating $20 million. In the end, Pinnacle was the only one of the top trading card manufacturers that didn't lay off workers during the baseball strike.[9]

Responsibility has value, not just in hard times, but at all times. It increases our abilities and gives us opportunities. One reason it does is that it causes us to take action, to make things happen. On the job, we need to take responsibility, not just for what we're assigned, but for the contribution we make. For example, if you're in business, at the end of every day you should ask yourself, *Did I make a profit for my employer today?* If the answer is no, then you may be in trouble. Take responsibility for being a contributor. Every worker needs to be an asset to the company, not an expense.

Author Richard L. Evans remarked, "It is priceless to find a person who will take responsibility, who will finish and follow through to the final detail—to know when someone has accepted an assignment that it will be effectively, conscientiously completed." When leaders find responsible people, they reward them with opportunities and resources that help them to become more effective.

4. Responsibility, Over Time, Builds a Solid Reputation

Responsible people enjoy an increasingly better reputation. And that is one of the greatest assets of sustained responsibility. Others discover what they can expect from you, and they know they can depend on you. You're solid.

In contrast, the longer you know a person who lacks responsibility, the *less* you trust him. It is not surprising to me that the better Andrew Todhunter got to know Dan Osman, the more reservations he had about him and what he was doing. A person may try to compartmentalize his life—taking responsibility in one area and shirking it in another—but in the long run it doesn't work. Irresponsibility, left unchecked, inevitably grows and spreads into other areas of a person's life.

A general from American history whose reputation continued to grow was Dwight D. Eisenhower. In fact, his reputation became so strong that it got him elected president. Though he was only an average president, he was an excellent general. One reason was his willingness to take responsibility for his decisions.

During World War II, Eisenhower was responsible for planning the D-Day invasion of Normandy, France. Giving the okay for the assault was a painful decision, one he knew that would lead to the deaths of many servicemen. Yet he also knew that if it was successful, it would be a pivotal point in the war against the Nazis.

Pat Williams, in his book *American Scandal*, writes that in the hours prior to the assault, Eisenhower handwrote a press release that would be used in the event of the invasion's failure. It read,

Our landings have failed . . . and I have withdrawn the troops. My decision to attack at this time and this place was based upon the best information available. The troops, the air, and the Navy did all that bravery and devotion to duty could do. If any blame or fault attaches to the attempt, it is mine alone.[10]

Eisenhower had determined that he would take responsibility for whatever happened. That mind-set earned the admiration of his fellow officers, his soldiers, and citizens alike.

If you want others to trust you, to give you greater opportunities and resources to develop and strengthen your talent, and to partner with you, then embrace responsibility and practice it faithfully in every area of your life.

TALENT + *RESPONSIBILITY* = A TALENT-PLUS PERSON PUTTING THE TALENT-PLUS FORMULA INTO ACTION

There's no way for me to know your personal history in regard to responsibility. Maybe assuming responsibility has been a problem for you. Or you may have a strong sense of responsibility, and you never drop the ball. Either way, please review the following steps to help you become a talent-plus person when it comes to responsibility:

1. Start Wherever You Are

Greek philosopher Aristotle observed, "We become what we are as persons by the decisions that we ourselves make." Each time you make a responsible decision, you become a more responsible person. Even if your track record hasn't been good up to now, you can change. Successful people take personal responsibility for their actions and their attitudes. They show response-ability—the ability to choose a correct response, no matter what situation they face. Responsibility is always a choice, and only you can make it.

If being responsible has not been one of your strengths, then start small. You can't start from anyplace other than where you are. I think you'll find that when it comes to responsibility, the best helping hand you will ever find is at the end of your arm.

2. Choose Your Friends Wisely

Since I've devoted an entire chapter to relationships and how they influence talent, I don't need to say very much here. Heed the advice of trainer and consultant Kevin Eikenberry, who says, "Look carefully at the closest associations in your life, for that is the direction you are heading." If you have started your journey on the road to responsibility, just make sure that you have the right traveling companions. You will find it difficult or impossible to be responsible when you spend most of your time with irresponsible people.

3. Stop Blaming Others

The sales manager of a dog food company asked his sales team how they liked the company's new advertising program.

"Great!" they replied. "The best in the business."

"What do you think of the product?" he asked.

"Fantastic," they replied.

"How about the sales force?" he asked.

They were the sales force, so of course they responded positively, saying they were the best.

"Okay then," the manager asked, "so if we have the best brand, the best packaging, the best advertising program, and the best sales force, why are we in seventeenth place in our industry?"

> "My philosophy is that not only are you responsible for your life, but doing the best at this moment puts you in the best place for the next moment."
>
> —Oprah Winfrey

After an awkward silence, one of the salesmen stated, "It's those darned dogs—they just won't eat the stuff!"

If you want to be successful and to maximize your talent as a talent-plus person, you need to stop blaming others, take a good look in the mirror, and take responsibility for your own life. Television host Oprah Winfrey says, "My philosophy is that not only are you responsible for your life, but doing the best at this moment puts you in the best place for the next moment."

Ron French of the Gannett News Service writes that failing to take responsibility has become pervasive in America:

> Ducking responsibility has become an American pastime. We all have learned to play the blame game, where the seven deadly sins are acceptable syndromes, and criminals are victims. From life-long smokers suing tobacco companies, to students rationalizing cheating, we've become a nation of whiners and cry babies. "It's part of the American character nowadays," says Charles Sykes, A Nation of Victims. "We've gone from a society of people who were self-reliant to a people who inherently refuse to accept responsibility."

People who think others are responsible for their situation assign the blame to various individuals, institutions, or entities. Some fault society or "the times." Some point at the system or "the man." (Criminals serving time in prison are notorious for blaming others and declaring their innocence.) Others rail against the previous generation as the cause of their problems. But do you know why? Cartoonist Doug Larson observed, "The reason people blame things on previous generations is that there's only one other choice."

> "Do what you can with what you have, where you are."
>
> —Theodore Roosevelt

Some of the best advice you could follow on this subject came from President Theodore Roosevelt: "Do what you can with what you have, where you are." That's all any of us can do. Don't make excuses. Don't look for others to blame. Just focus on the present and do your best. And if you make a mistake or fail, find whatever fault you can inside yourself and try to do better the next time around.

4. Learn Responsibility's Major Lessons

There are four core lessons we need to learn if we want to display the kind of responsibility that makes us talent-plus people. The lessons are simple and obvious. They are also very difficult to master:

Recognize that gaining success means practicing self-discipline. The first victory we must win is over ourselves. We must learn to control ourselves. You can use any incentive you want to do this: the desire to follow moral or ethical values, rewards for delayed gratification, even the threat of public exposure. Business executive John Weston commented, "I've always tried to live with the following simple rule: Don't do what you wouldn't feel comfortable reading about in the newspaper the next day." Every time you stop yourself from doing what you shouldn't or start yourself doing what you should, you are strengthening your self-discipline and increasing your capacity for responsibility.

What you start, finish. There are two kinds of people in the world: those who do and those who might. Responsible people follow through. If they make a commitment, they see it through. They finish. And that is how others evaluate them. Are they dependable or not? Can I rely on them? Writer Ben Ames Williams observed, "Life is the acceptance of responsibilities or their evasion; it is a business of meeting obligations or avoiding them. To every man the choice is continually being offered, and by the manner of his choosing you may fairly measure him."

Know when others are depending on you. Talent does not succeed on its own. (I'll discuss that in detail in the next chapter.) If you desire to be successful, you will need others. Sometimes you will have to depend on them. And there will be times they need to depend on you. In my book *The 17 Indisputable Laws of Teamwork*, I write about the Law of Countability, which says, "Teammates must be able to count on each other when it counts."

The first step in making yourself the kind of person others can depend on is being dependable. The second is taking the focus off yourself and becoming aware that others are depending on you. Having the *intention* to be responsible isn't enough. Your *actions* need to come through.

Don't expect others to step in for you. The following challenge was issued to the 1992 graduating class of the University of South Carolina by Alexander M. Saunders Jr., chief judge of the South Carolina Court of Appeals:

> As responsibility is passed to your hands, it will not do, as you live the rest of your life, to assume that someone else will bear the major burdens, that someone else will demonstrate the key convictions, that someone else will run for office, that someone else will take care of the poor, that someone else will visit the sick, protect civil rights, enforce the law, preserve culture, transmit value, maintain civilization, and defend freedom.
>
> You must never forget that what you do not value will not be valued, that what you do not remember will not be remembered, that what you do not change will not be changed, that what you do not do will not be done. You can, if you will, craft a society whose leaders, business and political, are less obsessed with the need for money. It is not really a question of what to do but simply the will to do it.

Many people sit back and wait for someone else to step up and take responsibility. Sometimes that is because of weak character—laziness, lack of resolve, and so on. But more often it comes from poor judgment or low self-esteem. People believe that someone else is more qualified or better situated to stand up and make a difference. But the truth is that most of the people who make a difference do so not because they are the best for the job but because they decided to try.

5. Make Tough Decisions and Stand by Them

When he was mayor of New York City, Rudy Giuliani kept a sign on his desk that stated, "I'm responsible." In his book *Leadership*, he writes,

> Throughout my career, I've maintained that accountability—the idea that the people who work for me are answerable to those we work for—is the cornerstone, and this starts with me . . . Nothing builds confidence in a leader more than the willingness to take responsibility for what happens during his watch. One might add that nothing builds a stronger case for holding employees to a high standard than a boss who holds himself to an even higher one. This is true in any organization, but it's particularly true in government.[11]

That mind-set served him well during the crisis of 9-11 in 2001. He had to make many tough decisions very quickly. And whether they were right or wrong, he stood by them. His tough-minded responsibility coupled with strong leadership served the people well during that difficult time.

> "You cannot escape the responsibility of tomorrow by evading it today."
>
> —Abraham Lincoln

President Abraham Lincoln said, "You cannot escape the responsibility of tomorrow by evading it today." Easy decisions may make us look good, but making tough ones—and taking ownership of them—makes us better.

6. Live Beyond Yourself

There is one more aspect of responsibility that I want to share with you. It will make you a talent-plus person beyond the level of those who simply take responsibility for themselves. It is the idea of taking responsibility beyond yourself by serving others. In a speech to the Massachusetts legislature on the eve of his presidency, John F. Kennedy said,

For of those to whom much is given, much is required. And when at some future date the high court of history sits in judgment on each one of us—recording whether in our brief span of service we fulfilled our responsibilities to the state—our success or failure, in whatever office we may hold, will be measured by the answers to four questions. First, were we truly men of courage[?] . . . Secondly, were we truly men of judgement[?] . . . Third, were we truly men of integrity[?] . . . Finally, were we truly men of dedication[?][12]

Self-serving people regard their talent and resources as what they own. Serving people regard their talent and resources as what's on loan.

Holocaust survivor Elie Wiesel, who won the Nobel Peace Prize in 1986, spent the years after his time in the Nazi concentration camps trying to give back to others. He taught as a professor at Boston University. He also traveled extensively giving talks and sharing the wisdom he gained from his life experiences. One of the questions he asked young people was, "How will you cope with the privileges and obligations society will feel entitled to place on you?" As he tried to guide them, he shared his sense of responsibility to others:

What I receive I must pass on to others. The knowledge that I have must not remain imprisoned in my brain. I owe it to many men and women to do something with it. I feel the need to pay back what was given to me. Call it gratitude . . . To learn means to accept the postulate that life did not begin at my birth. Others have been there before me, and I walk in their footsteps.

Practicing responsibility will do great things for you. It will strengthen your talent, advance your skills, and increase your opportunities. It will improve your quality of life during the day and help you to sleep better at night. But it will also improve the lives of the people around you.

If you want your life to be a magnificent story, then realize that you are its author. Every day you have the chance to write a new page in that story. I want to encourage you to fill those pages with responsibility to others and yourself. If you do, in the end you will not be disappointed.

Talent + Responsibility
Application Exercises

1. How good are you about taking care of the small stuff? That really is the prerequisite for being given responsibility for the big stuff. And even if you are being entrusted with huge responsibilities, you must not neglect details in your primary area of responsibility. You also never outgrow the need for responsibilities for small things with the people closest to you, such as your spouse or children. Give yourself a review. Are you taking care of the details in your job? How about at home? How often do you forget small things that are big things for your family members? It can be as big as forgetting an anniversary or birthday, or it can be as small as not picking up dry cleaning or being late for a child's game or recital. If you're neglecting small things, then get back to the basics.

2. Which of the major responsibility lessons are the toughest for you to live out with consistency?

    *   *Practicing self-discipline*—denying yourself for the sake of something or someone more important. If this is your trouble area, seek assistance from someone who can lend expertise, give you some guidelines, and help you motivate yourself. If you're lacking discipline fiscally, find someone to help you put together a budget. If your health is an issue, see a doctor. If you're overweight, talk to a trainer and a nutritionist.

    *   *Following through*—taking responsibilities to completion. If you have a tendency to quit, give yourself relatively small goals that require you to stretch. Start in areas where you have passion.

Then with a few wins under your belt, begin tackling other areas of your life.

- *Knowing when others are depending on you*—being there for others. People with this problem area usually lack people skills or are too self-centered. If people skills are your problem, then read a book like Dale Carnegie's How to Win Friends and Influence People or my book Winning with People. If you are too self-focused, then volunteer to help people in serious need.

- *Stepping forward*—not expecting someone else to do what's important to you. You've already done exercises to help you tap into your passion areas, identify your core values, and so on. Review them and determine whether you are taking action in these areas. If you're not, take a bold step. Volunteer, give financially, join an organization, or start your own. Do something by the end of this week.

3. Most people have a tough decision in their jobs or personal lives that is waiting to be made. They put it off and put it off. What's yours? Why aren't you taking action? Write the reasons so that you know without a doubt what they are. Now write down the advantages of making the decision. Are there any clear, concrete, and compelling reasons for putting off the decision? If so, write them down. At this point, you know in your heart what you should do. Do it, and stand by it.

13

TEAMWORK MULTIPLIES YOUR TALENT

In the Academy Award–winning movie *Rocky*, boxer Rocky Balboa describes his relationship with his girlfriend, Adrian: "I've got gaps. She's got gaps. But together we've got no gaps." What a wonderful description of teamwork! It doesn't matter how talented you may be—you have gaps. There are things you don't do well. What's the best way to handle your weaknesses? Partner with others who have strengths in those areas. If you want to do something *really* big, then do it as part of a team.

EXTRAORDINARY TEAMWORK

In the previous chapter, I mentioned that I recently toured the aircraft carrier USS *Enterprise*. I got that opportunity when my friend, Tom Mullins, invited me to make the trip along with him and a few others. It started when we landed aboard the aircraft, which was already at sea. For twenty-four hours, we received the VIP treatment, touring every part of that magnificent ship. The entire experience was fantastic, but the highlight for me was sitting with Rear Admiral Raymond Spicer, commander of the *Enterprise*'s carrier strike group, and watching F/A-18 Hornet jets taking off and landing at night. What an incredible sight!

There was beauty in the way the jets shot off the deck and others landed, coming to a halt in a mere two seconds. But what struck me even more was the number of people who seemed to be involved in the process and the teamwork that was required. When I asked Admiral Spicer about it, he put me in contact with Lt. Commander Ryan Smith, the V2 Division Officer, who explained the process to me. He said,

> The pilot is seated at the controls of an F/A-18 Hornet as the jet is accelerated from 0 to nearly 160 mph in the span of less than three seconds. As the aircraft climbs away from the carrier, she raises the landing gear and is suddenly alone in the black of night. There are few examples of solitary combat in today's era of modern, networked warfare, but an aviator seated in the cockpit of one of today's Navy fighters still seems like an example in which the accomplishment of a particular objective is entirely dependent on the talent, skill, and effort of one particular, highly trained individual. However, the singular act of catapulting a jet off of the end of one of these carriers is the result of the complex orchestration of scores of individuals, each with a mastery of his or her own specific task. It is the efforts and coordination of these individuals, most of whom are just barely high school graduates, which serve as a truly inspiring example of teamwork.[1]

He then went on to explain the process. Hours before that jet taxis to the catapult for launching, it is being inspected by a team of mechanics and technicians from the Aircraft Squadron. While the pilot is receiving a briefing on the mission, including weather, target information, radio procedures, and navigational information (all of which are produced by teams of sailors), the aircraft is going through an equally rigorous period of preparation. The preflight routine ends only when the pilot has reviewed the aircraft's maintenance records and inspected the aircraft for flight.

Exactly thirty minutes prior to the aircraft's launch time, a specific sequence of steps begins that is always followed with precision. The aircraft carrier's air boss calls for engine starts, a test to make certain that the jets are in proper working order, while the pilot runs through his pre-taxi checks. The aircraft's plane captain is listening to the engines and watching the movement of each control surface as the pilot does his checks. Once it is determined that everything is okay, the aircraft is then topped off with fuel by a crew from the carrier's Fuels Division.

Meanwhile, the aircraft handling officer, seated in flight deck control and using a tabletop model of the carrier's flight deck with scale models of the individual aircraft to keep track of everything, reviews the launch sequence plan with the deck caller. The aircraft handling officer radios the deck caller, telling him which aircraft are reported to be "up" and ready to taxi.

The deck caller leads three separate teams of plane directors and other sailors from the carrier's Flight Deck Division, and each team is responsible for a different area of the flight deck. These teams ensure that each aircraft to be launched is safely unchained, directed around other parked aircraft (often with only inches of clearance), and put in line to be launched—sometimes as the deck of the carrier is pitching and rolling. When the deck caller gets the word from the aircraft handling officer, he leads the plane directors to distribute the aircraft among the four catapults facilitating the fastest possible departure of all the aircraft from the flight deck. As the time of the launch approaches, the directors bring each aircraft to the throat of a catapult, and the jet blast deflector is raised once an aircraft has taxied over it.

On deck, final maintenance checkers walk alongside the aircraft and inspect each panel and component as crew members from the Catapult and Arresting Gear Division hook the aircraft up to the catapult mechanism and ready it for launch. Below deck, other teams are using hydraulics and other equipment to control steam from the nuclear reactor that will be used to power the catapult.

At this time, ordnance personnel arm the aircraft's weapons.

The catapult officer then confirms the weight of the aircraft with the pilot. He also makes note of the wind over the deck and ambient conditions. He performs calculations to determine the precise amount of energy needed to achieve flight.

Even with all of this preparation, no jet would be able to take off if the ship weren't in the proper position. The ship's navigational team, which makes calculations to determine the required speed and heading, has relayed information to the bridge, and by now the ship has completed its turn and has accelerated to proper speed on its directed course.

The aircraft is almost ready for launch. The catapult officer signals to the operators, and the aircraft is hydraulically tensioned into the catapult. At this point, the pilot applies full power to the aircraft's engines and checks to be sure the aircraft is functioning. If the pilot determines that the aircraft is ready for flight, he signals the catapult officer by saluting him. If the catapult officer also receives a thumbs-up from the squadron final checker, he will then give the fire signal to a catapult operator who depresses the fire button and sends the aircraft on its way.

What's amazing is that three more aircraft can be launched right behind it in less than a minute, each having gone through that same procedure. And in just a matter of minutes, that same flight deck can be prepared to receive landing aircraft, one coming on final approach just as the previous one is taxied out of the landing area.

TEAMWORK TRUTHS

I can think of few things that require such a high degree of precision teamwork with so many different groups of people as the launching of a jet from an aircraft carrier. It's easy to see that teamwork is essential for the task. However, a task doesn't *have* to be complex to need teamwork. In 2001 when I wrote *The 17 Indisputable Laws of Teamwork*, the first law

I included was the Law of Significance, which says, "One is too small a number to achieve greatness." If you want to do anything of value, teamwork is required.

Teamwork not only allows a person to do what he couldn't otherwise do; it also has a compounding effect on all he possesses—including talent. If you believe one person is a work of God (which I do), then a group of talented people committed to working together is a work of art. Whatever your vision or desire, teamwork makes the dream work.

Working together with other people toward a common goal is one of the most rewarding experiences of life. I've led or been part of many different kinds of teams—sports teams, work teams, business teams, ministry teams, communication teams, choirs, bands, committees, boards, you name it. I've observed teams of nearly every type in my

> Teamwork makes the dream work.

travels around the world. And talking to leaders, developing teams, counseling with coaches, and teaching and writing on teamwork have influenced my thinking when it comes to teams. What I've learned I want to share with you:

1. Teamwork Divides the Effort and Multiplies the Effect

Would you like to get better results from less work? I think everyone would. That's what teamwork provides. In his book *Jesus on Leadership*, C. Gene Wilkes describes why teamwork is superior to individual effort:

- Teams involve more people, thus affording more resources, ideas, and energy than an individual possesses.

- Teams maximize a leader's potential and minimize her weaknesses. Strengths and weaknesses are more exposed in individuals.

- Teams provide multiple perspectives on how to meet a need or reach a goal, thus devising several alternatives for each situation. Individual insight is seldom as broad and deep as a group's when it takes on a problem.

- Teams share the credit for victories and the blame for losses. This fosters genuine humility and authentic community. Individuals take credit and blame alone. This fosters pride and sometimes a sense of failure.

- Teams keep leaders accountable for the goal. Individuals connected to no one can change the goal without accountability.

- Teams can simply do more than an individual.

It's common sense that people working together can do more than an individual working alone. So why are some people reluctant to engage in teamwork? It can be difficult in the beginning. Teams don't usually come together and develop on their own. They require leadership and cooperation. While that may be more work on the front end, the dividends it pays on the back end are tremendous and well worth the effort.

2. Talent Wins Games, but Teamwork Wins Championships

A sign in the New England Patriots' locker room states, "Individuals play the game, but teams win championships." Obviously the Patriot players understand this. Over a four-year period, they won the Super Bowl three times.

> Individuals play the game, but teams win championships.

Teams that repeatedly win championships are models of teamwork. For more than two decades, the Boston Celtics dominated the NBA. Their team has won more championships than any other in NBA history, and at one point during the fifties and sixties, the Celtics won eight championships in a row. During their run, the Celtics never had a player lead the league in scoring. Red Auerbach, who coached the Celtics and then later moved to their front office, always emphasized teamwork. He asserted, "One person seeking glory doesn't accomplish much; everything we've done has been the result of people working together to meet our common goals."

It's easy to see the fruit of teamwork in sports. But it is at least as important in business. Harold S. Geneen, who was director, president, and CEO of ITT for twenty years, observed, "The essence of leadership is the ability to inspire others to work together as a team—to stretch for a common objective." If you want to perform at the highest possible level, you need to be part of a team.

3. Teamwork Is Not About You

The Harvard Business School recognizes a team as a small number of people with complementary skills who are committed to a common purpose, performance goals, and approach for which they hold themselves mutually accountable. Getting those people to work together is sometimes a challenge. It requires good leadership. And the more talented the team members, the better the leadership that is needed. The true measure of team leadership is not getting people to work. Neither is it getting people to work hard. The true measure of a leader is getting people to work hard together!

I've studied exceptional team leaders and coaches. Here are what just a few say about getting people to work together:

PAUL "BEAR" BRYANT, legendary Alabama football coach: "In order to have a winner, the team must have a feeling of unity. Every player must put the team first ahead of personal glory."

BUD WILKINSON, author of *The Book of Football Wisdom*: "If a team is to reach its potential, each player must be willing to subordinate his personal goals to the good of the team."

Lou Holtz, coach of college football national championship teams: "The freedom to do your own thing ends when you have obligations and responsibilities. If you want to fail yourself— you can—but you cannot do your own thing if you have responsibilities to team members."

Michael Jordan, most talented basketball player of all time and six-time world champion: "There are plenty of teams in every sport that have great players and never win titles. Most of the time, those players aren't willing to sacrifice for the greater good of the team. The funny thing is, in the end, their unwillingness to sacrifice only makes individual goals more difficult to achieve. One thing I believe to the fullest is that if you think and achieve as a team, the individual accolades will take care of themselves. Talent wins games, but teamwork and intelligence win championships."[2]

All great teams are the result of their players making decisions based on what's best for the rest. That's true in sports, business, the military, and volunteer organizations. And it's true at every level, from the part-time support person to the coach or CEO. The best leaders also put their team first. C. Gene Wilkes observes,

> Team leaders genuinely believe that they do not have all the answers— so they do not insist on providing them. They believe they do *not* need to make all key decisions—so they do not do so. They believe they *cannot* succeed without the combined contributions of all the other members of the team to a common end—so they avoid any action that might constrain inputs or intimidate anyone on the team. Ego is *not* their predominant concern.

Highly talented teams possess players with strong egos. One secret of successful teamwork is converting individual ego into team confidence, individual sacrifice, and synergy. Pat Riley, NBA champion coach, says, "Teamwork requires that everyone's efforts flow in a single direction. Feelings of significance happen when a team's energy takes on a life of its own."

4. Great Teams Create Community

All effective teams create an environment where relationships grow and teammates become connected to one another. To use a term that is currently popular, they create a *sense of community*. That environment of community is based on trust. Little can be accomplished without it.

On good teams, trust is a nonnegotiable. On winning teams, players extend trust to one another. Initially that is a risk because their trust can be violated and they can be hurt. At the same time that they are giving trust freely, they conduct themselves in such a way to earn trust from others. They hold themselves to a high standard. When everyone gives freely and bonds of trust develop and are tested over time, players begin to have faith in one another. They believe that the person next to them will

> "The mark of community . . . is not the absence of conflict. It's the presence of a reconciling spirit."
>
> —Bill Hybels

act with consistency, keep commitments, maintain confidences, and support others. The stronger the sense of community becomes, the greater their potential to work together.

Developing a sense of community in a team does not mean there is no conflict. All teams experience disagreements. All relationships have tension. But you can work them out. My friend Bill Hybels, who leads a congregation of more than twenty thousand people, acknowledges this:

The popular concept of unity is a fantasy land where disagreements never surface and contrary opinions are never stated with force.

Instead of unity, we use the word *community*. We say, "Let's not pretend we never disagree. We're dealing with the lives of 16,000 people [at the time]. The stakes are high. Let's not have people hiding their concerns to protect a false notion of unity. Let's face the disagreement and deal with it in a good way."

The mark of community . . . is not the absence of conflict. It's the presence of a reconciling spirit. I can have a rough-and-tumble leadership meeting with someone, but because we're committed to the community, we can still leave, slapping each other on the back, saying, "I'm glad we're still on the same team." We know no one's bailing out just because of a conflicting position.

When a team shares a strong sense of community, team members can resolve conflicts without dissolving relationships.

5. Adding Value to Others Adds Value to You

"My husband and I have a very happy marriage," a woman bragged. "There's nothing I wouldn't do for him, and there's nothing he wouldn't do for me. And that's the way we go through life—doing nothing for each other!" That kind of attitude is a certain road to disaster for any team—including a married couple.

Too often people join a team for their personal benefit. They want a supporting cast so that they can be the star. But that attitude hurts the team. When even the most talented person has a mind to serve, special things can happen. Former NBA great Magic Johnson paraphrased John F. Kennedy when he stated, "Ask not what your teammates can do for you. Ask what you can do for your teammates." That wasn't just talk for Johnson. Over the course of his career with the Los Angeles Lakers, he started in every position during championship games to help his team.

U.S. president Woodrow Wilson asserted, "You are not here merely to make a living. You are here in order to enable the world to live more amply, with greater vision, with a finer spirit of hope and achievement.

You are here to enrich the world, and to impoverish yourself if you forget the errand." People who take advantage of others inevitably fail in business and relationships. If you desire to succeed, then live by these four simple words: *add value to others*. That philosophy will take you far.

TALENT + TEAMWORK = A TALENT-PLUS PERSON
PUTTING THE TALENT-PLUS FORMULA INTO ACTION

All talented people have a choice to make: do their own thing and get all the credit, or do the team thing and share it. My observation is that not only do talented people accomplish more when working with others, but they are also more fulfilled than those who go it alone. My hope is that you choose teamwork over solo efforts. If that is your desire, then do the following:

1. Buy into the Law of Significance

Earlier in this chapter I mentioned the Law of Significance from *The 17 Indisputable Laws of Teamwork*: "One is too small a number to achieve greatness." In 2002, when I was teaching on the laws, I challenged members of the audience of ten thousand: "Name one person in the history of mankind who alone, without the help of anyone, made a significant impact on civilization."

A voice from the crowd yelled, "Charles Lindbergh—he crossed the Atlantic Ocean in a plane by himself."

The crowd cheered.

"That's true," I responded, and the crowd cheered louder, thinking I had been stumped. "But did you know," I continued, "that Ryan Aeronautical Engineering designed and built the plane? And did you know that ten millionaires financed the trip?" The crowd exploded. "Are there any more suggestions?" I asked.

I want to give you the same challenge. Think of any significant accomplishment that appears to be a solo act. Then do some research and you will find that others worked with the individuals or supported them so that they could do what they did. No one does anything significant on his own. One is too small a number to achieve greatness. If you buy into that idea, then you will embrace the concept of teamwork. And that will be the foundation upon which you multiply your talent and take it to the highest level. No one can become a talent-plus person without it.

2. Include a Team in Your Dream

Journalist and radio host Rex Murphy asserts, "The successful attainment of a dream is a cart and horse affair. Without a team of horses, a cart full of dreams can go nowhere." Teamwork gives you the best opportunity to turn your vision into reality. The greater the vision, the more need there is for a good team.

> Teamwork gives you the best opportunity to turn your vision into reality.

But being willing to engage in teamwork is not the same as actively pursuing a team and becoming part of it. To succeed, you need to get on a team and find your best place in it. That may be as its leader, or it may not. Rudy Giuliani says,

> In reality, a leader *must* understand that success is best achieved through teamwork. From the moment you are put into a leadership position you must demonstrate ultimate humility. A leader must know his weaknesses in order to counterbalance them with the strengths of the team. When I became the Mayor of New York, I had both strengths and weaknesses. For instance, I did not have very much experience in economics. I found members for my team that had experience and great talent in the field of economics. When every member of the team is operating in his or her strengths, your organization will flourish. When crisis comes you will have the people in place to manage every situation with excellence.

If you're not certain about where you ultimately belong on a team, don't let that stop you from engaging in teamwork. Find others who are like-minded in their attitudes and passion, and join them.

3. Develop Your Team

If you are a leader on your team, then you must make it your goal to develop your teammates or players. That process begins with having the right people on the team. It's said that people are known by the company they keep. But it can also be said that a company is known by the people it keeps. Jack Welch, former chairman and CEO of General Electric, observed, "If you pick the right people and give them the opportunity to spread their wings—and put compensation as a carrier behind it—you almost don't have to manage them." That's why Patrick Emington said, "It is the greatest folly to talk of motivating anybody. The real key is to help others to unlock and direct their deepest motivators."

The process continues with your doing whatever you can to help people grow and reach their potential. You must do your best to see the abilities of others and help them recognize and develop those abilities. That's what all good leaders do. They don't just become talent-plus people. They help others to become talent-plus people.

4. Give the Credit for Success to the Team

The final step to becoming a talent-plus person in the area of teamwork is to give as much of the credit as you can to the people on the team. In his book *Good to Great,* Jim Collins points out that the leaders of the best organizations, what he calls "level-5 leaders," are characterized by humility and a tendency to avoid the spotlight. Does that mean those leaders aren't talented? Of course not. Does it mean they have no egos? No. It means they recognize that everyone on the team is important, and they understand that people do better work and do it with greater effort when they are recognized for their contribution.

If you consider what top leaders and former CEOs say about this, you'll recognize a pattern:

RAY GILMARTIN OF MERCK: "If I were to put someone on the front cover of *Business Week* or *Fortune*, it would be . . . the person who heads up our research organization, not me. Or I would put a team of people on the cover."

LOU GERSTNER OF IBM: "I haven't done this [created the company's turnaround]. It's been 280,000 people who have done it. We took a change in focus, a change in preoccupation, and a great talented group of people . . . and changed the company."

DAN TULLY OF MERRILL LYNCH: "It's amazing what you can do when you don't seek all the credit. I find nothing is really one person's idea."

WALTER SHIPLEY OF CITIBANK: "We have 68,000 employees. With a company this size, I'm not 'running the business' . . . My job is to create the environment that enables people to leverage each other beyond their own individual capabilities."

If you want to help your team go farther and help team members to sharpen their talent and maximize their potential, when things don't go well, take more than your fair share of the blame, and when things go well, give all of the credit away.

One person who has captured my attention lately has been Bono, singer for the rock band U2. I must admit, I'm late in discovering him. His music isn't really my cup of tea. But his passion, leadership, and activism really impress me. In 2005, he was named a Person of the Year by *Time* magazine, along with Bill and Melinda Gates.

There's no doubting Bono's talent. His success in the musical world is obvious. He has penned many hit songs, and U2, which has been together for thirty years, is one of the most successful bands in history. Together the band members have sold more than 170 million albums.[3]

In recent years, Bono has expanded his efforts beyond the world of music. He has become an advocate for African aid and economic development. And he's not just a celebrity lending his name to a cause. Senator Rick Santorum said of him, "Bono understands the issues better than 99% of the members of Congress."[4] And Bono has relentlessly worked at partnering with other people to further the causes he's passionate about. He has met with heads of state, economists, industry leaders, celebrities—anyone who has the potential to add value to the people he desires to help.

Where did Bono learn to rely on others, to be part of a team and enlist the aid of others? Rock stars are supposed to be self-absorbed, iconoclastic, isolated, and indifferent to others. That is what happens to many famous people, and it's the reason many music groups don't stay together. Bono comments,

> There's moments when people are so lost in their own selves, the demands of their own life, that it's very hard to be in a band . . . People want to be lords of their own domain. I mean, everybody, as they get older . . . rids the room of argument. You see it in your family, you see it with your friends, and they get a smaller and smaller circle of people around them, who agree with them. And life ends up with a dull sweetness.[5]

What is Bono's secret, after having been a rock star for more than twenty-five years? He learned teamwork in the band. Bono recognizes his need for others and, in fact, says he can't imagine having been a solo artist. He admits:

> The thing that'll make you less and less able to realize your potential is a room that's empty of argument. And I would be terrified to be on my own as a solo singer, not to have a band to argue with. I mean, I

surround myself with argument, and a band, a family of very spunky kids, and a wife who's smarter than anyone. I've got a lot of very smart friends, a whole extended family of them . . . You're as good as the arguments you get. So maybe the reason why the band hasn't split up is that people might get this: that even though they're only one quarter of U2, they're more than they would be if they were one whole of something else. I certainly feel that way.[6]

I can't think of a better way to say it myself. A talented person who is part of a team—in the right place on the right team—becomes more than he ever could on his own. That's what it means to be a talent-plus person.

Talent + Teamwork
Application Exercises

1. How do you think of your talent? Is it something you own or something on loan? Why do you desire success? Do your goals primarily benefit you, or are you simply an instrument being used to benefit others? Do some soul-searching. If you think everything is all about you, you will never be a good team player.

2. What kinds of experiences have you had with teams? Think about how your experience with teams during various phases of your life has impacted your thinking. Write down the kinds of teams you were a part of as a child, as a teenager, and as a young adult. Now try to recall the significant moments, milestones, and experiences with each team. Were they primarily positive or negative? If you had some bad experiences along the way, they may be coloring your thinking and making you reluctant to engage in teamwork. Process through those experiences on the emotional level, and work on seeing the current benefits of being part of a team.

3. How strong is the sense of community on a team of which you are currently a part? Do people trust one another? Do they count on one another when it counts? If not, why not? First, take responsibility for your part in any weakness in the team, and try to make amends for past failures. Work at regaining people's trust. If you have been let down by someone else on the team, go to that person privately and talk about it. Try your best to repair the relationship and start building again.

4. How can you add value to others on your team? Think of three people on your team who you believe have high potential *and* could benefit from talent, skills, or experience you have to offer. Write out a plan for each, outlining how you could help him or her. Then approach each individual with an offer to train or mentor him or her.

5. For the next two weeks, make a commitment to yourself to take no credit for anything that goes right. Praise your employees, coworkers, colleagues, and family members for their contribution. Note the difference it makes in their performance and your relationship with them. I believe that once you've tried it, you will enjoy giving the credit away so much that it will become a regular part of your life.

THE LAST WORD ON TALENT

Early in 2006, I read a report from *Money* magazine that claimed we were experiencing a worldwide talent shortage:

> ZURICH, SWITZERLAND (REUTERS)—Employers are having difficulty finding the right people to fill jobs despite high unemployment in Europe and the United States, a survey by U.S.-based staffing firm Manpower showed Tuesday.
>
> The survey conducted late in January showed that 40 percent of nearly 33,000 employers in 23 countries across the world were struggling to find qualified job candidates.
>
> "The talent shortage is becoming a reality for a larger number of employers around the world," Manpower's CEO and Chairman Jeffrey Joerres said.[1]

And in what is the number one talent shortage, according to the report? Sales. They wanted more good salespeople.

Every few years, we hear similar statements about certain professions. But the reality is that there never has been nor will there ever be a talent shortage. Talent is God-given. As long as there are people in the world, there will be plenty of talent. What's missing are people who have made the choices necessary to maximize their talent. Employers are really looking for talent-plus people. By now I trust you agree that the key choices we make—apart from the natural talent we already possess—set us apart from others who have talent alone.

William Danforth, who became the owner of the Ralston Purina Company, found a secret of success when he was a young man:

When I was sixteen, I came to St. Louis to attend the Manual Training School. It was a mile from my boardinghouse to the school. A teacher who lived nearby and I would start for school at the same time every morning. But he always beat me there. Even back then I didn't want to be beaten, and so I tried all the shortcuts. Day after day, however, he arrived ahead of me. Then I discovered how he did it. When he came to each street crossing he would run to the other curb. The thing that put him ahead of me was just "that little extra."

Talent-plus people give a little extra. You see it in the choices they make that multiply and maximize their talent. Because they have given more to *develop their talent*, they are able to give more to others *with their talent*.

I want to encourage you to make the thirteen choices described in this book. And every day remind yourself about how these choices can help you:

1. Belief lifts my talent.
2. Passion energizes my talent.
3. Initiative activates my talent.
4. Focus directs my talent.
5. Preparation positions my talent.
6. Practice sharpens my talent.
7. Perseverance sustains my talent.
8. Courage tests my talent.
9. Teachability expands my talent.
10. Character protects my talent.
11. Relationships influence my talent.
12. Responsibility strengthens my talent.
13. Teamwork multiplies my talent.

Whatever talent you have you can improve. Never forget that the choices you make in the end make you.

Choose to become a talent-plus person. If you do, you will add value to yourself, add value to others, and accomplish much more than you dreamed was possible.

NOTES

WHEN IS TALENT ALONE ENOUGH?

1. Malcolm Gladwell, "The Talent Myth," *New Yorker*, 22 July 2002, http://www.gladwell.com/2002/2002_07_22_a_talent.htm.

2. Robert J. Kriegel and Louis Patler, *If It Ain't Broke . . . Break It!* (New York: Warner Books, 1991), 11.

CHAPTER 1

1. Mark Kriegel, *Namath: A Biography* (New York: Viking), 15.

2. Ibid., 13–14.

3. Ibid., 14.

4. Ibid., 47.

5. Ibid., 234.

6. Used with permission. Copyright 2004–5, Joel Garfinkle. All rights reserved. *Dream Job Coaching*, http://www.dreamjobcoaching.com/articles/court-martial.html.

7. Kriegel and Patler, *If It Ain't Broke . . . Break It!*, 44.

8. Martin Seligman, *Learned Optimism: How to Change Your Mind and Your Life* (New York: Pocket Books, 1998), 99.

9. Kriegel, *Namath*, 57.

10. From Walter D. Wintle, "The Man Who Thinks He Can," *Poems That Live Forever*, comp. Hazel Felleman (New York: Doubleday, 1965), 310.

11. August 26, 1996: Christopher Reeve speaks at the Democratic National Convention," Floor Speeches, PBS, http://www.pbs.org/newshour/convention96/floor_speeches/reeve.html, accessed 2 August 2006.

12. Harvey Mackay, "Be a Believer to be an Achiever," Pioneer Thinking, http://www.pioneerthinking.com/achieve.html, accessed 2 August 2006.

13. Robert H. Schuller, *Tough Times Never Last, But Tough People Do!* (New York: Bantam, 1984), 204, emphasis added.

CHAPTER 2

1. Ana Figueroa, "Rueben Martinez: Barber and Book Lover," *AARP Segunda Juventud*, April/May 2005, http://www.aarpsegundajuventud.org/english/nosotros/2005-AM/05AM_bookshop.html.

2. "Life and Times" (transcript), KCET News, 11 November 2004, http://www.kcet.org/lifeandtimes/archives/20041109.php.

3. Marco R. della Cava, "Barber Grooms Love of Books," *USA Today*, 10 October 2004, http://www.usatoday.com/life/books/news/2004-10-10-barber-genius-grant_x.htm.

4. Ibid.

5. Interview of Rueben Martinez by Brancaccio, NOW, 28 January 2005, http://www.pbs.org/now/printable/transcriptNOW104_full_print.html.

6. Figueroa, "Rueben Martinez: Barber and Book Lover."

7. Http://www.humanmedia.org/program_martinez.php3.
8. "Life and Times," KCET News.
9. Della Cava, "Barber Grooms Love of Books."
10. Tara Burghart, "MacArthur 'Genius Grants' Awarded," *Seattle Times*, 28 September 2004, http://seattletimes.nwsource.com/html/nationworld/2002048058_genius28.html.
11. Figueroa, "Rueben Martinez: Barber and Book Lover."
12. Kriegel and Patler, *If It Ain't Broke . . . Break It!*, 259.
13. Richard Edler, *If I Knew Then What I Know Now: CEOs and Other Smart Executives Share Wisdom They Wish They'd Been Told 25 Years Ago* (New York: Berkley 1995), 185.

CHAPTER 3

1. "Northridge Earthquake," Wikipedia, http://en.wikipedia.org/wiki/1994_Northridge_Earthquake.
2. "Lessons for Post-Katrina Reconstruction: A High-Road vs. Low-Road Recovery," 6 October 2005, Economic Policy Institute Briefing Paper #166, 2, http://www.epi.org/content.cfm/bp166.
3. Ibid.
4. "Past Projects: Santa Monica I-10 Freeway," C. C. Myers, Inc., http://www.ccmyers.com/completedprojects.cfm?ID=8.
5. "Lessons for Post-Katrina Reconstruction," 4.
6. "Les Brown," http://www.lesbrown.com/about_les.htm, accessed 2 August 2006.
7. Proverbs 6:6–11 *The Message: The New Testament in Contemporary English*, by Eugene H. Peterson. Copyright © 1993, 1994, 1995, 1996, 2000.
8. http://littlecalamity.tripod.com/Quotes/L.html, accessed 2 August 2006.
9. Edgar A. Guest, "To-morrow," *A Heap O' Livin'* (Chicago: Reilly and Lee, 1916).

CHAPTER 4

1. Donald E. Demaray, *Laughter, Joy, and Healing* (Grand Rapids: Baker Book House, 1986), 34–35.

CHAPTER 5

1. Stephen E. Ambrose, *Undaunted Courage: Meriwether Lewis, Thomas Jefferson, and the Opening of the American West* (New York: Simon and Schuster Paperbacks, 1996), 68.
2. Ibid., 27.
3. Ibid., 76 (emphasis added).
4. Ibid., 59.
5. Richard Dillon, *Meriwether Lewis: A Biography* (New York: Coward-McCann, 1965), 30.
6. Ambrose, *Undaunted Courage*, 77.
7. List was created using information from Ambrose, *Undaunted Courage*, pages 87–92.
8. Ibid., 126.
9. Ibid., 114.
10. James P. Ronda, "Lewis and Clark Expedition," Microsoft Encarta Online Encyclopedia 2005, http://encarta.msn.com.
11. Ambrose, *Undaunted Courage*, 14.
12. Don Deveridge Jr. and Jeffrey P. Davidson, *The Achievement Challenge: How to Be a 10 in Business* (Homewood, IL: Irwin Professional, 1987).
13. The New American Standard Bible ®, Copyright © The Lockman Foundation 1960, 1962, 1963, 1968, 1971, 1972, 1973, 1975, 1977. Used by permission. (www.Lockman.org).

14. Kahleen M. Gisenhardt, "Making Fast Strategic Decisions in High-Velocity Environments," *Academy of Management Journal*, Vol. 32, No. 3 (Sept. 1989), 543–76.

CHAPTER 6

1. Fred Kaplan, *Dickens: A Biography* (Baltimore: Johns Hopkins University Press, 1988), 50.
2. Ibid., 59.
3. Ibid., 58.
4. Ibid., 62.
5. Jane Smiley, *Charles Dickens* (New York: Lipper/Viking, 2002), 26.
6. Kaplan, *Dickens*, 60.
7. Ibid., 64.
8. Smiley, *Charles Dickens*, 3.
9. Ibid., 16.
10. *Reader's Digest*, January 1992, 91.
11. Jon Johnston, *Christian Excellence* (Grand Rapids: Baker Book House, 1985), 30.

CHAPTER 7

1. Vonetta Flowers with W. Terry Whalin, *Running on Ice: The Overcoming Faith of Vonetta Flowers* (Birmingham, AL: New Hope Publishers, 2005), 25.
2. "Tom Hanks," Box Office Mojo, http://www.boxofficemojo.com/people/chart/?view=Actor &id=tomhanks.htm, accessed 8 May 2006.
3. "Tom Hanks Earns His $25 Million Salary, but Not Jim Carrey," 6 May 2006, http://sg.news.yahoo.com/060506/1/40lm9.html, accessed 8 May 2006.
4. Adapted from Max Isaacson, *How to Conquer the Fear of Public Speaking and Other Coronary Threats* (Rockville Centre, NY: Farnsworth Publishing, 1984), 77.
5. Howard Goodman, "I Don't Regret a Mile," used by permission /Rick Goodman, Goodman and Associates, P.O. Box 158778, Nashville, TN 37215.
6. "One List," *Houston Chronicle*, 1 January 2001, 2D, http://www.chron.com/CDA/archives/archive.mpl?id=2001_3270661, accessed 10 May 2006.
7. George E. Vaillant, *Aging Well: Surprising Guideposts to a Happier Life from the Landmark Harvard Study of Adult Development* (New York: Little, Brown and Company, 2003), 285.
8. Bruce Nash, *The Football Hall of Shame* (New York: Pocket Books, 1991), 21–22.

CHAPTER 8

1. Winston S. Churchill, "Reflections at Century's End: Man of the Millennium?" The Churchill Centre, http://www.winstonchurchill.org/i4a/pages/index.cfm?pageid=818, accessed 17 May 2006.
2. "10 Facts About Churchill," Churchill Museum and Cabinet War Rooms, http://churchillmuseum.iwm.org.uk/server/show/nav.00i002, accessed 17 May 2006.
3. Douglas S. Russell, "Lt. Churchill, 4th Queen's Own Hussars" (lecture), Boston, 28 October 1995, The Churchill Centre, http://www.winstonchurchill.org/i4a/pages/index.cfm?pageid=638, accessed 17 May 2006.
4. "Malakand Field Force," The Churchill Centre, http://www.winstonchurchill.org/i4a/pages/index.cfm?pageid=176, accessed 2 August 2006.
5. "Churchill, 4th Queen's Own Hussars," The Churchill Centre, http://www.winstonchurchill.org/i4a/pages/index.cfm?pageid=638, accessed 2 August 2006.
6. Churchill, "Reflections."

7. John C. Maxwell, *Winning with People: Discover the People Principles That Work for You Every Time* (Nashville: Thomas Nelson, 2004), 221.

8. Pat Williams, *American Scandal: The Solution for the Crisis of Character* (Shippensburgh, PA: Treasure House, 2003), 290.

CHAPTER 9

1. Giorgio Vasari, *The Lives of the Artists*, trans. Peter Bondanella (Oxford: Oxford University Press, 1991), 284.

2. "The Moon and the Sky," American Museum of Natural History, http://www.amnh.org/exhibitions/codex/astronom.html, accessed 30 May 2006.

3. "Bill and Melinda Gates Bring Leonardo da Vinci's Codex Leicester to Life," http://www.microsoft.com/BillGates/news/codex.asp, accessed 29 May 2006.

4. Emily Morison Beck, ed., *Bartlett's Familiar Quotations* (Boston: Little, Brown, and Company, 1980), 152.

5. Philip B. Crosby, *Quality Is Free* (New York: Penguin, 1980), 68.

6. J. Konrad Hole, *Diamonds for Daily Living* (World Press, 1996).

7. Proverbs 26:12, New King James Version®. Copyright © 1982 by Thomas Nelson, Inc. Used by permission. All rights reserved.

8. Eric W. Johnson, ed., *A Treasury of Humor* (New York: Ivy Books, 1990), 304.

9. Anonymous.

10. Dan Sullivan and Catherine Nomura, *The Laws of Lifetime Growth: Always Make Your Future Bigger Than Your Past* (San Francisco: Barrett-Koehler Publishers, 2006), 17.

11. Anonymous.

CHAPTER 10

1. "Dr. Hwang Woo Suk," *Time*, http://www.time.com/time/asia/2004/personoftheyear/people/hwang_woo_suk.html, accessed 3 June 2006.

2. "Hwang Woo-Suk," Wikipedia, http://en.wikipedia.org/wiki/Hwang_Woo-Suk, accessed 3 June 2006.

3. Ibid.

4. "10 Questions for Dr. Hwang Woo Suk," *Time*, 5 December 2005, http://www.time.com/time/asia/magazine/printout/0,13675,501051212-1137709,00.html, accessed 3 June 2006.

5. Nicholas Wade and Choe Sang-Hun, "Researcher Faked Evidence of Human Cloning, Koreans Report," *New York Times*, 10 January 2006, http://www.nytimes.com/2006/01/10/10clone.html, accessed 3 June 2006.

6. Steven Ertelt, "Hwang Woo-Suk Apologizes for Faking Embryonic Stem Cell Research," Lifenews.com, 11 January 2006, http://www.lifenews.com/bio1274.html, accessed 3 June 2006.

7. "Disgraced Korean Cloning Scientist Indicted," *New York Times*, 12 May 2006, http://www.nytimes.com/2006/05/12/world/asia/12korea.html, accessed 3 June 2006.

8. Stan Mooneyham, *Dancing on the Strait and Narrow* (San Francisco: Harper and Row, 1989), 1–2, 68.

9. "Bobby Jones (golfer)," Wikipedia, http://en.wikipedia.org/wiki/Bobby_Jones_%28golfer%29, accessed 6 June 2006.

10. Stephen Covey, *The Seven Habits of Highly Effective People: Restoring the Character Ethic* (New York: Simon and Schuster, 1989), 21.

11. Alexander Solzhenitsyn, *One Day in the Life of Ivan Denisovich* (New York: Signet, 1998), 88.

12. Laura L. Nash, *Good Intentions Aside: A Manager's Guide to Resolving Ethical Problems* (Boston: Harvard Business School Press, 1993), 125.

CHAPTER 11

1. Dan Haseltine, "Foreword," in Dave Urbanski's *The Man Comes Around: The Spiritual Journey of Johnny Cash* (Lake Mary, FL: Relevant Books, 2003), xiv.
2. Urbanski, *The Man*, 50.
3. Ibid., 51.
4. Ibid., 53–54.
5. Johnny Cash with Patrick Carr, *Cash: The Autobiography* (New York: Harper Paperbacks, 1997), 229.
6. Ibid., 232.
7. "Tribute to June by Rosanne Cash," http://www.johnnycash.com/june/may18.html, accessed 13 June 2006.
8. Cash, *Autobiography*, 314.
9. Les Parrott, *High Maintenance Relationships* (Wheaton, IL: Tyndale, 1997).
10. http://home.comcast.net/~b.learn/bob.htm, accessed 13 June 2006.

CHAPTER 12

1. Http://www.climber.org/data/decimal.html.
2. Http://www.supertopo.com/rockclimbing/route.html?r=loeabear.
3. Andrew Todhunter, *Fall of the Phantom Lord: Climbing and the Face of Fear* (New York: Anchor Books, 1998), 44.
4. Craig Vetter, "Terminal Velocity," *Outside*, April 1999, http://outside.away.com/magazine/0499/9904terminal.html, accessed 14 June 2006.
5. Ibid.
6. Todhunter, *Fall*, 43.
7. Ibid., 78.
8. Tony Campolo, *The Covenant Companion*, April 1998.
9. *Business Ethics*, November/December 1996.
10. Williams, *American Scandal*, 174–75.
11. Rudolph W. Giuliani with Ken Kurson, *Leadership* (New York: Hyperion, 2002), 69–70.
12. Speech to Massachusetts legislature (9 January 1961), quoted on www.mass.gov/statehouse/jfk_speech.htm, accessed 4 August 2006.

CHAPTER 13

1. Lt. Commander Smith's description was so complex and detailed that I asked him to e-mail it to me so that I could describe it accurately in this book.
2. Michael Jordan and Mark Vancil, *I Can't Accept Not Trying* (San Francisco: Harper, 1994).
3. "U2," http://en.wikipedia.org/wiki/U2, accessed 21 June 2006.
4. Josh Tyrangiel, "The Constant Charmer," *Time*, 26 December–2 January 2006, 50.
5. Michka Assayas, *Bono in Conversation with Michka Assayas* (New York: Riverhead Books, 2005), 151.
6. Ibid., 152.

THE LAST WORD ON TALENT

1. "Worldwide 'Talent Shortage' Seen by Employers," *Money*, 21 February 2006, http://money.cnn.com/2006/02/21/news/international/jobs_manpower.reut/index.htm.

ABOUT THE AUTHOR

JOHN C. MAXWELL is an internationally recognized leadership expert, speaker, and author who has sold more than 12 million books. His organizations have trained more than 1 million leaders worldwide. Dr. Maxwell is the founder of Injoy Stewardship Services and EQUIP. Every year he speaks to Fortune 500 companies, international government leaders, and organizations as diverse as the United States Military Academy at West Point and the National Football League. A *New York Times*, *Wall Street Journal*, and *Business Week* best-selling author, Maxwell was one of 25 authors named to Amazon.com's 10th Anniversary Hall of Fame. Two of his books, *The 21 Irrefutable Laws of Leadership* and *Developing the Leader Within You*, have sold more than a million copies each.

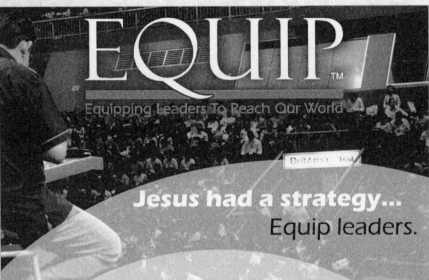

John Maxwell's
REAL
Leadership Series

RELATIONSHIPS 101
ISBN 0-7852-6351-9

EQUIPPING 101
ISBN 0-7852-6352-7

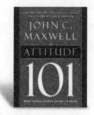

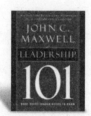

ATTITUDE 101
ISBN 0-7852-6350-0

LEADERSHIP 101
ISBN 0-7852-6419-1

THOMAS NELSON
Since 1798

thomasnelson.com

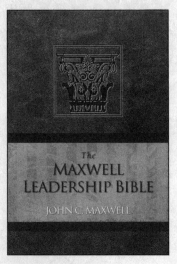

ISBN: 0-7180-1344-1

The *Maxwell Leadership Bible* shows us what God's Word has to say about leaders and leadership. Executive Editor John C. Maxwell has assembled biblical teaching to equip and encourage leaders and those who serve with them, to meet 21st-century challenges by using the time-tested and irrefutable principles of leadership that God has shown us in the Bible.

THOMAS NELSON
Since 1798

thomasnelson.com

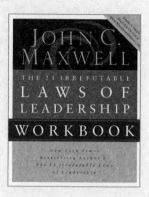

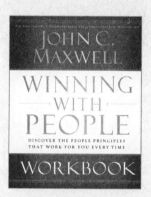
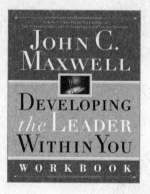

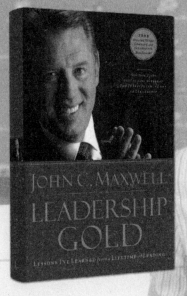

BOOKS BY DR. JOHN C. MAXWELL
CAN TEACH YOU HOW TO BE A **REAL** SUCCESS

RELATIONSHIPS

Be a People Person

Becoming a Person of Influence

Relationships 101

The Power of Influence

The Power of Partnership in the Church

The Treasure of a Friend

Ethics 101

Winning with People

25 Ways to Win with People

EQUIPPING

Developing the Leaders Around You

Equipping 101

The 17 Indisputable Laws of Teamwork

The 17 Essential Qualities of a Team Player

Partners in Prayer

Your Road Map for Success

Success One Day at a Time

Today Matters

Talent Is Never Enough

ATTITUDE

Be All You Can Be

Failing Forward

The Power of Thinking Big

Living at the Next Level

Think on These Things

The Winning Attitude

Your Bridge to a Better Future

The Power of Attitude

Attitude 101

Thinking for a Change

The Difference Maker

The Journey from Success to Significance

LEADERSHIP

The 21 Indispensable Qualities of a Leader

The 21 Irrefutable Laws of Leadership

The 21 Most Powerful Minutes in a Leader's Day

Developing the Leader Within You

Leadership 101

Leadership Promises for Every Day

The 360 Degree Leader

The Right to Lead